**Date: 5/14/19**

**616.89 HEA**
**Headcase : LGBTQ writers and**
**artists on mental health and**

# Headcase

# Headcase

## LGBTQ Writers and Artists on Mental Health and Wellness

Edited by Stephanie Schroeder

and

Teresa Theophano

OXFORD
UNIVERSITY PRESS

# OXFORD

## UNIVERSITY PRESS

Oxford University Press is a department of the University of Oxford. It furthers the University's objective of excellence in research, scholarship, and education by publishing worldwide. Oxford is a registered trade mark of Oxford University Press in the UK and certain other countries.

Published in the United States of America by Oxford University Press
198 Madison Avenue, New York, NY 10016, United States of America.

© Oxford University Press 2019

Library of Congress Cataloging-in-Publication Data
Names: Schroeder, Stephanie, editor. | Theophano, Teresa, editor.
Title: Headcase : LGBTQ writers and artists on mental health and wellness /
edited by Stephanie Schroeder, Teresa Theophano.
Description: New York, NY : Oxford University Press, [2019] |
Includes bibliographical references and index.
Identifiers: LCCN 2018020915 (print) | LCCN 2018024432 (ebook) |
ISBN 9780190846602 (updf) | ISBN 9780190846619 (epub) |
ISBN 9780190846596 (hardback)
Subjects: LCSH: Sexual minorities—Mental health. | Gender
identity—Psychological aspects. | BISAC: MEDICAL / Mental Health.
Classification: LCC RC451.4.G39 (ebook) | LCC RC451.4.G39 H43 2019 (print) |
DDC 616.890086/6—dc23
LC record available at https://lccn.loc.gov/2018020915

1 3 5 7 9 8 6 4 2

Printed by Sheridan Books, Inc., United States of America

# CONTENTS

# ILLUSTRATIONS

# FOREWORD

## *Kai Cheng Thom*

I am several months behind deadline on writing this foreword: first, there were the implications of a mental health crisis of my own, then there was the deluge of catch-up emails, work obligations, other writing deadlines. The usual story: I am crazy, but capitalism marches on. There were phone calls from friends and friends of friends in the middle of the night, queer and trans people I love and some I barely know, searching for any kind of support that felt both relevant and safe—always someone on the brink of a breakdown, a depressive or manic episode, a suicide.

Dear queer readers, let's be honest: often, that someone was me. And sometimes that someone is you.

Beneath the winding road that leads to the "queer community" (scare quotes because queer community so often feels like a mythical place—somewhere we talk about but rarely find, somewhere just beyond the rainbow) there is the shadow we call mental health, mental illness, trauma, madness, and a hundred other whispered names. For all our words, we still struggle to speak of it: shame, the legacy of over a century of pathologization, stigma and psychiatric abuses, still clenches its bony hand around our throats.

Audre Lorde, the patron saint of queer women of color, once wrote that our silence will not protect us. Sigmund Freud, an ambiguous figure at best to many LGBT persons, wrote of language's "magical power" to transform emotion and heal the psyche's wounds. Those of us who are therapists, poets, artists, storytellers know: speaking the truth has always been our greatest power.

In *Headcase*, Stephanie Schroeder and Teresa Theophano have woven an ambitious tapestry of diverse LGBTQ voices, professional and academic disciplines, and storytelling mediums. The anthology traces the past and present of psychiatry's oppression of queer sexualities and identities, reflects on the contemporary state of queer psychotherapeutic and mental health services, and lays bare the emotional and spiritual intersection of queerness and madness through trenchant personal narratives. Balanced throughout the collection are a wide span of racial, gendered, and generational perspectives—a sorely needed shift from a paradigm of mental health writing and activism that tends to center White, cisgender, middle-aged individuals.

One great strength of the anthology is that Schroeder and Theophano have chosen to situate academic, literary, and artistic contributions alongside one another, on equal footing. Thus, Arlene Istar Lev's review of historic and contemporary therapeutic practices with queer and trans people speaks in dialogue with Juan Antonio Trujillo's searing narrative excavation of the borderline personality construct, which in turn resonates with Guy Glass's heartbreaking evocation of conversion therapy in the excerpt from his play. These are but a few of the varied forms and subjects that comprise the shimmering, kaleidoscopic vision of this collection.

Tellingly, the editors have also chosen to place both "victims" and "healers" of mental dis-ease on equal footing: In *Headcase*, poet and practitioner, client and clinician, speak as a chorus in a subversion of the rigid crazy patient–wise therapist boundaries that are endorsed by Western colonial mental health disciplines. In the space where "mental health professionals" can strip away their professional accoutrements and bare their vulnerabilities, where those who have been pathologized as "mental health patients" seize control of their own narratives, a truer and more human relationship emerges.

*Headcase* speaks to the chaotic intensity that is queer mental health and illness in a world that both fetishizes and despises us. Despite some historic gains won by queer and trans mental health advocates of the past decades, the times remain dangerous and crazy-making for the vast majority of us—and what ground has been gained is in danger of being quickly lost as neo-fascist and White supremacist movements march toward political resurgence.

So, we struggle on, somehow. We fall behind on our work, we disappoint the ones we love, we set up makeshift crisis hotlines in our bedrooms at night. We survive, often in fear and silence.

A few months ago, I consulted a fellow trans woman therapist—the only other trans woman therapist I am acquainted with in North America, actually—on a clinical case with which I was struggling. In my work on this case, with a young trans client whose life story resonated intensely with my own, I worried that my strong protectiveness and affection for this client might in some way blind my judgment. Settler colonial and cis-normative therapeutic training had taught me that strong feelings were weakness, a contagion that might infect those I have dedicated my life to supporting.

I was, in a word, afraid: afraid of my own past, my trauma, my madness. And I was ashamed that this young client could evoke such intense feelings in me, a trained social worker and therapist who had supposedly attained the type of stability and dispassion that mainstream mental health so deeply values.

My trans woman peer listened to my fears. She heard me out compassionately and critically, evaluating each fear with care. And then she told me that it is our responsibility and our privilege as survivors of the system who have found our way to the other side of power to love our clients—our communities, our selves—fearlessly.

When I reflect on the overarching impact of this anthology, I believe that this is what *Headcase* brings to the discourse on queer and trans mental health: fearless love. Fearless love of our madness. Fearless love, and the language we need to speak a new reality into being.

# ACKNOWLEDGMENTS

I am indebted to my friend and co-editor Teresa Theophano for asking me to work with her on this important book, trusting my judgment and instinct throughout the process, and remaining friends afterward.

From the first email exchange with our editor at Oxford University Press, Dana Bliss, I knew we had a trustworthy professional as well as a supporter and admirer on our side. Dana gently, but firmly, guided us through the process of editing and producing *Headcase*; first, by accepting our prospectus, and then cheering us on every bit of the way. Dana's insistence on adding clinicians to the mix of pieces has made the collection much stronger. I also appreciate his acceptance of our bottom line of keeping the book free of academic jargon. Additionally, Dana's assistant, the extremely knowledgeable Andrew Dominello, was an important support for me in the process. He was a fan of the book from the start and fielded my random questions, always being more than helpful.

I have to hand it to my friend and former PR client Nancy Blaine, who, on top of transitioning out of her editing job at Oxford to found her own local business, made sure our book proposal reached Dana, albeit through a very circuitous channel.

I am grateful for every contributor to this book: you each bring such a unique and necessary perspective to the topic of LGBTQ mental health. Thank you so much for hanging in there with us for the duration.

Liz Margolies, an early advisor, helped with standards around vetting clinical submissions, provided other appreciated input, and was supportive in numerous ways throughout the process. My sister, Ann Schroeder, proved a trusty second set of eyes and valuable sounding board for me during this project. She was so much more than an editorial advisor and I will be forever grateful for her assistance. My partner, Lisa Haas, provided technical assistance instrumental in assembling the final manuscript. Along with insight, warmth, and caring throughout the several-years-long process, she was also immensely supportive in many other ways. I also want to thank Sophie Keir who has been extremely supportive of *Headcase* from inception and has kept up with the demands of our project even while in the process of grieving her beloved companion and artistic partner and *Headcase* contributor Kate Millett.

I could not have finished this book without any of the above-mentioned folks, and many others I did not mention. Thank you all!

—Stephanie Schroeder

I have such gratitude for our wonderful editorial team at Oxford University Press. Dana Bliss and Andrew Dominello have championed and strengthened *Headcase* every step of the way. Stephanie Schroeder has been a dream co-editor, and I can't think of anyone with whom I'd rather collaborate. Thank you to all of our fabulous contributors. It takes such courage to "come out" as LGBTQ+ and mad. I am touched by and thankful for each and every one of you. Thanks to Liz Margolies of the National LGBT Cancer Network for her insightful technical assistance and huge heart.

Thanks to my loving and supportive parents, Shelli Shaw, Dimitri Theophano, and Marc Shaw, and my brilliant, witty, and warm Aunt Janet Theophano. They have shown up for me through thick and thin during the course of this book's development (and beyond).

I have the best friends and chosen family in the world, and their support, encouragement, feedback, and advice have helped immeasurably with this project and with my life in general!: Tessa Bronner, Michelle Brotman, Chelsea Ebin and Jack Vimo, Helen Fourness, Stephanie Gilman and Judy Yu, Andy Hale, Keith Kahla, my platonic/work husband Pony Knowles, Lauren Lydiard and Jake Campbell, Krissy "Jude" Mahan, Roseann Marulli, Abby Nathanson, Robyn "Dude" Overstreet, Sary Rottenberg, D. Schiff, my down-the-hall family Jean Shepherd and Jack Skelton, Phoenix Schneider, Greg Stephens and Chris Silva, CB Stewart, my punk-rock little sister Sara Takacs, Monica Terry, the legendary Jay Toole, and, last but absolutely not least, Johanna and Brad Wood. Jennye Patterson supported this project when it was still a twinkle in my eye. Much appreciation to Tom Weber at SAGE and to Dr. Jack Pula for all you do.

—Teresa Theophano

# CONTRIBUTORS

**Guy Albert**, PhD, is a licensed psychologist and Jungian analyst working with adolescents, adults, and couples in Berkeley, California. He's an adjunct faculty for JFK University, a former adjunct faculty for Sofia University, and a former clinical director for Pacific Institute. Dr. Albert is an analyst member of the C. G. Jung Institute of San Francisco. He is also a member of the American Psychological Association, the California Psychological Association, and Gaylesta, the Psychotherapy Association for Sexual and Gender Diversity. Dr. Albert has been active in the fight against the practice of conversion therapy, including support for the passage of SB 1172, the first bill in the world that protects minors from being subjected to conversion therapy in California. He is currently co-coordinating a national effort to have all major US healthcare associations sign a joint statement warning against the potential harms and unethical nature of conversion therapy.

**Crista Anne** is a passionate advocate for sexual freedoms, inclusive pleasure-based sex education, and reproductive justice. As a Professional Oversharer, she uses memoirist blogging and decades of experience working in sexuality to educate via shared experience. "Internet famous" for her #OrgasmQuest, she loves to spark conversations around sexuality, queer parenthood, and mental health. Proudly, she is an Advisory Board Member at the Effing Foundation for Sex-Positivity and Leadership for the Woodhull Sexual Freedom Summit. A native Wisconsinite, she is based on the East Coast of the United States where she lives with her partners and children and their dogs.

**Kelly Barth** lives in Lawrence, Kansas, with her wife, landscape painter Lisa Grossman. She is a clerk and social media manager at The Raven Book Store. *My Almost Certainly Real Imaginary Jesus* is her first book.

**Gabriella M. Belfiglio** lives in Brooklyn, New York, with her partner, son, and four cats. She teaches self-defense, conflict resolution, karate, and tai chi to people of all ages throughout the five boroughs of New York City. Gabriella won second place in the W. B. Yeats Poetry Contest. Her work has been published in many anthologies and journals including *The Shanghai Literary Review, Radius, The Centrifugal Eye, The Potomac Review,* and *Lambda Literary Review.* Her website is www.gabriellabelfiglio.info

**Lynn Breedlove** helps outsiders live in a world that wants them dead by creating punk songs, essays, novels, solo shows, and screenplays and advertising for his latest trans-portation entrepreneurial endeavor. He's always working on a new form. Currently: poetry (45 poems about love and war) and memoir. He fronts bands The Homobiles and Commmando, and runs Homobiles, the nonprofit ride service, and Lickety Split Trans AF Delivery. Breedlove believes in the scientific fact that love is energy, infinite and unstoppable, as it cannot be destroyed, only transformed.

**Donald V. Brown, Jr.** is a doctoral student in Critical Social Psychology at The Graduate Center, City University of New York, where he is a Presidential MAGNET Fellow. His research interests include social identity development and maintenance over the life span, intersectionality as theory and method, and identity development in postsecondary contexts. More broadly, Donald is concerned with questions of social categorization and its scientific, societal, and personal consequences. He has previously worked on projects in the Center for Intersectionality and Social Policy Studies, under the leadership of Kimberlé W. Crenshaw, at Columbia Law School. For the past seven years, in addition to academic pursuits, he has served as a higher education professional at New York University—most recently as Associate Director of Student Services for Global Public Health. He holds a master's degree in higher and postsecondary education from Teachers College, Columbia University, in addition to a bachelor's degree in neuroscience.

**Michael Brown** is a published poet based in Cambridge, England. His audiobooks became popular after film star Sigourney Weaver reviewed them. He is currently working on a science fiction novella and is a researcher at Cambridge University.

**Antoine B. Craigwell** is Founder, President, and CEO of DBGM, Inc. He is originally from Guyana. As a journalist, Antoine graduated from Bernard Baruch College of the City University of New York, and, in 2008, he earned awards from the New York Association of Black Journalists. He has written for *FORTUNE Small Business* magazine, *Out In Jersey* magazine, *The Bilerico Project, The Bronx Times Reporter,* and *The New York Amsterdam News;* was the assistant editor with *The Network Journal;* and has been a contributor to mainstreet.com. Antoine produced the documentary "You Are Not Alone" (www.yana-thefilm.com) and facilitates multiple forums on depression in Black gay men. He founded DBGM, Inc. (www.dbgm.org) in 2013, and presents workshops on the convergence of HIV and mental health; he has been a keynote speaker at several national and international conferences and provides training in cultural competency for LGBTQ peoples of color. DBGM hosts the annual LGBTQ Peoples of Color Mental Health Conference.

**J. M. Ellison** is a writer, a teacher and scholar, and a grassroots community activist. They are also a doctoral student in Women's and Gender Studies at the Ohio State University. J. M. is interested in using stories both fictional and true to build community, document social movements, and imagine a liberated world. Their work has been featured in the *Baltimore Review, Lunch Ticket, Story Club Magazine*, and many other publications. From 2007 to 2010, they lived in Palestine. They are currently in the process of publishing a graphic novel about their experiences. J. M. believes that storytelling is integral to healing, transformation, resistance, and survival. Their fiction, nonfiction, and academic work is available at http://jmellison.net.

**Eliza Gauger** is a writer, artist, and the creator of occult psychotherapy project Problem Glyphs, sci fi collaboration with Warren Ellis DEEP MAP PILOTS, doom space metal comic Black Hole Wizard with writer Simon Berman, and the reimagining of the cult underground webcomic, Jerkcity HD. They are represented and collected in Seattle, San Francisco, Berlin, Munich, and New York. Upcoming illustrations and stories by Gauger will appear in Queers Destroy Science Fiction! and Queers Destroy Horror! by LIGHTSPEED Press, as well as guest pages in BARTKIRA. Gauger is indifferent about their pronouns, and passionate about drawing the perfect aquiline nose.

**Guy Fredrick Glass** is a psychiatrist who is also a playwright. A graduate of the University of Pennsylvania School of Medicine, Guy served on the executive board of the Association of Gay and Lesbian Psychiatrists and was in private practice for many years in New York City. A growing interest in theater led him to write *Doctor Anonymous*, a play about gay conversion therapy and the events leading up to the removal of homosexuality from the *Diagnostic and Statistical Manual of Mental Disorders (DSM)*; his play was produced in Los Angeles in 2014 and published by Heartland Plays. In 2015, he received his MFA in theater from Stony Brook University. Guy is Clinical Assistant Professor at the Center for Medical Humanities, Compassionate Care and Bioethics at Stony Brook School of Medicine, and a Fellow of the College of Physicians of Philadelphia, where he is on the steering committee for the Section on Medicine and the Arts.

**Louisa Hammond** is an artist based in Manchester, England. Louisa is passionate about raising awareness of what it is like to live with an invisible illness. Her chosen medium is textiles—specifically machine and hand embroidery. Her artwork has, in the past, explored her personal experiences of having a mental health condition. Through her artwork and current practice, she focuses on the experiences of other people with lived experience of mental illness. This body of work has been developed through research gathered by studying for a master's degree in embroidery at Manchester Metropolitan University. Louisa is passionate about working with people who are vulnerable and less represented. She would like to share their perspectives and raise awareness about mental health issues with an aim to destigmatize possible prejudices she has faced personally, as a person living with a long-term invisible illness.

**Lance Hicks** is a clinical social worker and community organizer born and raised in Detroit, Michigan. He identifies as Black, mixed, trans, and queer. Since 2005, Lance has been a street outreach worker, a crisis interventionist, a mental health therapist, a youth program coordinator, and an education mentor for oppressed youth across Southeast Michigan. In his free time, Lance spends time with his friends and chosen family, writes, take pictures, and nerds out over neurobiology and traumatology.

**Christian Huygen**, PhD, is a clinical psychologist and the executive director of Rainbow Heights Club, a psychosocial support agency for LGBT adults living with serious mental illness. Ninety percent of the Club's clients stay free of hospitalization each year, and the agency's services are provided at no cost to the client. In 2012, Dr. Huygen was appointed to the Multicultural Advisory Committee of the New York State Office of Mental Health. He organized three conferences on LGBT affirming behavioral health services and developed a training program for mainstream care providers. The curriculum has been presented to thousands of individuals who work at hundreds of agencies, clinics, hospitals, and residences. Along with Dr. Barbara Warren, Dr. Huygen successfully advocated for the inclusion of questions about sexual orientation and gender identity in the New York State Office of Mental Health's statewide patient surveys and records for both inpatients and outpatients, to better understand the prevalence and needs of LGBTQ people living with mental illness.

**Benjamin Klas** lives in Minnesota with his partner and their son. He spends his days block printing, playing the ukulele, parenting, and writing, although not necessarily in that order. His works have appeared in a handful of literary magazines and a collection by queer authors.

**Bill Konigsberg** is the award-winning author of four young adult novels. *The Porcupine of Truth* won the PEN Center USA Literary Award and the Stonewall Book Award in 2016. *Openly Straight* won the Sid Fleischman Award for Humor and was a finalist for the Amelia Elizabeth Walden Award and Lambda Literary Award in 2014. His debut novel, *Out of the Pocket*, won the Lambda Literary Award in 2009. His most recent novel, *Honestly Ben*, received three starred reviews from *Publishers Weekly*, *Booklist*, and *School Library Journal*. He lives in Chandler, Arizona, with his husband Chuck and their Australian Labradoodles Mabel and Buford.

**Arlene Istar Lev**, LCSW-R, CASAC, CST, is a social worker and family therapist who is the founder and clinical director of Choices Counseling and Consulting (www.

choicesconsulting.com) and TIGRIS: The Training Institute for Gender, Relationships, Identity, and Sexuality (www.tigrisinstitute.com) in Albany, New York. She is a part-time lecturer at the University at Albany, School of Social Welfare and is the Project Director of the Sexual Orientation and Gender Identity Project (SOGI). She is also an adjunct professor at Smith College School for Social Work and Empire College. Lev is also the Board President for Rainbow Access Initiative, Inc., which provides low-cost therapy to LGBTQ individuals. She has authored numerous journal articles and authored two books: *The Complete Lesbian and Gay Parenting Guide* and *Transgender Emergence: Therapeutic Guidelines for Working with Gender-Variant People and Their Families,* winner of the APA (Division 44) Distinguished Book Award, 2006. She has spent many hours on both sides of the proverbial couch.

**Fidelindo A. Lim** has worked as a critical care nurse for 18 years. Concurrently, he has been a faculty member at New York University Rory Meyers College of Nursing since 1996. Dr. Lim has published numerous articles on various topics including clinical practice, geriatric nursing, nursing education issues, LGBT health disparities, reflective practice, men in nursing, and Martha Rogers and Florence Nightingale, among others. He is particularly interested in bridging gaps in nurse engagement and practice excellence in the clinical setting. To this end, his work as a Nurse Educator in a Magnet-designated hospital currently provides sustainable, staff-focused educational support. In further recognition of his excellence in the classroom, the NYU Meyers student body has honored him with various teaching awards over the years. Dr. Lim is also a founding member of New York City Men in Nursing, an organization for which he hosts a monthly professional development series.

**Nikkiesha N. McLeod** is a writer, singer/songwriter, and musician. They began playing the steel-pan at the age of twelve, when they convinced their parents to let them join the neighborhood steelband orchestra, Panasonic Connection. Currently, Nikkiesha is working on their first EP, scheduled to debut this year. They were a co-founder of the grassroots feminist zine *OutLaw Sister Riff,* which focused on issues affecting women and young girls, and have been a recipient of Howard University's John J. Wright Award for poetry, a finalist in the Hollin's Poetry Festival, and a co-award recipient for the City College English Department Adrian Schwartz Award for Women's Fiction. Nikkiesha's work has appeared in the literary journal *[sic],* in *Tom Tom Magazine,* and on the online literary and artistic expression of queer and trans people of color forum Black Girl Dangerous. Nikkiesha blogs at coceyea.wordpress.com

**Stephen Mead,** as a writer and artist publishing for the last three decades, has finally gotten around to getting links to his poetry still online at various zines available in one place: stephenmead.weebly.com/links-to-poetry-on-the-line-stephen-mead.

His latest Amazon release is entitled "Our Spirit Life," a poetry/art meditation on family heritage, love, and the evanescence of time. For Christmas 2014, he released a sound collage song cycle, "Threnody for a Forgotten Plague," a series-in-progress dealing with the early days of the AIDS pandemic, free to listen to via amazingtunes. com/stephenmead/albums/24122. Currently, he is seeking a publisher for two other projects: *A Thousand Beautiful Things*, an esoteric book about living in two hallways and four small rooms; and "According to the Order of Nature (We too are Cosmos Made)," a text–image hybrid which looks at the language used against the LGBT community since the dawn of LGBT oppression and turns it on its head.

**Kate Millett** was an American feminist writer, educator, artist, and activist. Born in St. Paul, Minnesota in 1934, Millett was educated at the University of Minnesota, Oxford University, and Columbia University, where she obtained her PhD with Distinction. Best known for her groundbreaking book *Sexual Politics*, long credited as the "bible of the Second Wave feminist movement," Millett is the author of twelve other books including *The Loony-Bin Trip*, a deeply personal account of her struggle against involuntary confinement and a diagnosis of manic depression. As an artist with a career spanning some sixty years, Millett exhibited her art and sculpture internationally, and, in 1978, she founded an art colony for women. Millett was a tireless advocate for women's rights and the rights of the mentally ill. Described by *The New York Times* as one of the most important Americans of the twentieth century, Millett died in Paris in September 2017.

**Calvin Rey Moen** wrote his first fantasy story at the age of four and then lost it somewhere. His mom is still sad about that and brings it up all the time. His most recent fantasy story was published in *JONATHAN* (since renamed *CALLISTO*), a journal of queer fiction. He received a master of fine arts degree in creative writing but gets uncomfortable when talking about it. Calvin works as an educator and advocate for cognitive liberty and against institutional force and coercion. He also writes songs about starting fires, queer sex, and ghosts, and he performs as half of the synth-pop-post-rock duo badweatherfriend.

**Thomas Mondragon**, LMFT, has a private practice in West Hollywood, California, focused on the principles of gay-centered and affirmative psychotherapy. He has extensive clinical experience in dual-diagnosis substance abuse treatment. He is also a founding instructor in Antioch University Los Angeles' LGBT Specialization, the first program of its kind devoted to academic and clinical instruction in LGBTQ affirmative theory and practice necessary for effective therapeutic work and psychological healing with LGBTQ clients. He was instrumental in creating two training sites for LGBT Specialization students to gain clinical experience—one serving the LGBTQ HIV-impacted community, and the other, Colors LGBTQ Youth

Counseling Center, serving a diverse spectrum of LGBTQ youth in Los Angeles. As affiliate faculty in Antioch's Masters of Arts in Clinical Psychology program, Thomas has taught classes including LGBT Affirmative Psychotherapy, Intercultural Transpersonal and Depth Psychology and Gay Male Identity: Sex, Love, Intimacy & Other Community Issues.

**Tanisha Neely** is a passionate yogi, writer, and teacher. She is the founder and director of RESILIENT Yoga, a nonprofit organization committed to empowering people to reduce stress, be well, and face the challenges of life with resilience through the practice of yoga. Tanisha also serves as Associate Faculty in English at Indiana University—Purdue University Indianapolis (IUPUI) and Marian University, where she teaches composition and literature.

**James Penha**, a native New Yorker, has lived for the past quarter-century in Indonesia. He has been nominated for Pushcart Prizes in fiction and poetry, and his LGBTQ speculative story "Leaves," also set in Indonesia, was a finalist for the 2017 Saint & Sinners Literary Festival Short Fiction Contest. His essay "It's Been a Long Time Coming" was featured in *The New York Times* "Modern Love" column in April 2016. Penha edits *TheNewVerse.News*, an online journal of current-events poetry.

**Joseph Ruggiero**, PhD, is a clinical psychologist who graduated from Fordham University's doctoral program. He has worked in the field of addiction for more than twenty years. As Assistant Clinical Director of the Addiction Institute of Mount Sinai, he oversees all outpatient programs at Mount Sinai West Hospital. In addition, he is a co-founder and director of the Crystal Clear Program, which addresses the issue of methamphetamine use in gay and bisexual men. He has co-authored an article about the program and has given many talks at conferences, grand rounds, and other forums. Ruggiero has made several television appearances to inform people about this concern, and he maintains a private practice.

**Stephanie Schroeder** is a writer based in New York City. She has published works in *The Guardian, Curve Magazine, Brooklyn Magazine, Healthline, Life of the Law, Lambda Literary Review*, and many other outlets. Her nonfiction work has been anthologized in *That's Revolting: Queer Strategies for Resisting Assimilation, Here Come the Brides: Reflections on Lesbian Love and Marriage*, and *Easy to Love, But Hard to Live With: Real People, Invisible Disabilities, True Stories*. Schroeder is also the author of the memoir *Beautiful Wreck: Sex, Lies & Suicide* (2012). She works part-time as a peer advocate at a mental health shelter for homeless women ages forty-five and older. Find additional information about Stephanie and her writing at stephanieschroederauthor.com

**Kevin Shaw** lives in London, Ontario, where he completed a PhD in Canadian Literature at Western University. His poems and essays have appeared in *The Malahat Review, Plenitude, Contemporary Verse 2, The Fiddlehead,* and *The New Quarterly.* He received *Arc Poetry Magazine*'s Poem of the Year award and the Grand Prize in the *PRISM international* Poetry Contest. He is the author of *Smaller Hours* (2017).

**Gabrielle Jordan Stein** is a New York City-based interdisciplinary artist. She is a queer, chronically ill sex workers' rights activist, a public health student, a full-spectrum doula, a yoga teacher, a writer, an internationally exhibited and award-winning visual artist, and a plant mom. Her play, work, and research all explore the intersections of tenderness and pain.

**Teresa Theophano** is a New York State-licensed social worker and freelance writer/ editor who co-founded the New York City Queer Mental Health Initiative (QMHI), an LGBTQ mental health peer support network in collaboration with the Brooklyn Community Pride Center, in July 2014. Since graduating from Hunter College School of Social Work with an MSW the same year that her book *Queer Quotes* (2004) was published, she has worked and volunteered with LGBTQ communities at numerous organizations including Rainbow Heights Club, the New York City LGBT Community Center, and Queers for Economic Justice. Additionally, she has taught as an adjunct professor at the New York City College of Technology—part of the City University of New York—and she completed a year-long training program at the Institute for Integrative Nutrition, as well as graduate courses in public health. Teresa has been involved in social justice movements for more than two decades and is interested in further exploring radical and holistic approaches to mental health. She currently serves on the board of directors of a queer homeless youth program, Trinity Place Shelter. Her writing has appeared on websites such as xojane.com and glbtq.com and in anthologies including *The Queer Encyclopedia of the Visual Arts* (2004) and *Queerly Loving* (2017).

**Kai Cheng Thom**, MSW, MSc Couple & Family Therapy, is a writer, performer, and psychotherapist based in Montreal and Toronto, unceded Indigenous territories. She is the author of the award-winning novel *Fierce Femmes and Notorious Liars: A Dangerous Trans Girl's Confabulous Memoir,* as well as the poetry collection *A Place Called No Homeland* and the children's book *From the Stars in the Sky to the Fish in the Sea.* Kai Cheng has been published widely on issues of gender, race, and mental health.

**Juan Antonio Trujillo**'s academic and creative work explores intersections between Latinx identity, queerness, and his upbringing in a devout Mormon family. As full-time faculty in the School of Language, Culture, and Society at Oregon State

University, Tony offers courses on minoritized language communities and the role of foodways in constructing ethnic identity. He has published scholarly articles on queering the Spanish as a Heritage Language classroom and the dynamics of the mixed Anglo/Latinx college language classroom, and he is a regular reader of poetry and creative nonfiction with the Portland-based Latinx writers collective Los Porteños. His short autobiographical documentary *Companions: Lessons from Gay Mormon Missionaries* was an official selection for Ethnografilm 2015 and winner of best LGBT film at the 2015 Oregon Independent Film Festival.

**J. R. Sullivan Voss** is a non-binary transgender artist living and creating in the DC Metro area. He has participated in recent local art shows with mixed-media work, writes occasional poetry, regularly crafts, and can be reached online with the handle @doitforthesulz on Instagram and offline at various local venues displaying his work. Sullivan believes in the power of art to connect and heal and encourages the readers of this book to create something every day, no matter how small or insignificant it may seem. The world can always use more voices, not less.

**Kathryn Wagner** is a staff psychologist at the Washington DC VA Medical Hospital. She received her PhD in clinical psychology at Duquesne University in Pittsburgh and completed a postdoctoral residency in LGBT Healthcare at a VA setting. Her clinical interests include LGBT-affirming psychotherapy and psychotherapy with minority populations. She has previously published in both psychology and creative writing journals and enjoys research that centers on the intersection of psychology, queer, and disability studies.

**Asher J. Wickell** is a specialist in change-work and transitions of many kinds, a one-time girl and approximate man, whose best answer to gender is: *it's complicated.* Said another way, he's a marriage and family therapist, which is a cool job, but a seriously dated title. Personally and professionally, he strives to center curiosity, creativity, and flexibility and to support others in doing the same. Asher holds an abiding interest in ambiguity—in the tense, in-between places that he regards as origin points of radical and redemptive change. He suspects this has to do with being a therapist in possession of his own SPMI (severe and persistently mentally ill) diagnosis and also being queer in Kansas. In particular, Asher sees the complex, conflictive parts of our humanity as unique sites for engaging and transforming traumatic experience, negotiating and navigating good consent, and exploring new dynamics in our gendered, sexual, and relational lives.

**Paula J. Williams** is a person-centred psychotherapist, supervisor, and trainer living in Scotland. She has extensive experience in working with GSDR issues and working for several LGBTQI organizations as a counselor and supervisor, and she has presented at a number of LGBTQI conferences. She specializes in trauma, offering trauma support to organizations such as the courts and first responders, as well as critical incident support in addition to her work with survivors of interpersonal trauma. She believes the primary question in therapy should not be "What's wrong with you?" but "What happened to you?" and her current professional interests are focused on questions of identity, power, and sociopolitical context and its influence on both client and therapist. When not working, she is a singer in a folk band and loves to dance.

**Chana Wilson** is a storyteller, retired psychotherapist, and former radio producer. She is the author of the award-winning memoir *Riding Fury Home,* from which "Not Our Fault" was adapted. In her twenty-five years in private practice, Wilson was an LGBTQ-affirmative psychotherapist. She currently blogs on the Huffington Post in "Queer Voices." Her essays and stories have appeared in multiple anthologies, as an editor's pick on *Salon,* and in online and print journals. You can hear excerpts of her 1974 radio interview with her lesbian mother on her website on the "Listen" page: www.RidingFuryHome.com. Since the mid-eighties, Wilson has been playing percussion with the women's samba band Sistah Boom. With their wild samba beat, they energize San Francisco's Dyke March, Gay Pride, and now women's and resistance marches.

**Lucy Winer** is a pioneering documentary filmmaker whose award-winning work has helped bring LGBT topics to mainstream audiences for more than thirty years. Her directing credits include *Greetings from Washington D.C., Silent Pioneers, Golden Threads,* and the groundbreaking, four-part public television series *Positive: Life with HIV.* Winer's most recent film, *Kings Park: Stories from an American Mental Institution,* chronicles her commitment to a state hospital at age seventeen following a series of suicide attempts and her subsequent journey to understand her own history and ultimately that of the mental healthcare crisis in the United States today. In "Knowing Reynolds," Winer reframes the subject matter of *Kings Park* in the context of a queer love story. Her past writing credits include two one-act plays written for a lesbian feminist theater troupe in the 1970s. Learn more at http:// kingsparkmovie.com

**Sara Zaanti** works in the mental health arena, is a dedicated advocate and voice for those with mental illness, and looks forward to the day that they can write about parenting with a mental illness and not have to use a nom de plume. Sara is genderqueer/transmasculine and lives with their wife and two teenage children in New York City.

# INTRODUCTION

*Stephanie Schroeder and Teresa Theophano*

Because we have found that being queer in a straight world can be downright crazymaking, we have chosen to use the term "headcase" as a reclamation. This anthology explores the evolution of queer identity as it interfaces with mental health, details experiences that foster resilience and stress-related growth among individuals, and examines what comes *after* sexual/gender minority status is disentangled from its historical association with the concept of mental illness.

Reclamation in lesbian, gay, bisexual, transgender, and queer (LGBTQ) communities has come in many forms. Terminology such as "queer," "dyke," and "fag" has been embraced by different segments of our communities, while some under the LGBTQ umbrella have categorically rejected these words. The pink and black triangles used by the Nazis to identify and shame male homosexuals and "asocials" (including lesbians) in the concentration camps have become queer and feminist symbols of solidarity and strength. The Stonewall Rebellion is a touchstone for the modern-day LGBTQ rights movement, though, of course, LGBTQ people have existed throughout history and rebelled in their own ways. LGBTQ folks these days are "queering" traditions and institutions: marriage, the family, workplaces, monetary systems, literature, art, and much more, including how we discuss and view people living with mental health issues.

Both of us are out queer women living with what has been described as mental illness. As a social worker and a peer advocate, respectively, we believe that the "craziness" of many members of LGBTQ communities is at least partly a response to the homophobia and transphobia—arguably forms of madness itself—in the world around us. This point is being driven home all the more at the time of this writing in January 2018, one year into Donald Trump's presidency, as we continue to face the loss of protections that were precarious to begin with. Our communities have been scrambling to ensure their own safety.

Does the infrastructure of our mental healthcare system consider which factors are chemical and which are environmental when people in our communities feel like we are "going nuts?" Some of us simply cannot carry out the functions of our day-to-day lives unless we remain actively engaged in ongoing professional treatment. At the same time, it is foolish to deny the ways in which infrequently challenged cultural phenomena of hetero- and cis-normativity contribute greatly to our depression, anxiety, and other psychological difficulties. Real or perceived minority status and subsequent disenfranchisement make us vulnerable to being labeled as sick. This leads us to ask, really, who is a headcase here: those who are pathologizing us or we who are being pathologized.

We are apprehensive about an increasing prevalence of diagnosed mental illnesses, which have already been especially high in LGBTQ communities in the current political climate. As organizers and advocates, we interpret this as both a reflection of the extent to which heterosexism and cissexism are ingrained into our culture and as a clarion call for appropriate, culturally competent care to become much more widely available. By this we mean treatment that takes into account the marginalization of LGBTQ people while affirming our strengths, resilience, and identities.

We initially conceptualized *Headcase* in 2014 as a curated collection of personal pieces including essays, poems, illustrations, and photographs by writers and artists both established and new. We wanted the anthology to explore themes of mental health, mental illness, and experiences of mental healthcare systems by members of LGBTQ communities. In early 2016, we expanded the scope of the anthology to include perspectives from members of LGBTQ communities with clinical expertise and professional mental health credentials. We sought to broach the topics of mental health and mental illness in LGBTQ communities from myriad perspectives to present a broader, more in-depth, and balanced conversation. We have made a concerted effort to create a bridge between consumers and clinicians, choosing not to solicit clinical contributions that would replicate the traditional "arm's length," detached, and ostensibly objective professional mode of writing about, speaking to, and treating consumers. We took this approach to reach a broader audience that includes lay readers, consumers, academics, mental health providers, and medical professionals both within and outside of LGBTQ communities.

We chose final submissions to include in the anthology based on subject matter, strength of writing or artwork, and demographics, to ensure an inclusive array of contributors. As two White cis women, we remain conscious of not only our day-to-day privilege, but also the privilege of being in a position to get our work published. Thus, we aimed to include voices that are sorely missing from the literature.

We chose general categories for the table of contents of this book, yet all of the pieces in *Headcase* could fall into any of the five categories we created since these contributions are simultaneously highly personal and truly universal. They are "Stories of Survival" and also "Conversations About Mental Health and Wellness," along with "Poetics of Mental Health and Wellness," as well as part of the other categories.

*Headcase*'s expressive reflections on LGBTQ mental health and wellness comprise a vanguard of today's writing and art on those topics. Myriad texts and artwork within the collection question whether existing models of mental healthcare support, services, and especially diagnosis are useful to our contributors and the LGBTQ communities surrounding them.

Some contributors find current definitions of wellness and health limiting and exclusionary. J. M. Ellison's "Bad Penny" reframes as a mental health issue living under extreme political oppression. Ellison posits that those privileged to never experience—or witness—such severe and ongoing oppression firsthand may not understand the psychological repercussions.

A number of *Headcase*'s writers and artists illustrate how they create community and find support among peers and other like-minded folks. We hope seeing their work will help others think about new ways to create and live the lives they crave, regardless of the labels they may be assigned by mental health professionals.

To that end, Sullivan Voss's thirteen-panel comic "Sisyphus (or: Rocks Fall and Everyone Dies)" is a striking tale of one peer's treatment, paralleling exhaustive efforts to become well with the endless task of Sisyphus in Greek mythology. An art diary reflecting on a genderqueer person's multiple psychiatric hospitalizations, the work chronicles the ways in which these experiences impacted Voss's views on gender, race, class, and mental health. Voss's work is a singular visual contribution among the many substantive narratives in this anthology.

Meanwhile, the need for clinical cultural competence is explored in a number of *Headcase* contributions, including Arlene Istar Lev's "Queer-Affirmative Therapy." Lev, a psychotherapist, professor, and writer, explores what it means to be truly queer- and trans-affirmative in psychotherapy practice. Her essay touches on how LGBTQ behavior and identity have been historically pathologized, and she offers guidance for practitioners as well as advice for clients in therapy seeking competent, respectful care. Thomas Mondragon, a psychotherapist in private practice as well as an affiliate faculty member at Antioch University, teaching an LGBT specialization in a master's program in clinical psychology, emphasizes the importance of seeing and hearing the pain of LGBTQ clients who have experienced trauma, oppression, and discrimination because of their sexual orientation and/or gender identity in his essay, "Liberating The Big Pink Elephant in the Therapy Room." Mondragon further discusses the healing power of an understanding, culturally competent therapist who reinforces the incredible resilience and multiple strengths of LGBTQ clients.

Other contributions represent not only the lived experience of peers, but also partnerships between peers and practitioners and the accounts of mental health professionals who disclose their dual status. "Informed Consent," Ash Wickell's internal monologue about a day in the life of psychotherapy practice for a Kansas-based trans therapist with his own mental health concerns, is a powerful testimony about the delicate balance a therapist with dual status must preserve and the boundaries he must maintain with his clients—and the fears and fantasies of both parties.

Some of our practitioner contributions question the omnipotent role of the clinician and suggest ways in which LGBTQ providers and recipients of mental health services might work together. They articulate our own belief in a collaborative approach to patient goals that places the specific needs of LGBTQ individuals and communities at the center of both clinical practice and health activism.

As many LGBTQ mental health professionals frequently point out, homosexuality was not removed from the American Psychological Association's mental health "bible," the *Diagnostic and Statistical Manual of Mental Disorders* (*DSM*), as a diagnosable mental illness until 1973. This is particularly relevant as transgender communities gain further visibility: Gender Identity Disorder, with which transgender people must be diagnosed in order to legally receive gender-affirming treatments and surgeries, was removed from the *DSM IV* and replaced with Gender Dysphoria in the *DSM V*, released in May 2013. Psychologist Guy Albert and psychiatrist and playwright Guy Glass both provide history about the *DSM* and its continued use in their respective contributions, "Fix Me Please: I'm Gay" and "*Doctor Anonymous*: A Play, and a Lesson in Medical Ethics."

Meanwhile, Chana Wilson's poignant essay "Not Our Fault" lends a personal perspective to such salient issues of historical trauma and mistreatment of LGBTQ clients. Wilson, a psychotherapist in private practice as well as an award-winning writer, details in her piece her mother's battle to become well after experiencing forced institutionalization and multiple invasive treatments to "cure" her of her homosexuality in the 1950s. Suffice it to say that living through this harrowing period alongside her mother inexorably altered both of their lives, and Wilson frames their survival in beautifully articulated prose.

Our own essays in *Headcase* reflect our struggles to become and remain well. Both of us are fortunate enough to be ensconced in a loose-knit radical queer community that supports us in our personal and professional lives in New York City. Teresa spent time years ago working at Rainbow Heights Club (RHC) in Brooklyn—the country's only government-funded support and advocacy program, known as a "clubhouse," for LGBTQ people with psychiatric disorders. Club members sometimes spoke to her about being among "their kind," and she realized that, while wary of the divisiveness identity politics can create, she related to this and even began to embrace it.

As Teresa details in her essay "The Family Legacy Ends Here," her two ill-fated attempts to discontinue her mental health treatment in years past were debilitating;

as staff at RHC, she discovered a workplace setting in which being queer as well as a consumer was no cause for shame. Teresa found that learning how many people have avoided hospitalization because of the program, and how consumers felt a sense of "coming home" and being among one's peers without judgment or pressure to conform, was a revelation. RHC has been a striking exception to what seems an unfortunate rule in clinical approaches to the LGBTQ consumer population, as the program's executive director Dr. Christian Huygen details in his essay "On Listening to Clients."

Huygen notes that the structure of RHC entails a collaborative decision-making process between club members and staff, and he supports and facilitates the participation of club members and other stakeholders in city- and statewide advocacy work. "Recipients of care are the experts on what helps and what doesn't," Huygen writes, and he explicates his commitment to ensuring consumer voices are heard and their ideas are effectively utilized.

Stephanie has developed a great deal of her own expertise in discerning what helps and what doesn't. Diagnosed with bipolar disorder at age thirty-seven after two suicide attempts, she had been engaged in weekly psychotherapy for many years when these events occurred. No therapist with whom she had worked possessed the insight, skill, or cultural competence to identify and understand the attenuating effects of the societal oppression, anti-LGBT sentiment, and intimate partner violence in Stephanie's life. When she was hospitalized for a third suicide attempt and then rejected for treatment because she made "too much money" despite subsisting on unemployment insurance, Stephanie became an aggressive self-advocate, directing her own mental healthcare and securing her prescribed medications even while lacking health insurance.

In her personal-political essay "Crowdsourcing My Antipsychotic," Stephanie describes the harsh reality she has faced interacting with the US mental healthcare system. An outspoken advocate in the New York City LGBTQ community, she is known for assisting others in finding affordable mental healthcare, including resources for free or low-cost prescription medication.

While we both believe that medication can be a useful component of treatment, we also observe how traditional mental health treatment modalities can fail to adequately address crucial social and environmental factors—such as racism, classism, and ableism—in addition to lesbian, gay, bisexual, and especially queer and trans identity. As a social worker, Teresa notes that while social work's historical focus on the needs of marginalized communities should ensure that the profession remains inextricably linked to issues of social justice, its activist aspects sometimes get lost in the milieu of clinical practice. We encourage all readers, whether or not they are social workers or consider themselves activists, to lead advocacy efforts in their communities and on their own behalves. The appendix to this book includes information on grassroots organizations such as the US-based Icarus Project, the NYC Queer Mental Health Initiative, and the UK's MindOut, all of which help facilitate connection and the building of peer-led movements.

These types of movements, and alternatives and challenges to the medical model and traditional methods of diagnosis, are the focus of contributor Calvin Rey Moen's "Surviving Science, or: How I Learned to Stop Worrying and Love Being Mad and Queer." Moen has organized with the Icarus Project, works within the psychiatric survivors' movement, and urges readers to examine common views of mental illness, puncturing the notion that acceptance, support, and healing must be externally driven and professionally mediated. He narrates his self-acceptance as a young trans activist within the framework of radical madness and in the face of familial rejection.

It is stories like these that will help us open up a larger conversation and create a space in which people can share their experiences and go deep into topics that are so rarely discussed openly. We need to document our lives in our own language, framing our issues in ways that make sense to us and to our peers; the world needs an expanded, written record of them. *Headcase* is a starting point and a way in which we can further chip away at the stigma and shame that has colored many of our lives. We believe this book can be a springboard for more scholarly investigation and publication, altering social attitudes, public policy changes, and programmatic shifts regarding the experiences of peers and consumers as well as clinicians who have dual status.

We look to mental healthcare professionals to commit not only to providing affirmative, culturally competent care, but to listening carefully to the voices of those on the receiving end of their services and helping ensure that those voices are amplified. This is why we have spent so much time, love, and care putting together *Headcase*: to ensure this book speaks volumes for those of us who are able to speak up as well as those who have not yet found their voice, but will, we hope, one day be able to join in this important conversation.

—Teresa Theophano and Stephanie Schroeder,
New York City, January 2018

# DISCLAIMER

All opinions are those of the individual contributors and not Oxford University Press. Given the personal nature of many of these pieces, and out of respect for the privacy of people involved, we have endeavored to disguise the identities of individuals, companies, and groups and organizations discussed.

# Headcase

## PART I

# Conversations About Mental Health and Wellness

# 1

## FALLING BETWEEN THE CRACKS OF QUEER AND BLACK

*Tanisha Neely*

Invisible hands grab me without warning. First, there's the squeezing of my chest and the feeling of being smothered. Then the leaping of my heart up my throat and its crashing back down into the pit of my stomach like a meteor landing. It's hard to tell if what follows next is happening all at once or a quick sequence of events: hot flash, cold sweat, tingling toes, trembling hands, rapid breath, and a racing heart trying in vain to outrun a raging sea of mixed emotions.

* * *

I have a general discomfort with sentiments. They overwhelm me. Even the ones that are supposed to feel good are uncomfortable. I'm told that emotions are a necessary part of the human experience. This may be true; however, I personally find only a few of them useful. Fear is the most useful of them all. I can always rely on it to ground me in the present moment, make me pay close attention and do whatever is necessary to survive my current situation.

When it happened, I can't recall. It could have been after my child eyes watched my mother's lover beat her head into the concrete from our upstairs apartment window. Or maybe it was after witnessing the violent murder of my neighbor who sat slumped under a San Diego palm tree for hours before an ambulance arrived to take him away in the bag. All I know is that, at some point in my young life, I began to identify as a rational species and concluded that I must be a surviving descendant of the planet Vulcan. It took my father years to help me master the Vulcan salute.

Fear is among the strongest and most violent of the emotions.
—Captain Spock

* * *

When I board my plane from Geneva, Switzerland, I am deliriously tired after ten fourteen-hour work days compounded by moving in and out of various time zones. I'm heading back in time to Indianapolis, Indiana, where I belong. I try hard not to think of the eleven-hour flight in my cramped coach seat.

The plane plateaus and a flight attendant comes around to offer us an early lunch. I order a glass of Merlot with my turkey sandwich to calm my nerves, hoping that I'll sleep through most of the flight. No luck. Instead, I feel light-headed and sick to my stomach. Then, for no reason that I can think of, my heart jumps like someone has snuck up from behind and scared the shit out of me! I'm hot. I can make breathing motions, but I can't feel any air coming into me.

I haphazardly climb over my neighbor to get to the center aisle, thinking that standing and a trip to the restroom might help me feel better. As I make my way to the back of the plane, I find a line of passengers waiting for the loo. I, too, stand there waiting, heart palpitations gaining speed. I look around for a place to lean and catch a glimpse of the cabin door, briefly imagining it bursting open and sucking me into the atmosphere, then plunging me into the icy Atlantic. At the entrance of the plane's galley, my hot sweaty hands find cool metal counters with semi-round edges to hold on to. My eyes connect with the eyes of the flight attendant across from me moments before my body gives in to the weight of gravity pulling me through the floor into a silent black sea of nothing. In the distance, I can hear a faint voice calling me.

"Ma'am? Can you hear me? Ma'am? Ma'am?!"

I want to verbally answer her, but I am silently screaming on the inside. Am I dying? No! No, no, no, no, no! Tamiko is waiting for me. Babe!? I have babies. I have four babies. My babies! Michael!? Anne!? Abby!? Goober!?

* * *

Tamiko appears in the hospital emergency room to find me half asleep and entangled in wires monitoring my heartbeat and oxygen intake. She looks at me with a pity that still disturbs me. With no regard for the wires, she leans over to lay her head on my chest and the weight of her body halfway over mine. My fingers grab the roots of her locks. I take note of her naturally arched eyebrows and the heavy black lashes that line the lids of her deep-set eyes that are always searching me. Small dark moles gather along her cheek bones like a constellation of little black stars on her cocoa-colored face. She is self-conscious about them, and occasionally talks of having them removed.

My EKG is fine. My oxygen intake is fine. My iron levels are fine. My blood sugar is fine. The ER doctor expresses concern about my stress levels. Other than that, I am the picture of health and released with orders to rest and follow-up with my family doctor.

\* \* \*

"If everything is fine, then why don't I *feel* fine?" I ask Dr. S. during my follow-up visit. "I haven't been out of the house in days. I'm scared to leave home. They never happen at home. But I can't stay home forever. I have a job to do, soccer games to attend, a wedding to plan, people to take care of. . . . "

DIAGNOSIS: Generalized Anxiety Disorder (GAD) with symptoms of Agoraphobia

Dr. S. gives me a prescription for a sedative used to treat seizures, panic disorder, and anxiety in exchange for my promise to see a counselor and work on reducing my stress levels. I've always been fearful of drugs, especially habit-forming ones, due to my mother's history of addiction. But today, I go straight to the pharmacy to have the prescription filled and take my first dose in the car with no water. They taste like sugar-free Smarties.

I spend a few days adjusting to the drowsiness. Eating before I take them helps. Each day, life feels a little more livable. But the medication alone does not return to me a sense of well-being. Right now, it's as a pharmacologic crutch to help me make the journey toward "wellness," whatever that means, wherever that is.

\* \* \*

Being home feels strange. Foreign. Like being in a hotel made up to *look* like my home. Nothing feels real. Not even Tamiko and the kids. I go through the motions of hugging, kissing, and cooking for these strangers living in this hotel with me. Each day the strength of the black hole, a depressive force hovering over me since I could remember, grows. Normally, I am mindful enough to keep from being sucked into it. My strategies for survival: yoga, cooking, music, sex, sunlit windows, and orange everywhere.

\* \* \*

I am apprehensive about making an appointment to see a psychiatrist. I had seen a licensed clinical social worker off and on in my twenties to work through the process of coming out and identifying as a queer Black woman while married with children. But this situation is unlike any other I've experienced. I am not dealing with a person or a concrete problem that can be reasoned with or solved. I am dealing with a phantom in my head that can disable me physically and emotionally at any given moment without my permission. I am dealing with a direct assault on my power, resilience, and image of myself as a "Strong Black Woman." I am dealing with an attack on my we that is coming from inside of *me*.

The Black community in which I was raised doesn't necessarily stigmatize mental health issues or getting professional help. Instead, it glorifies the myth of the "Strong Black Woman" and worships her ability to suffer in silence and beauty. It praises her for carrying backbreaking burdens and enduring crushing abuse while continuing to hold her head up high and smile. Ironically, the Black community responds to mental illness in the same way it responds to homosexuality. It isn't real. And if it is, you bet' not tell nobody but God.

Once, while talking to my children's grandmother on the phone about how I'd been feeling, I was commanded to "Snap out of it and pull yourself together!" and told, "You can't let your kids see you like this." With time, I come to understand that there is no honor or healing to be found in pretending to be stronger than I really am. With time, I learn to insist on my freedom to fall apart if I need to, fully believing that if I can look life in face without fear and see things for what they really are, I can make sense of my broken pieces and put myself back together in a healthier and more sustainable way.

My first appointment is with a well-respected psychiatrist, Dr. B., who is also a Black woman. I make the mistake of believing that since we are both women of color, she will be able to connect with me in a more personal way. However, when I mention my wife, she pauses to clarify. "So, you are in a homosexual relationship?" she asks in perfect English laced with a Nigerian accent. Her stoic use of the word "homosexual" to describe my relationship instantly turns me cold. Am I crazy? Well, technically, yes. I am. So I could be misinterpreting her, right? For all I know, she could simply be clarifying my relationship status (although she doesn't stop to clarify much else). There is no further discussion about my relationship with Tamiko.

As the interview progresses, I also make the mistake of telling her that I have *at times* taken more medication than prescribed by my primary care physician when my anxiety attacks are unmanageable. Instead of addressing why my anxiety attacks were peaking in intensity after a year of being stable, she attempts to refer me to a state-funded drug rehabilitation center in the inner city that serves a large population of poor Black patients for "detox." As an educated, upper-middle-class professional who lives in the suburbs and has private insurance, I am confused.

Detox! From what? I am flooded with reminders of the racist and classist undertones often encountered when it comes to dealing with "addiction." I know from personal experience that America's misguided war on drugs has been a war on people—people of color in particular. Growing up, I watched my mother go in and out of court-mandated twelve-step programs and noticed that when people of color have issues with addictive behaviors, we are demonized in ways that White people are not. I noticed how people of color in need of treatment are criminalized and humiliated while White people with privilege are treated as real patients in need of medical care.

My mother Vivian was well into her fifth month when Mercy Hospital staff told her she was pregnant with me, her first-born baby girl. I imagine that the news of my existence disturbed her at the time, considering she had been rushed there for passing out after injecting an opioid cocktail in her veins. Regardless, I arrived uninvited into her life when she was twenty-one years old. Her love was soft and cold like fresh snow. Even as a little girl, I knew her, and I knew that it was not always her intent to be distant and hurtful. While she was never entirely cured of her many heartbreaks and addictions, as we both grew, she learned to manage them and love me with a limp.

I often underestimated my mother's intelligence and love for me, as many young people do. In my "giftedness," I looked down on her home-grown wisdom, adding insult to her many injuries, especially when I corrected her eleventh-grade southern English. And, of course, I blamed her for everything. I blamed her for being poor. I blamed her for being uneducated. I blamed her for being depressed, abused, addicted, and unable to keep a man. But, most of all, I blamed her for being weak.

Her sister was weak, too! Or so I thought. In the early '90's, my aunt Mini left my baby cousins Lamar (age two) and Marcella (age three) home alone while she went on a late-night crack hunt. I remember the day my mother told me they had both died in a house fire. I remember the rage. I remember the guilt. I remember my aunt's imprisonment and the discovery of her untreated schizophrenia. I remember her unsupported release back into the world. I remember the day my sister called to tell me Aunt Mini was found murdered in a San Diego alley.

\* \* \*

I am a Black woman. However, unlike my mother Vivian and my aunt Mini, I have socioeconomic advantages. I am college-educated in the field of medical science and clinical research, and my individual income is significantly higher than that of the average working-class American household. I am not subjected to the perpetual angst of living in crime-infested neighborhoods anymore. I understand how to evaluate a suggested course of medical treatment through research and to respectfully disagree with my doctor and others in authority. As such, I refuse rehab, explaining to Dr. B. that I did not see any addiction issues to address. On the contrary, my fear of addiction kept me from drinking until I was twenty-seven years old. While I agree that I am currently dependent on medication to manage my chronic anxiety disorder, I see no difference between my chemical dependency on anti-anxiety medication and my father's chemical dependency on insulin, which his own body no longer makes. She finally concedes and refers me to an outpatient treatment facility closer to my own home.

Over the course of my treatment, I am pushed multiple combinations of sedatives, selective serotonin reuptake inhibitors (SSRIs), other antidepressants, antipsychotics, and antihypertensives. My refusal to take most of these drugs is not uncommon. Mental Health America notes that "African-Americans were less likely to take an antidepressant for treatment of depression; only 34% would take one if it were prescribed by a doctor."

Many people of color still have a deep distrust of the medical community. Why wouldn't we? America's history of biological warfare and medical abuse against people of color is well documented. We have not forgotten the Tuskegee Airmen Experiments in which Black men serving America's military were unknowingly inoculated with syphilis and left to die untreated, so scientists could see how the disease progressed and use that knowledge to cure White Americans. Nor have we forgotten how Black women were involuntary sterilized and forced to undergo many experimental procedures without the benefit of anesthesia, antibiotics, or wound care. This, too, was done in the name of science, so that the knowledge earned through our pain could be used to perfect lifesaving procedures for the benefit of White Americans.

\* \* \*

The kids think it's cool that I see a psychiatrist.

Goober (age twelve): "Are they going to put one of those jackets on you?"
Abby (age thirteen): "I've always wanted to see a psychiatrist. I think it would be cool to lay on a couch and tell somebody my problems."
Anne (age sixteen): "You get to see a psychiatrist? Why didn't you tell me? Can I interview them for my biomedical science class?"
Michael (age nineteen): "My mother IS crazy! Now I can tell everybody I get it from you."

\* \* \*

I am an hour and a half late to the day program this morning. Given my propensity to be fucked by the universe, I decide to check on my short-term disability claim. As I fear, my claim has been denied and is now in appeal. Who appealed it? I don't even remember getting a decision letter for this claim, so I know I didn't. Or did I? My mind is mush much of the time. Maybe I did get something and overlooked it, again. How could I overlook something so important? I have no income. The holidays are coming, and I have gone from $72,000 a year to qualifying for food stamps.

Why am I acting like such an invalid? This is why Tamiko "lovingly" took away my debit card from the joint account that I keep overdrawing. This is why Abby micromanages me to ensure that I get her to soccer practices on time. This is why Goober checks that the stove is off after I am done cooking. This is why I cry myself into another anxiety attack.

I try to accomplish at least one thing a day. Today, my one thing is picking up a short-term disability form from my doctor's office and mailing it to the insurance company. If I can manage this, they will make my credit card payments for me as long as I am unemployed. I *need* to do this so that I can prove that I'm not totally incapacitated. I drive two minutes up the road to the doctor's office only to find that I never submitted the form for completion. Later, I find it sitting under a pile of mail on my desk.

I walk into group therapy a little after noon. Marla is talking about problems with her children. Dr. T. encourages Chantel to talk about her challenges with her stepson who lies, disrespects her, talks back, blames her for everything, and takes no responsibility. I am reminded of my son Michael. I miss my baby boy. Fucking asshole!

I break open. And just like that, I shatter with the splendor and frailty of a sparkling crystal glass that has been pitched against a wall. I cry and cry and cry myself into another anxiety attack in front of everyone. I am still crying and breathing and crying when the group leaves the room for lunch. Dr. T. stays behind to give me a supportive hug. I don't usually hug strangers. But he has a strong grip and the kindest blue eyes. I stay for a while. Then I go eat lunch alone with Dr. A.

* * *

Once upon a time, the church was a therapeutic place. There, I could clap my hands, play tambourine, sing healing hymns and songs of thanksgiving, off key, without judgment. There, I could break down to my knees and purge my heart in prayer and supplication. There, someone would carry me to the altar if they had to and help me lay my burdens down. But we can't go there anymore. Tamiko, who is now my wife and a founding member of her predominantly Black church, sang in the choir and taught Sunday school for years before being exiled for breaking the "don't ask don't tell" rule by coming out as a lesbian and publicly announcing our wedding engagement. I'd left the Black church years before due to their suppression of women and their blatant homophobia. Still, I visited CC Baptist Church with Tamiko and Mama Neely on occasion. And with mixed emotions I'd enjoy the singing, dancing, and praying while dreading what nonsense would come out of the preacher's mouth during the sermon. "That's not love. That's lust!" was his only understanding of our relationship.

\* \* \*

In another group session at the day program, we are talking about managing our relationships when I mention my "wife" on multiple occasions in the same manner that other patients in the group reference situations with their spouses or significant others. I can see the group, including a Black man who is involuntarily there to deal with anger management issues, quickly absorb the shock of my bluntness and then move on to the issue of discussion without comment. No one is ever rude. Never an ugly stare.

During a break, Dr. T. asks me in private, "Does it ever occur to you that other people might be uncomfortable with how you discuss your relationship with your *wife*?"

"Should it?"

\* \* \*

My disability claim is denied because the underwriters say my medical condition isn't bad enough to prevent me from working in some capacity, even at McDonald's. My unemployment claim is denied because I am unable to work or accept work at this time for medical reasons. My medical insurance lapses. The state of Indiana does not legally recognize my relationship with Tamiko so she is unable to carry me on any of her insurance plans. I am uninsured now and therefore released from treatment untreated.

\* \* \*

Freedom is strangely ephemeral. It is something like breathing; one only becomes acutely aware of its importance when one is choking.
—William E. Simon

\* \* \*

My journey toward healing leads me to Canada for my first Art of Living retreat. Tamiko and I drive eight hours to Mississauga, Ontario, a suburb of Toronto, to spend three days with Art of Living students and teachers, mostly from India. Here, I expand on my yoga practice of pranayama or "breath control" and learn how it is scientifically correlated with the reduction of stress and anxiety. Here I practice the breathing technique known as *Sudarshan Kriya*, which "uses specific, natural rhythms to get you unstuck" mentally, physically, and emotionally. Here, I sit in lotus on my mat, my own little boat, for hours, learning to "Be like a baby and breathe from the belly."

Guru instructs me in the art of living without fear. To be still and see. To experience my interconnectedness with everything and everyone. To let go of all the things that devour my happiness: chronic anger and resentment, the desire to control, perfectionism, the need to be right, and perpetual worry over things that I can't change. To practice Santosha, being with what is.

\* \* \*

I manage.

I manage to sleep.

I manage to eat regularly.

I manage to pray, meditate, and set good intentions for each day.

I manage to be with others in social spaces with less fear and apprehension.

I manage to forgive myself more and judge myself less.

I manage to forgive others more and judge others less.

I manage to find a pharmacy discount on my anxiety medication and pay for it while uninsured.

I manage to find a family of faith that accepts me and my family without reservation.

I manage to find a school to support me in my yoga practice.

I manage to breathe my way out of most anxiety attacks.

But nothing prevents them from coming.

# 2

# QUEER AFFIRMATIVE THERAPY

*Arlene Istar Lev*

I have been practicing as a social worker and family therapist for thirty years, and my work has always been with LGBTQ people: my people, my community, my home. When I went to graduate school in the 1980s with the explicit intention of working within the emerging lesbian, gay, and feminist communities, there were few mentors to be found in mainstream academia (and a number of enemies who quickly found me).

## A SHORT HISTORY LESSON

Searching for knowledge about positive queer therapy, I found a small extant body of scholarship written by a cohort of out gay and lesbian professionals—voices of sanity amid a cacophony of pathology. I have vivid memories of Xeroxing their articles page by page while standing at an institutional copy machine with a large bag of dimes—it cost ten cents a page, and each journal issue had to be signed out individually since the journal (there was only one) on homosexuality was kept under lock and key. One had to be brave indeed to ask for it by name and to face the librarian with her raised eyebrow. The journal explored issues like coming out as homosexual and bias, stigma, and violence against homosexuals—the operative word was homosexual, as "gay" was still considered slang and not yet in professional usage. I could not, back then, envision a time when queer theory would be a scholarly pursuit, or when I could chat daily with the esteemed journal authors on Facebook and call them colleagues.

We were still crawling out of the early psychotherapeutic theories that assumed people with alternative sexual and gender identities were suffering from severe psychopathologies. Freud (never as homophobic in his ideology as his followers) based his psychosexual theories in the heterosexist belief that male–female pair-bonding was the developmental norm for adult sexual behavior. These theories became the foundation for various treatments aimed at treating and attempting to "cure" homosexual and gender-nonconforming behaviors. These reparative therapies, based in psychoanalysis and behavioralism, included aversion therapy and also worked in conjunction with medical interventions such as lobotomies, castrations, sterilizations, and electroshock treatments. We were not all outraged by these treatments; indeed, some queers sought out these treatments to save us from our desires. In was not until psychologist Evelyn Hooker published her 1957 paper "The Adjustment of the Male Overt Homosexual"—dispelling with science the myth that homosexuals (i.e., gay men) were inherently mentally ill—that curative treatment strategies would even be challenged.

In the 1960s, political activism and social science research converged to challenge the belief system that homosexual behavior was abnormal. Researchers such as Alfred Kinsey, Clellan Ford, Frank Beach, George Weinberg, and Stephen Morin began to promulgate the then-controversial theory that homosexual behavior was a normal variation of human sexual behavior. At the same historical juncture, the gay liberation movement began gaining momentum. In 1967, the National Institute on Mental Health developed a Task Force on Homosexuality, and, by 1971, gay rights activists including Frank Kameny and Barbara Gittings were protesting at meetings of the American Psychiatric Association (APA) and taunting presenters who recommended using aversion therapy to treat homosexual behavior. Prominent clinicians including Judd Marmor, Robert Stoller, Richard Green, and John Money began to lend support to the idea that homosexuality should not be labeled a mental illness. These reformers who risked their careers to support the nascent sex and gender movement later became the focus of much controversy as the movement expanded away from staid research and professional theorizing about queer bodies.

In 1972, Dr. Henry Anonymous (John Fryer, MD), a closeted gay male psychiatrist, wore a mask to disguise his face and used a voice distortion machine to present at a panel discussion at an APA meeting. Dr. Fryer had already lost jobs due to his homosexuality, and, despite the great threat to his career, he spoke out to support this controversial theory that homosexuality should be depathologized. One year later, homosexuality was officially removed from the APA's *Diagnostic and Statistical Manual* (DSM), paving the way for psychotherapy that was affirming of gay and lesbian people. This process was not without controversy, and, as Ronald Bayer documents in his 1981 book *Homosexuality and American Psychiatry: The Politics of Diagnosis,* was accomplished more by emerging gay rights protests than standard scientific inquiry.

In 1973, when homosexuality was removed from the DSM, I was fourteen years old and in love with my best girlfriend, who we secretly named Charlie. I wrote impassioned monologues in my journal about what was to become of me if I was indeed, as suspected, a "lesibean." (I had never seen the word lesbian in print and therefore

FIGURE 2.1   Dr. John Fryer (Dr. Henry Anonymous) with Frank Kameny and Barbara
Gittings, 1972 APA Convention.

Manuscripts and Archives Division, The New York Public Library. "Gittings, Kameny, and Dr. H. Anonymous
on panel #2" New York Public Library Digital Collections. Accessed November 16, 2017. http://
digitalcollections.nypl.org/items/510d47e3-8315-a3d9-e040-e00a18064a99

had no idea how to spell it.) Although decades younger than Dr. Anonymous, I, too,
wore a mask. The DSM decision did little to change my daily life on the working-class
streets of Brooklyn, but gay liberation was slowly seeping its way onto my color television screen and into books I could find at my local library.

Around the same time that homosexuality was removed from the DSM, gender
identity diagnoses were added. This can seem confusing, especially when we take
into account that the same men who developed the DSM diagnosis for gender identity were the strongest advocates for the removal of homosexuality from the DSM,
as well as the earliest professional pioneers supporting trans people desiring medical
transition. Hindsight is 20/20, but it was thought at the time that the inclusion of a
diagnosis would legitimize transgender identity and provide a path for medical treatment and legitimization. It has proven to be a mixed blessing.

## THE DEVELOPMENT OF GAY AFFIRMATIVE
## PSYCHOTHERAPY

In the 1970s, numerous books denounced the supposition that gay people had significantly more psychopathology than heterosexuals (there was still mostly silence
around bisexuality, and lesbians were subsumed under the supposedly inclusive

nomenclature of "gay"). In 1972, for example, Del Martin's *Lesbian/Woman* and *Out of the Closets: Voices of Gay Liberation*, edited by Karla Jay and Allen Young, both made this argument. In the following years, scholarly books such as Alan Bell and Martin Weinberg's *Homosexualities* (1978) and more popular works such as Dennis Altman's *Homosexual: Oppression and Liberation* (1973) documented the lived lives of lesbian and gay people, showing them to be emotionally healthy but experiencing enormous psychosocial strain from a repressive culture long before terms like "minority stress" existed.

The psychotherapeutic community's negative view of same-sex relationships was identified as exacerbating the problems faced by queer people. Don Clark's *Loving Someone Gay* (1975) and Betty Berzon's *Positively Gay* (1979) marked the first books written by out gay and lesbian psychotherapists. These books advocated the use of psychotherapeutic techniques to improve the lives of lesbian and gay people without stigmatizing them or regarding homosexuality itself as pathological. *The Journal of Homosexuality* (the one under lock and key at my University library) was founded by Bill Cohen in 1974; the editor-in-chief was Charles Silverstein, followed by John De Cecco. In 1982, Haworth Press published a seminal issue of the *Journal of Homosexuality* entitled *Homosexuality and Psychotherapy: A Practitioner's Handbook of Affirmative Models*. Edited by John Gonsiorek, this issue included groundbreaking articles by such scholars and therapists as Eli Coleman, Martin Rochlin, Barbara McCandlish, and Bronwyn Anthony on psychotherapy with lesbian and gay clients. One article, written by Alan Malyon, specifically used the term "gay affirmative" psychotherapy, introducing a new model that supported homosexual relationships as inherently healthy and a normative expression of human sexuality.

Gay affirmative therapy was based on certain fundamental concepts, including the idea that homosexuality was not a psychopathology and that lesbian and gay people did not suffer from mental illness as a result of their homosexuality per se. Additionally, gay affirmative therapy postulated that homosexuality was a normal variation in human sexuality and that there is a normative developmental process of coming out for lesbians and gay men that is obstructed by societal homophobia. Gay affirmative therapy purported that therapists who espouse negative views toward homosexuality cannot be effective clinicians with gay or lesbian clients. Gay affirmative therapy required psychotherapists to become sensitized to the role of homophobia in the psyches of gay men and lesbians so they could recognize the difficulties associated with the internalization of homophobia. "Gay" was used as an inclusive term for both lesbians and gay men, but it was rare that lesbian issues were specifically addressed or that differences in gay and lesbian coupling and communities were highlighted.

Gay affirmative psychotherapy was not a new school of therapy per se, but one that utilized the diverse theories and techniques available across psychotherapeutic modalities within a framework that supported the unique developmental processes of lesbian and gay people. Historically, its great significance is that it was the first therapeutic movement to acknowledge the harm done to lesbian and gay people through heterosexist socialization and institutional homophobia. The unconditional affirmation of same-sex relationships by psychotherapists was intended to serve as a counterbalance to the negative sociocultural and familial environments within which most queer people mature and live. Thus, gay affirmative psychotherapy was supposed to ameliorate the negative impact of growing up gay in an oppressive society, as well as to assist the gay or lesbian client in a coming-out process that actualized a healthy homosexual identity. Central to gay affirmative therapy is the attempt to enhance the dignity and self-respect of clients by establishing a supportive and accepting atmosphere.

## BEYOND JUST GAY: LESBIAN, BISEXUAL, AND TRANSGENDER AFFIRMATIVE PSYCHOTHERAPIES

Gay affirmative psychotherapy did not, in its early manifestations, recognize the need to establish specific therapeutic contexts for exploring lesbian, bisexual, or transgender identity development. Models of lesbian affirmative therapy did not blossom until the mid-1980s, with the publication of Marny Hall's *The Lavender Couch: A Consumer's Guide to Psychotherapy for Lesbians and Gay Men* (1985) and the Boston Lesbian Psychologies Collective issue of *Lesbian Psychologies* in 1987, a book that transformed my emerging career, enabling me to see myself as a *lesbian therapist*. Lesbian affirmative models generally still utilized the term "gay affirmative," although they recognized its limitations— particularly how it emphasized male experience and identity. Bisexual identity development was not documented professionally until 1993 with Fritz Klein's *The Bisexual Option* and Martin Weinberg, Colin Williams, and Douglas Pryor's 1994 *Dual Attraction: Understanding Bisexuality.* Professional publications that depathologized transgender identity development began with Mildred Brown's *True Selves* (1996), Gianna Israel's *Transgender Care* (1998), and Randi Ettner's *Gender Loving Care* (1999). My book *Transgender Emergence: Therapeutic Guidelines for Working with Gender-Variant People and Their Families* (2004) was the first clinical book to assert that transgender people were not mentally ill and that gender transitions impacted all within the family system. Looking back on these books today, few scholars or activists would find them "affirming," as they are steeped in language that may now seem oppressive; the tone of the books is defensive as these professionals with a Sisyphean task tried to normalize what had been so pathologized.

Within a postmodern worldview, gay affirmative therapy may appear to be a historic relic that was once necessary to counterbalance the homophobia of the extant therapeutic systems. It did, however, establish a necessary foundation: a therapeutic model that recognized same-sex identity and relationships as potentially healthy and natural. The work to depathologize bisexuality and trans identities would not be possible without the existence of gay affirmative psychotherapy. Certainly, a more contemporary queer affirmative therapy must have a broader understanding of sex and gender identity development and the intersectionalities of cultural/racial/ethnic contexts and must take into account the numerous pathways and outcomes for healthy human psychosexual identity formation. Although the term "gay affirmative" does not do justice to the wide array of sexual and gender identities and sexual minority communities included under the banner of postmodern queer LGBTQQIAP identities, the basic need for psychotherapeutic models that embrace and support diverse sexual and gender expressions remains urgent. We must, however, go beyond just affirmative models.

## DECONSTRUCTING PATHOLOGY

Throwing off the yoke and stigma of pathology allowed for legal, political, and clinical transformations that could never have been granted a "mentally ill" population. Marriage equality, "gay" adoption, and the increasing civil rights protections in housing and employment owe much to the depathologization of homosexuality. We are beginning to see the same civil rights struggles and gain for transgender rights. Although still listed in the DSM as Gender Dysphoria, in recent years, transgender identity has gone from obscurity to mainstream in the media and has become part of evolving civil rights struggles (and the inevitable backlash).

Anyone committed to being a therapist must engage with the history of how sexual and other minorities have been mistreated within the helping professions. The field of psychology and the psychiatric system in general has been permeated by Eurocentric, patriarchal, racist, sexist, and heteronormative thinking that has done enormous damage to the mental health of women, people of color, and queer people. We must examine the use of language and labeling—including such terms as "mental illness" and "psychiatric disorder"—and their utility in working with LGBTQ people.

In my role as a social work educator, I teach master's-level students how to utilize the DSM; as a feminist and holistic practitioner, I also teach them to be very wary of labeling. Diagnosis is a political tool. It has been used to medicate angry and powerless women and to take away our children. It has been used to hospitalize political activists and other radicals. In the not very distant past, women were routinely diagnosed with "hysteria," manifested by fainting, yelling, and depressive "fits" when they tried to step out of their limited female roles. They were "treated" with clitorectomies. In the latter part of the 1800s, African slaves were diagnosed with "drapetomania," believed to be a blood disorder. According to the diagnostic texts, this caused Black slaves to want to flee captivity; the disorder was "cured by whipping." Medical textbooks listed the size of men's heads to prove that people of African descent had smaller brains and were less intelligent than White people and that people with larger noses (Semitic people) harbored certain communicable diseases. If these examples—and these are only a quick soundbite—sound absurd or irrelevant, remember that some of them highlight the state of clinical medicine only about a century ago.

Changes in the DSM are not immune from political pressure and indeed are often informed by it. Homosexuality was removed from the DSM due to the activism of gay liberationists. Alcoholism is no longer viewed as a moral problem, but instead seen as a disease that can be treated. Feminists have challenged diagnostic labels like premenstrual syndrome that may pathologize normative female biological processes, as well as diagnoses like Borderline Personality Disorder that pathologize the traumatic reactions of survivors of sexual abuse, incest, and domestic violence. Increasing recognition of the role of trauma in mental illness has transformed treatment, including our treatment of sexual and gender minorities.

However, we must never lose sight of the fact that the psychiatric profession and psychopharmacological industry are institutionalized arms of a sexist, heterosexist, and transphobic patriarchal system. Researchers and clinicians such as Irving Bieber, Joseph Nicolosi, and Charles Socarides, and organizations such as the National Association for the Research and Therapy of Homosexuality (NARTH) and the Family Research Council, still view homosexuality as psychopathology and actively oppose gay and trans-affirmative psychotherapy models. We also cannot ignore the role that profit plays in the diagnosing and treatment of vulnerable populations. As managed care has become increasingly resistant to paying for services for adults, the industry is suddenly concerned about the mental stability of young children, and many psychiatric hospitals have suddenly refocused their entire treatment programs on the care of young people. How can we not look at the patriarchal system of labeling illness with some skepticism?

## BEYOND AFFIRMATION

So, what does it mean to be a therapist committed to working in the queer community if we start from an affirmative stance toward LGBTQ identities and recognize the limitations of labels and pathology as remnants of cisheteropatriarchal systems of oppression? Are there elements of diagnostic systems that remain useful to us in helping to heal human pain and suffering? How do we provide safe spaces for queer people to begin to heal from trauma and oppression that does not reinforce the rigid labels of pathology?

Nowhere have these questions been more salient than in examining how trans people are treated when attempting to access transition-related medical services. An indelible image from my childhood comes to mind: I'm watching *The Wizard of Oz* on television, and I see the merry travelers reach the Wizard's castle in Oz after a long and perilous journey. They are met at the door by a gatekeeper, who opens the peephole and, after a confusing interaction, essentially turns them away, saying, "You're wasting my time."

Therapists working in trans and gender-nonconforming communities are frequently viewed as this type of gatekeeper—a powerful figure who can determine entry and must be convinced, cajoled, bribed, or tackled into allowing admission. In the past, clients came prepared to their first session, armed with copious clinical reading material, armed to prove their transgender status. These days they quote from YouTube videos that have prepared them for my resistance and judgment. They are either terrified of me because I have the power to diagnose them or furious at me because they need me to diagnose them in order to receive medical care.

Developing a healing and trusting relationship that starts from the premise of power and exclusion is a challenge. How can I be a gatekeeper who is a gentle door "man," warmly inviting scared and vulnerable clients into my office, offering a safe haven from judgment and a pathologizing diagnosis, providing them a path forward for their own actualization?

Clients are right to be wary. Many therapists are ignorant about transgender people and the challenges they face; most therapists have had virtually no training on these issues. Some therapists still believe gender diversity is a disorder; a few, in their effort to refuse the yoke of being a gatekeeper, eschew any clinical assessment and approve all requests for medical referrals on principle. They ignore ethical guidelines and individual narratives, and they fail to provide any ongoing advocacy or emotional support. They write letters for approval regardless of a client's mental status or confusion about the future. In an effort to avoid being gatekeepers, they have become cheerleaders, supporting transition without listening carefully to individual human stories. If there is anything we are learning about gender in the twenty-first century it is that there are as many gender journeys as there are humans, and the same solution does not serve all.

Therapists working in the gender community are placed in an untenable position—caught between the requirements of Western medicine's bureaucratic machine on one hand and the burgeoning trans liberation movement on the other. The medical model has required diagnosis before medication can be provided, and the trans political community challenges a pathologizing model that diagnoses disease, mislabels identity, and implies illness. The politics of liberation, however empowering, do not often bear witness to the intensity of very personal human pain in the face of gender dysphoria. Informed consent may make access to services easier, but it may or may not provide the support some need to navigate the complications of transition within a transphobic culture.

Therapists are professionals with experience and expertise in understanding something about human pain, and our goal is to assist people in living healthier, more productive lives. As a family therapist, I believe that people are interconnected within a web of others; our actions and decisions impact one another. Transition is most definitely a family affair. I am also a feminist, a social worker, and a political activist, which means I cannot limit myself to psychological explanations of human behavior, but am committed to exploring the social, environmental, systemic, and political ramifications of oppression and why people experience the kind of pain they do.

These parts overlap inside of me, synthesizing a working analysis of my professional obligations. I believe that living in a binary gender system is no less than tyranny. I believe that everyone has a right to their own gender presentation and expression and that everyone has a right to access appropriate and expert medical care. I believe that our culture is at the beginning of a revolution and that the transgender movement is at the forefront of a truly feminist, nonsexist, and liberating social transformation.

However, I also believe that all of us are deeply wounded from the ravages of this racist, heteronormative, and patriarchal society. I believe that those of us who are "queer" by societal standards suffer greatly. At its worst, the system institutionalizes us, abandons us to poverty, and ultimately kills us. At its best, it gives us an opportunity to heal as we deconstruct the patriarchy's lies; we can reinvent ourselves in our own image. Good therapy can be a tool to help this process.

That I am a gatekeeper is undeniable—I have the power to write referral letters for hormones and surgery or to not do so. I have the power to diagnosis people with mental illnesses—and who among us is not afraid of some outside authority's power to decree them "mad?"

As one of the authors of the World Professional Association of Transgender Health's Standards of Care 7, I strongly advocated for the significant reduction of a gatekeeping role. These new guidelines make it much easier for a therapist to provide an assessment and referral to a physician, forgoing long evaluations or a need for psychotherapy. This a great advance in our field, assisting in easier access to quality medical care.

However, at times, assessment processes are more complex. We are seeing increased numbers of young clients, small children who live in very black-and-white worlds regarding gender ("If I like playing with Barbie dolls then I am a girl because only girls can play with dolls, right?"). Sorting out family messages of judgment about gender and transgender, societal sexism, and normative expressions of gender diversity and creativity from transgender expression and gender dysphoria is not a simple process. Adolescents sometimes present in therapy requesting medical treatment with no history of gender diversity or gender dysphoria but having had a new insight after having seen a series of YouTube videos. They are often accompanied by confused, angry, frightened parents who are sure this is just peer pressure. One teen went to camp and shared a bunk with a trans child; by the end of the summer, the entire bunk identified as trans. Although it is possible that all of these children are indeed trans, a thorough assessment before a medical referral seems ethically appropriate, although it may also feel oppressive and intrusive to the teen.

Adults seeking treatment are often in great pain—with spouses and children who are less than supportive, they fear losing their marriages, their jobs, and custody of their children. Sometimes people present with ongoing psychiatric issues such as severe depression, chronic alcoholism, extreme anxiety, or suicidality. Sometimes people present with developmental or cognitive issues that may impair their full understanding of gender transition. Will medical treatment for gender dysphoria increase or decrease their pain? It is easy to assume that treatment will always improve lives by easing dysphoria—but having worked with trans people for nearly thirty years, I have seen that sometimes, without proper support, mental health issues can actually increase dramatically. People have lost family and other social supports or become unemployed and homeless. Sometimes their bodily changes cause increased confusion and pain, or simply do not eliminate their gender dypshoria. Assisting people in developing support systems, understanding the lifelong physical effects of medical treatment, and helping them negotiate complex bureaucratic medical and legal systems so they do not lose their jobs or children must be part of the gender therapist's work. Otherwise we may inadvertently cause more harm rather than lessening pain.

Is it ethical to write a hormone letter for a person assigned male at birth without his wife's knowledge? If a patient is abusing substances, are they capable of informed medical consent? Can someone who is psychotic or dissociative fully understand the ramifications of their decisions? How does trauma impact dysphoria? Or sexism? Or pubertal development? If I refuse to write a referral letter for a client who wants to take hormones without their wife's knowledge, or is clearly exhibiting psychotic symptoms that make me concerned about their ability to examine the consequences of these major decisions, or whose traumatic history may be influencing their discomfort with their body or experience of gender, have I abandoned the political call to arms of the trans liberation movement? Do trans people not have a right to hormones much as a diabetic has a right to insulin? These are complex ethical dilemmas that I face every day, supporting people in their struggles to live more authentic lives.

I am aware that many clients do not recognize the enormity of these decisions' impact on their lives. As a helping professional, I have an obligation to help people assess whether their choices will relieve their pain or increase it. I am a therapist, not a lawyer or surgeon, and I must establish criteria to determine who is capable of making informed decisions about gender transition and who needs psychoeducation, addiction recovery, or medication management before they are able to make life-altering decisions. We can argue about one's legal rights to medical care; we can—and should!—discuss who gets to "keep" the gates, but we must also thoughtfully engage in dialogic relationships with our clients about the causes of a client's pain and the options and pathways for solutions.

Sometimes it is appropriate to just write the damn referral letter, and often I do this in a few sessions. Other times, it seems appropriate to question some of the un-examined issues in a client's life, to see that they have considered the impact of their decisions on, for instance, their loved ones or their employment. Sometimes people exhibit bona fide serious mental health issues that may be entirely separate from their gender issues or may manifest as a direct result of oppression. Simply referring someone for hormones or surgery without helping them develop the necessary support systems can sometimes increase their confusion and pain and ultimately exacerbate other mental health issues.

You may remember the scene at the end of the *Wizard of Oz* in which Toto pulls back the curtain. The wizard is hiding there and says, in what I think of as one of the great moments of cinema, "Please ignore the man behind the curtain." Good therapy is not just about clients exposing their vulnerabilities, but also about therapists authentically revealing themselves. Any therapist who is hiding behind diagnoses and clinical interpretations is just hiding behind a curtain. Any good therapist will open the curtain and show you his or her or their face, which may often include their concerns and observations. Clients, of course, are free to reject these observations, engage in thoughtful dialogue, or seek alternative care.

Trans people were born into a binary system in which they do not fit, and be-coming whole is no easy task. The work of deep healing is the best work we can do—not because transgender people are gender dysphoric or mentally ill, but because the system is crazy-making, and, at the root of our being, we all have a right to heal.

It has been suggested that coming home to one's true spirit is a shamanistic journey. In most spiritual traditions, before undertaking a spiritual quest, one seeks out a guide. One client called me a "transition assistant," and, indeed, this work is about assisting and guiding. I think of a guide as a skilled person who is prepared for all circumstances and who is familiar with the diversity of the terrain. Guides do not necessarily know everything that will be encountered, and they cannot know the inner path of the seeker, but they can often sense when danger is near. They may know how to prepare a shelter in a storm or lead the seeker to water. I learned many years ago to never go camping without carrying matches in sealed plastic bags. When clients are drenched in the rainstorm of job loss, partners' abandonment, complicated medical problems, or authoritarian doctors, I can pull out my matches and build a fire. I can provide warmth and listen to their pain. At best, I can offer experienced guidance, and, at the least, the warmth of human comfort.

LGBTQ affirmative therapy has come a very long way in the past few decades. Nothing is more important than finding a therapist who provides a safe space and feels comfortable—someone who clients can trust with their truths. Trans people do not need to settle for a gatekeeper, someone to whom they present a false self, who will judge and diagnose. Nor should trans people settle for a paper pusher who does not challenge or help them to see themselves more clearly. Therapists at best are guides who can travel with their clients on a sometimes perilous but often exhilarating journey. Queer folk deserve nothing less.

Affirmative models of therapy are accepted today within the mainstream of helping professions, and they have the institutional support of most major professional organizations, including the American Psychological Association, the American Psychiatric Association, and the National Association of Social Workers. All of these organizations have developed strong policy statements depathologizing homosexuality, supporting same-sex relationships and gay families, and supporting trans people—including LGBTQ people who work in the profession. However, affirmative psychotherapy has not yet been fully integrated within the psychological or social work professions, and even those psychotherapists who profess to be accepting often lack in-depth education on the psychosocial issues and needs of queer people. As a profession, we have a long way to go.

Affirmative care means that LGBTQ people are not inherently mentally ill because we are queer. It does not mean that we are inherently mentally healthy either. Research shows that we have higher levels of addictions and mental health problems when compared to heterosexuals. We must dismantle the stigma attached to "mentally ill" people, work toward humane treatment for all, and address the health disparities queer people encounter in accessing adequate resources for healing. Affirmative treatment for queer folk also means addressing some of the complex mental health issues we face, in part stemming from oppression and in part simply because we are human. A good therapist must be able to balance these issues while always treating our clients with human dignity.

# 3

## NOT ALL WOUNDS ARE VISIBLE

*Louisa Hammond*

I live and work in Manchester, UK, and studied Visual Arts at the University of Salford, from which I graduated in 2008. Since that time, I have been creating artwork and exhibiting in a variety of galleries, festivals, and public spaces. Getting involved in art-based projects around the destigmatization of mental illness is close to my heart. I was unexpectedly diagnosed with schizoaffective disorder in 2010, which became a very dramatic, turbulent time in my life. During my recovery, I was referred to art therapy sessions using a variety of media, including textiles. It was at these workshops at an art-for-health National Health Service (NHS) organization that I was inspired to begin producing artwork again. I feel that my practice has very much been impacted and inspired by this life-changing experience, and I aim to voice my knowledge of living with mental illness through what I create.

Although I have worked in a variety of media, using hand embroidery has become a natural tool to translate my thoughts. I enjoy drawing with thread to convey my ideas, and it is through this medium that I currently feel most at home. With the use of embroidery, I aim to magnify the beauty of readily available craft materials and the use of sometimes-unusual materials such as the Band-Aid in "Not All Wounds Are Visible." This is ultimately a personal aim to transform the ordinary into the extraordinary.

In "Not All Wounds Are Visible" I explored my personal experiences of mental illness and a general perception of the illness that I have been witness to when out of work and unwell. I've noticed a general opinion by others that mental illness can be inferior to physical illness and is somehow not taken as seriously. I feel that although my scars cannot be seen, the damage is just as long-lasting and significant to my life. Mental illness can be just as devastating as any physical illness, and the internal scars can even cut deeper, seriously affecting quality of life and ultimately leading to prejudice and stigma.

In "Not All Wounds Are Visible" the canvas is a Band-Aid instead of a traditional material, laid on top of bandages, a surface onto which it is hard to sew; it's almost impenetrable, but with each stitch I contemplated the message that emerged. The use of the red embroidery floss is a nod to open wounds. The delicate escaping threads are to convey the way symptoms can creep out into the open and become visible, though the core of the illness remains hidden.

Fueled by the notion of art being available as a therapy, I continue in my work to seek out and explore wellness through meditative reflection during the time-consuming act of actually making the embroideries. This has helped me on a personal path of recovery from mental illness. It's of great importance to me in my day-to-day life to take the time to reflect, concentrate, and produce something to maintain mental well-being.

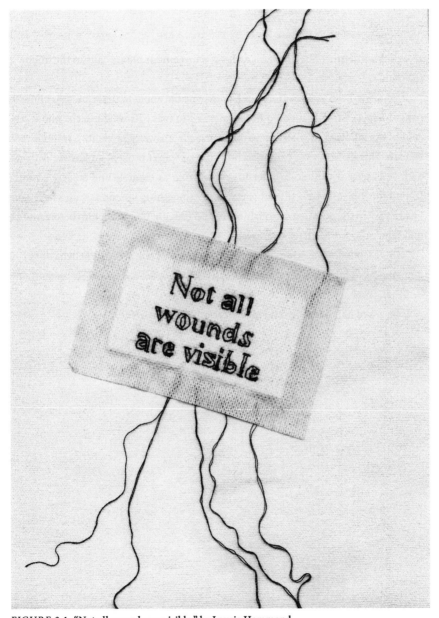

FIGURE 3.1 "Not all wounds are visible," by Lousia Hammond.

# 4

## BORDER/LINES

### *Juan Antonio Trujillo*

"Am I borderline?" he asked on one of his three-hour phone calls in the middle of the night.

If you have been in a relationship like the one I'm about to describe, you know the panic I felt—a panic that could not be allowed to make its way into the phone, that couldn't be allowed to interfere with getting my answer just right, a response that validated his question yet reassured him that he wasn't broken, an answer delivered with split-second timing in order to come across as credible and sincere. A millisecond too long and he'd think I was making something up; too fast and he'd claim I hadn't taken the question seriously or that I'd thought this about him before and not told him, or . . . wait, I have to answer.

"No," I replied. "but I think you might sometimes cope using BPD behaviors your mom modeled for you when you were little."

"That's probably true," he conceded.

If he asked me today, I would give him a different answer.

# ABANDONMENT

Frantic efforts to avoid real or imagined abandonment.

—DSM-5

Another gay Latino on campus?

A muted excitement started to build when I saw his OkCupid profile. There's no hiding in a town this small and this white when you're Latino and queer, so you might as well be proactive and make contact. I wrote a short greeting and hit send before I lost my nerve.

The quick reply was terse and formal but indicated that he'd be up for coffee. We decided on Wednesday. During negotiations, I mentioned the staged reading of *Standing on Ceremony: The Gay Marriage Plays* I'd be in on Sunday. He said he might make it.

He sat in the back row of the theater, five rows behind my therapist and her wife. Small town. I glanced at him a few times from my seat, but when I stood to read the adrenaline of the performance left me shamelessly projecting my lines in his direction. At intermission I made my way to the back. He shuffled over and pulled one hand out of his pocket just long enough to shake and introduce himself. Serious. Guarded. Intense.

My grad students suddenly popped up behind me and pulled me into the flow of people headed to the lobby for a beer.

We met in the student union on Wednesday and sat in two wing chairs with a small end table between them.

Sunday's plays dominated the conversation, in part because they facilitated so much of that initial getting-to-know-you dialogue. In a blatant act of typecasting the director had assigned me a part in *Strange Fruit*, the ultimately tragic story of a man who found love with another man late in life. This was me, 47 years old, still not out to my dad, and longing to find the connection described in the script. The playwright, Neil LaBute, was also a former BYU student and queer ex-Mormon. I had requested excommunication less than 6 months earlier.

The plays had their effect on him too.

"I made a decision when I got home." he said. "I don't know if you've logged into OkCupid since Sunday but I've updated my profile."

"No, I haven't looked."

"I changed it to say that I'm only looking for friends," he continued. "The plays really made me think and I've decided to try again with my boyfriend Gary in Boise."

In my mind I'd left myself an out, of course—wasn't this only supposed to be coffee? But the honest answer is that I immediately felt my hope for a connection drain from my body, leaving an all too familiar emptiness.

It was the emptiness of a self-imposed celibacy of over 25 years that followed that first burning touch of another man on my Mormon mission in Tijuana. It was the emptiness of believing my father wouldn't accept a 47-year-old gay son and the emptiness of my grandfather's funeral that spring. And it was the emptiness where Scott had been a month earlier, my best friend of 15 years and the man who finally made me say the words "I'm gay" in a completely unexpected mutual coming-out speech the year before. The one-sentence letter telling me he'd decided to never see me again was still sitting on my desk. This sounds more like an ending than a beginning.

We didn't stop talking when the half-hour coffee was up. We both missed the start of office hours and sometime past the hour mark we said goodbye. He left with the address for a local food security meeting in his pocket and later showed up and sat by me. We went home with a friend afterward and ate homemade pumpkin soup. By the end of the day we'd spent five and a half hours together and I knew he had his own emptiness. We were alone and we needed each other.

Within two weeks he had supervised my first pint of beer and consoled me over the sudden death of my cat, and I had stayed on the phone during his entire drive from Boise to eastern Oregon after a holiday fight with Gary. Within two months I knew not to fall asleep before 11:00pm so his call wouldn't wake me, and weeks later I had to change cell phone plans so I wouldn't run out of minutes. No, he didn't want to be my boyfriend, but did that matter? He knew my emptiness and he wasn't going to leave me.

## SPLITTING

A pattern of unstable and intense interpersonal relationships characterized by alter-
nating between extremes of idealization and devaluation.

—DSM-5

It felt more like a conference room than a patio as we took our seats at my new picnic table. My finger was starting to go numb, squeezed between the pages of my writing journal where I'd scribbled a formula from the internet for dealing with a BPD crisis:

1. Ask what happened
2. Listen without expressing judgment
3. Validate something
4. Ask if I can help
5. Give space

According to the web site, reaching step five means that the borderline person remains emotionally hostile and it's time to walk away—possibly forever. Of course, that wasn't going to happen, we were better together than that.

I started the incantation.

"You seem upset, would you tell me what's wrong?"

"How could you say that?" he replied, his voice trembling with hurt and rage. "You of all people. . . I'm not sure it's forgivable." He was talking about ducks.

We had watched my pet ducks together one afternoon and talked about avian pair bonding. A few days later he had gone on his first date with Mark. They met at a res-taurant and when both men got out of their cars, a small flock of wild mallards took flight from a corner of the parking lot. This was the sign from the universe he'd been looking for; he had found his life partner.

I kept solid eye contact so he wouldn't doubt my sincerity as I listened to him de-scribe his pain at my betrayal, which apparently had taken the form of a comment that ducks only form seasonal pair bonds—it's geese that mate for life. Thank God I hadn't reminded him that the reason the drakes had their own pen was to stop them from raping my chickens.

Validate, validate, validate. . . .

"I know how important the relationship with Mark is becoming to you, I'm sure I would feel hurt too," I responded once he had finished. "You know I make a lot of pedantic comments and I wasn't trying to say anything about you and Mark—I apol-ogize for hurting you."

Step four.

"Is there anything I can do for us to move past this?" I asked.

"I feel better about this after talking," he replied, "I think we might be able to continue some kind of friendship."

I felt myself start breathing again and finally let my finger slip from the page where I'd scripted my part of the conversation ahead of time.

No step five.

I spoke with Mark a few months later at a dance performance about their breakup. "Explosive," he told me, "stunningly intense."

Mark didn't have the formula.

## IDENTITY DISTURBANCE

Markedly and persistently unstable self image or sense of self.

—DSM-5

"I want to look like a skeleton," he had said, "I might have to perform almost naked and I should look like a corpse. Check out this guy on YouTube."

For nearly three months everyone had lived with the annoyance of him breaking into butoh rehearsal in the middle of conversation. Without warning he'd start staring into space and then an arm would slowly rise up and unfold into a bloom before fading and withering back down. "I'm practicing Ash Body," he'd inform us mid-cocktail with a calculatedly modest chuckle. "It's hard to explain, I'm not going to try."

As the rehearsal period went on I started to understand the process better. I learned that butoh lies somewhere near the intersection of dance, performance art, and meditation. In the tradition of butoh master Akira Kasai, the performer is trained to lose identity and become an empty vessel or corpse that is animated by another consciousness.

It was working. By the night of the performance, any nervousness about being on stage was subsumed by a deep identity crisis. Instead of complaints about our straight, white town or worries about the tenure process there were hours of circular monologues about a life on the wrong track. He was coming to see his genius for quantitative research as a burden imposed by the world on someone who should have been an artist—a dancer—and he needed confirmation from me.

Although the director decided they'd perform fully clothed after all, the performance was electric. The corpse I knew better than anyone kept opening new dimensions of himself to me as he weaved through the spotlights with his slow suriashi walk. I watched riveted as he collapsed to the ground and sat clawing at the floor around him, his identity conflict playing itself out in public on the black marley floor.

His part-time housemate Frank offered to drive him to celebrate over drinks, but to my surprise he asked me to take him.

"I love Frank, he's a great friend, but I need to be with someone who knows me like you," he explained once we were seated in the car.

"How was it, really?" he asked as we headed out of the parking lot.

I told him how moved I was by his piece, how impressed I was by his bravery and openness.

He thanked me and with the next breath began to sob. He didn't stop until we found parking just off Mississippi and went to join Frank for a whiskey.

# IMPULSIVITY

Impulsivity in at least two areas that are potentially self-damaging.

—DSM-5

"I don't think I'll ever have sex again," he announced, "I don't even like it." For a would-be dancer he was very uncomfortable with touching of any sort.

"I've already gone that route," I reminded him, "and I don't recommend it."

"Yeah, but this is different. I've been out since I was 16 and I never thought it was a sin to have sex. Everything changed after Gary."

He liked to remind me that I was far behind him on the development curve and still shackled by my Mormon conditioning. And he had made it clear that he wasn't up to helping me end my decades-long period of celibacy.

"Would it even be hot?" he had asked when I hinted at the idea. "What do you think you'd do if I slept with you?"

"How can I know," I told him. "I'd probably cry from relief or something."

"See, I think that crying would annoy me," he replied. End of discussion.

It was discouraging. If he wasn't able to see me as a boyfriend despite spending over 10 hours a week with me on the phone or in person, wasn't I at least as good for a lay as any of the many hundreds of guys he'd claimed to have been with? And now. . . celibacy.

When the usual late-night phone call didn't come, I knew. I knew and didn't need to ask, but he confirmed the next day anyway.

"It wasn't very satisfying," he reported. "I maybe touched two penises the whole time."

Swinging from vows of celibacy to anonymous bathhouse sex—I'm not sure where to look for that cycle on the development curve.

## SUICIDAL BEHAVIOR

Recurrent suicidal behavior, gestures, or threats, or self-mutilating behavior.

—DSM-5

"I can get everything I need at Home Depot," he told me over the phone. "They have those long flexible dryer vent hoses and duct tape. I could just pull the car into Frank's garage, he won't be back for a few days."

I tried to stay attentive to his words and delivery while simultaneously retrieving from memory the advice I got from my therapist the last time this happened. "Tell him how it would affect you," she had said. "Be direct."

Alright, I can do this.

He paused briefly and I jumped in.

"You know I'd be devastated if you killed yourself, right?" I told him with as much resolve and sincerity as I could convey through the overwhelming helplessness. I was a two-hour drive away from where he was housesitting. "I would not only be sad, I would be furious with you for leaving me like that."

"No, I won't do it right now," he responded. "It wouldn't be fair to Frank to come back and find me in his garage. And there's Maxi and Duke," he continued. "They need me."

"Maxi and Duke need you, but I do too," I said, knowing that this wasn't a compelling argument for him. He had told me before that the only thing standing between him and suicide was his dogs. Oh, he admitted that there were a couple of friends like Frank and me who would suffer if he killed himself, but he specifically refused to say that either of us were a real deterrent.

"Our deal from before is still in effect, okay?" I reminded him. "If you start feeling that you're going to hurt yourself I expect you to call me."

"Okay," he replied. He suddenly sounded exhausted.

It was around 2 a.m. when we said goodnight. I put the phone down next to me on the bed, making sure the ringer was turned on.

## AFFECTIVE INSTABILITY

Affective instability due to a marked reactivity of mood (e.g., intense episodic dysphoria, irritability, or anxiety usually lasting a few hours and only rarely more than a few days).

—DSM-5

"Where were you?" I asked. "You didn't call and I couldn't get ahold of you."

"I spent the last two days curled up in a ball on the floor," he responded.

"Can I help with anything?"

"No," he replied. "I'm up now. Don't tell Frank."

## EMPTINESS

Chronic feelings of emptiness.

—DSM-5

"Are you sure we should be friends?" he asked as he sat on the far end of the couch, my gray cat Buluu balanced on his thigh.

"Why would you ask that?" I could tell he was serious. What did he think I had done to him this time?

"I don't know if this friendship is good for either of us," he responded. "Any time we're together it's like there's a black vortex that opens up and pulls us in."

I thought about it for a second. "We're both pretty dark, you know that."

"I don't feel a vortex when I'm with Frank," he replied.

"Well I'm not going to take the blame. I'd love to do something besides sit on the couch and talk about work—I like to hike, go to shows. . . you do all of that with Frank," I countered. "You just use me to deal with all your dark shit so you can go and have fun somewhere else."

"I don't think so," he replied, "maybe . . . I'll think about that."

He worked on dislodging Buluu from his leg without her digging her claws into his pants.

"I've got to go, I still have one set of pushups to do," he said. "You should think about my question."

## ANGER

Inappropriate, intense anger or difficulty controlling anger (e.g., frequent displays of temper, constant anger, recurrent physical fights).

—DSM-5

"Am I *wrong* about this?" he asked, almost breathless with outrage. "I don't think I can keep working here."

That had been a rhetorical question but running the emotional regulation script is never a bad plan, right?

"Tell me what happened," I responded.

"The locks finally got changed on our new offices," he began, "and when I got my key from the office staff it didn't work."

"Okay, . . . "

"So, I went back to the secretary. She told me I had to go to the key shop and get it replaced."

I think we call them office specialists, I thought to myself, but I didn't want to get us sidetracked into another misogynistic MRA-fueled screed.

Validation time.

"Well, that's inconvenient," I responded calmly, "it's a pretty long walk. Did you get your key?"

"No! Why should I have to?" he raged. "*That's* what's wrong with this place."

"What is?" I asked.

"I asked if the key shop guy could just bring over the right key, and the secretary said no, we can't make him do that. He's the one who fucked up and now she acts like I'm an asshole for expecting him to fix his mistake?"

"Mmm hmmm, . . . "

"Can't you see what's wrong?" he said, with an almost rehearsed exasperation in his voice. "They think it's okay to send someone with an Ivy League PhD to fetch a key so that a guy who makes $15 an hour won't feel bad? *Really*? What about *me*? Am *I* less important than a locksmith who can't do his job right?"

"It doesn't seem like the best use of resources," I said. Sometimes validation doesn't come easy.

"Thank you!" he said jubilantly, "Somebody gets it! This is unacceptable. I've made a huge mistake coming here, I don't know how long I can stay. I should quit."

# PARANOIA

Transient, stress-related paranoid ideation or severe dissociative symptoms.

—DSM-5

He looked me straight in the eyes from across the sandwich crusts and potato chip fragments on the table, his face and his voice expressionless.

"What's with the crystal you gave me—with the spider web inside?" he asked.

"There's no spider web, they're fractures that make rainbows when you shine a light through them."

"Those aren't rainbows," he responded, "they're spider webs."

"They're rainbows."

"But the box lid design, *that's* a spider web," he insisted.

"I guess you could see it that way. It's the only little box the bookstore had," I replied. "It wouldn't have been my first choice."

"And the herbs inside?"

"It's that Fiji green tea blend, you saw me buy it," I said, finally starting to understand where this was going. "The box was too big so I tossed some in to cushion the stone, it's all I had in my office."

"Well, I took it to someone who knows about these things and that person confirmed that it was something else," he reported.

His eyes still showed no emotion while he paused to look for any sign of guilt in my expression.

"The spider webs, the herbs. . . you shouldn't have done it. I warned you to stay away from magick and binding spells," he continued. "You might get what you think you want but it won't be real."

"Um... I didn't do any binding spells," I replied, knowing that engaging would be futile. "If you don't want the crystal, just give it back. It cost $15 and I like it."

"So why did we both get flat tires last week? That's happened to me before when magick was involved," he responded. "Anyway, I don't think the crystal is real," he continued, "and maybe you didn't charge it on purpose, but I've talked to somebody and it will be disposed of safely," he said sternly.

We loaded the plastic baskets onto our tray and I grabbed the box of leftover coleslaw before we stood up together. We walked to the door and we said goodbye, both of us knowing that we'd had our last conversation together as friends.

We didn't hug.

# 5

## SA KANYANG SARILING MGA SALITA
## HEALTH, IDENTITY, AND ARTICULATIONS
## OF SELF

*Donald V. Brown, Jr., with Fidelindo A. Lim*

The tendency to locate mental illness solely within the individual is well-documented in the history of inquiry into various mental health topics. Though not explicitly stated as such, bodies of work on mental health are littered with the language of individual-level diagnoses based on clinicians' observations of aberrant behavior. Throughout their history, fields such as psychiatry have seen a shift in the consideration of environmental factors[1] as catalysts for declines or changes in mental health status (Schmidt, 2007). However, we still find in the latest edition of the *Diagnostic and Statistical Manual of Mental Disorders* (DSM-5) diagnostic materials that focus entirely on individuals, their observed behavior, and how that behavior validates a specific individual's future diagnosis.

The discourse on environmental influence exists, but has not gained the necessary traction to influence how the business of mental health is carried out. When we ask, "How are you feeling today?" it is more a question about *you* than an invitation to interrogate where your emotions may have originated.

Context[2] is stripped away.

We don't yet have the ability to know the thoughts and desires that animate the ebbs and flows of the human psyche. We, inclusive of both clinicians and laypeople, rely on what we see in order to make judgments about individuals and their adherence to prescriptions of normalcy—a barometer for society's allowance of their participation in quotidian engagements. With that in mind, especially in the context of Western medicine and mental health practice, it is important not to commit what we in social psychology would call a "fundamental attribution error."[3] Famously, Kurt Lewin[4] posited that behavior is a function of person in dynamic interaction with their environment. The psychosocial, interpersonal, and cultural environments within which individuals are embedded and with which individuals must contend to advance varying self-articulations are of vital importance to characterizing behavior as emergent from the individual or resultant from what the individual is experiencing within their particular, characteristic reality.

Of course this is not to say that conditions such as schizophrenia are not valid and should not be treated at the level of the individual. But when one considers the application of labels related to other mental health indicators such as suicidal ideation, depression, or the notion of one being "at risk"—especially as these labels vary in their employment across self-articulated identity groups—it is imperative that further reflection is encouraged.

One such self-articulation with which individuals may engage, either publicly or within themselves, is the collection of social identity[5] groups to which they belong, including sexual orientation and gender identity. In much the same way that sociocultural context is imperative to understanding mental health, one can also make note of the ways in which the construct of identity is destabilized when multiple, diverse voices speak to what it means to be gay or lesbian based on their situated knowledge. Culture[6] presents itself as a kind of scaffolding on which the fabric of identity, the fabric of mental health, lay.

Cultural origin and knowledge change the contours of what it means to be *well*, to present as *normal*, as well as what it means to be included (or excluded) from a certain group. Making note of these convergent phenomena is essential in truly meeting the needs of an LGBTQ population contending with realities that may be observed on the spectrum of mental wellness. What we see as flaw in individuals may indeed be flaw in interpretation, a misplaced gaze, or lack of understanding.

Context matters.

\* \* \*

As psychologists we can now do what others in fields such as history, anthropology, and sociology have been able to do—namely, use the study of an individual life as the means for revealing social structures and ideologies. We learn about society and culture as we learn about the particular unique person. (Suzanne Ouellette, *Portraits of Pioneers in Developmental Psychology*, 2012)

\* \* \*

Fidelindo Lim came to the United States at the age of twenty-two. He emigrated from the Philippines at a time when nurses were in great demand in America, and he was a new nurse. Having learned his craft in the Philippines and completed his studies in the late eighties, the beginning of his career coincided with high demands and low pay for American nurses. Foreigners took jobs in healthcare that many Americans didn't want. Fidelindo arrived in New York City against the backdrop of a raging

AIDS epidemic, economic hardships left at home, and with everything he knew about being a gay man coming directly from his experiences in the Philippines. In his own words, he makes note that being gay was linked directly to the performance of certain gender roles (i.e., whether a man is active or passive in sexual intercourse would determine if he is viewed as gay), a reality not undocumented in the literature on LGB Filipinos (Nadal & Corpus, 2013).

On more than one occasion I have had the privilege of speaking with my friend about his experiences, both coming of age in the Philippines and coming out in the United States. I have been fortunate in being allowed to record and share some of our conversations for further analysis and reflection. I believe that his words demonstrate the nature of culture in self-understanding as it relates to being gay and interpretation as it relates to mental health.

I think it is important to note that he might take issue with my employing the language of "coming out" here as he notes during a written exchange,

> there is plenty of evidence in the literature to support that coming out (or its antithesis) impacts the general well-being of LGBT persons. What I wanted to illustrate is that certain developmental markers in LGBT expressions may not apply to some cultures. I think partly the conspicuous absence of the coming out [process] in Filipino LGBT expression is the lack of vocabulary to articulate the process. LGBT identity and expression descriptors (e.g., "bakla" for gays and "tomboy" for lesbians) resonate with such negativity and stigma that I cannot even picture myself saying "I am gay" in my own dialect, but I have no problem saying it in English.[7]

We have discussed what it was like for him to be gay as he came to understand himself culturally as a Filipino man. Notably, it was in line with the collective, pervasive ideology in the Philippines at that time. One might consider Fidelindo's expressions as a metabolism of the social structure:

> to be gay means you possess within you the female virtues of subservience, loyalty, not expecting anything but serving the male counterpart in whatever relationship, you would call it. So, a gay person would be feeling the same way about himself [as a straight person does about gay people]. And it's, it's almost an affirmation that this is your gender role. So, you didn't question it. In fact, it validated who you thought and felt you were. If I didn't feel that way, maybe I am not gay, right? There was no reciprocity. There was one way it was expected; you didn't ask for anything else different because the role, the gender roles defined you as [serving] the guy, [making] them happy. So, there was no confusion. It

wouldn't drive you crazy because you were not confused about what is expected of you.

We have also spoken about the concept of gay relationships, as I believe relational patterns provide great insight into the construction of identities, primarily those that are most often nurtured through interpersonal engagement. Herein, we see a cultural foundation for expectations of self and others, healthy interpersonal interaction, and ways in which the cultural understanding of what is appropriate manifests in an individual's behavior, which is then observed by an outsider (e.g., friend, clinician, or otherwise).

Relationship did not exist in the context of a meaningful reciprocal manner. Gay people would express their emotions, either directly or indirectly, to a straight person and that person would know that you are attracted to them, but they would obviously not be able to reciprocate that. However, there's a chance that you might end up having sex with this person, okay, in different ways. So, you end up in a physical activity, sexual activity, with them. In that case it's usually a one way, a one-way thing wherein a straight guy drops down his pants, gets a blow job, and that's the end of it. He is not going to do the same thing to the gay guy . . . no discussion, none of that.

This excerpt seems to run counter to what we know to be true in America about the multiplicities of expression allowable to gay men and the limited expressions allowable for straight men. As I consider Fidelindo's transition from a context in which the preceding is held as cultural fact, it would seem that a host of mental health concerns might ensue. In the observed behavior, there is clearly an element of risk, undue self-sacrifice, and emotional detachment that may be characteristic of many mental illnesses. However, what the medical model might characterize as related to illness, Filipino culture might associate with normalcy or acceptable behavior (Tuliao, 2014). In all of these excerpts there is the pressing reality of cultural dynamics circulating in the spaces between the words. Simultaneously, knowledge is spoken about him as an individual but also as an individual who exists within a particular place at a particular time.

As I have noted previously, you cannot rightly appreciate the picture without the frame or marvel at the tapestry without an examination of the threads that compose its image.

When I came [to the United States] I was naïve of the idea that two gay guys could be romantically and sexually equal. I was not thinking about that. In 1990 if I saw a good-looking guy walking down the street, I would assume he was straight. Although he might be gay, I didn't associate a good-looking male person with being gay. It didn't occur to me at that time. Being gay means to be effeminate and you would not be attracted to a gay, effeminate male person. So, I am here and see a lot of good-looking people, they look good and they look heterosexual. . . . And, they're masculine, they conform to the image of the heterosexual male. In the Philippines, gay people did not date. When I came here I was still in this framework.

The striking conflation of sex, gender, and sexual orientation here seems to point to a kind of mental lapse in self-articulation. Truly, it would give pause to many contemporary, Western LGB folks as problematic, yet it is truly reconciled within Fidelindo. Indeed it seems that as the external culture is internalized, then carried to a new place in which the internal no longer matches the external, it necessitates shifting labels and potentially the application of labels that might signify mental illness. One might expect a lack of self-esteem or depression to be emergent, one might even try to read beneath the quoted text for those indicators in order to make the association between unhealthy behavior and an unhealthy body or mind.

What we do observe is that the social determinants of mental health we look for as precursors of certain conditions (David, 2010), within particular populations (e.g., gay Filipinos) may in fact reveal something else about a person, something more real, than their level of risk for decline in mental health or individual avoidance of the mental healthcare system (such as a lack of help-seeking behavior, which is typically associated with the Filipino and Asian-American populations).

You didn't question your lot in life because it would be immoral to question God [in the Philippines]. You didn't struggle because you accepted. When you accept it is resiliency building . . . in the gay perspective of things this is somehow protective . . . the Filipino characteristics[8], I think, have protective value in terms of mental health. This may not be unique to the Philippines because I think other immigrant populations have the same. It may not just be the Philippines, but I can't say.

\* \* \*

What, you might ask, does a young, Black American man have to say about the realities of Filipino American life for an older adult? What can a US citizen contribute to a conversation about immigrant mental health? How can someone who has never seen a patient or client make claims about what is important for mental health practitioners to know? In essence, it seems, the answer is inherent in the question(s). The categories employed to divide and set the conversation as one of ignorance versus expertise are, in fact, as futile as the labels applied to those who populate those categories. If I have learned nothing else over the course of life and study, I have learned that it is our shared fate and humanity that elevates us, not the porous boundaries of the groups to which we, either by choice or force, pledge allegiance. There is something universal in our shared understanding of the inherent uniqueness of one another as a result of the origins from which we have all emerged—inclusive of culture. We would do well to acknowledge this as a global community facing the challenges of the coming era.

The intention throughout this piece has been an attempt to trouble established pathways of understanding mental health. In providing the preceding qualitative data, I hope that, in some small part, I have shifted your thinking about how social realities and culture not only shape the nature of health within bodies, but they also shape the interpretation from the perspective of the person under observation. Additionally, those forces shape the interpretation of the information one receives. What we see as problematic may actually form the foundation for resiliency as it relates to mental health—the more culturally diverse one is, the more he or she might be inclined to thrive in situations others may find troubling (F. Lim, personal communication, April 17, 2016). Fidelindo makes note that, perhaps, a further elaboration of resiliency as protective is necessary in the mental illness/wellness literature. "I think resiliency is poorly understood or supported by clinicians. I think this speaks to the continued focus on cure rather than wellness in the practice of medicine or psychiatry" (F. Lim, personal communication, April 17, 2016). Focusing on resiliency will hopefully distance clinicians from pathologizing LGB persons and situate them as strengthened rather than disadvantaged by their multiple identities.

If clinicians look for something, they'll find it. It is important to make note of what is missed when one's gaze is not sufficiently widened or informed enough to take in all of the information present in another person's observed behavior.

Though the focus here is on an individual life and a particular context, its core lessons are applicable, within acceptable bounds, to work with underrepresented groups or subcultures. There are certainly things that carry over as important to remember when engaging patients or clients in a mental health context. As Ouellette notes, the individual life is the vehicle for greater understanding of our shared social reality.

# NOTES

1. It is important to note here that employment of the term "environment" can often be misleading as it is used in relation to a host of factors that have influence on individuals. Environment could consist of "infectious agents, pollutants, and other exogenous factors that influence the individual's physical surroundings. Environmental threats to mental health include these traditional parameters—along with pharmaceutical and illicit drugs, injuries, and nutritional deficiencies—but also consist of psychosocial conditions that relate to the individual's perceptions of the social and physical world" (Schmidt, 2007, p. A404–406). In this chapter, environment is used primarily to describe the cultural and interpersonal environment, the world of social norms and expectations, linked to place.

2. The term "context" is another that warrants further explanation. Here and throughout the paper context refers to the social, historical, national, political, interpersonal, and cultural milieu within which individuals are located, at present. Certainly it is understood that all of these things are dynamic and all bear witness to and influence each other.

3. The fundamental attribution error, also known as the correspondence bias or attribution effect, is the tendency to attribute observed characteristics/behaviors to a person's disposition rather than to the environment. One of the earliest demonstrations of this effect was in a classical social psychology experiment, published in a 1967 article by Edward E. Jones and Victor A. Harris. Though it is useful for the considerations of the current paper, it should be said that this effect is not without critique in the scientific community. The practical value is most useful here, over and above the scientific.

4. Kurt Lewin was a German-American social psychologist. He is most well-known today for his commitment to action research and applied psychology. He developed the equation $B = f(P, E)$—where B is behavior, P is person, and E is environment—as a counterpoint to the debate of nature versus nurture. He put forward that nature and nurture worked together to explain an individual's behavior.

5. A person's social identity is the information they derive about the "self" based on group membership, which is shared with others. Groups that could influence or contribute to one's social identity might include race, class, gender, etc. Social identity has historically been thought to correlate with self-esteem.

6. For several exceptional and necessarily critical definitions of the meaning of culture as a dynamic force, over and above traditions and customs, see the work by Per Gjerde. Notably his paper *Culture, Power, and Experience: Toward a Person-Centered Cultural Psychology* published in Human Development, which provides a strong foundation for engagement with this construct.

7. The provided data was collected for a course in the study of lives. It is provided here with permission from Fidelindo Lim, who appears in the authorship credit for this chapter. He speaks his own words and lived truth as a contribution to this work.

8. In this part of the interview, Fidelindo makes note of several characteristics of Filipinos that he personally sees manifested in his own life. He agrees with a growing body of work on Filipino psychology that notes characteristics such as *getting along, debt of gratitude,* and *filial piety* as important markers of Filipino social relations.

# REFERENCES

David, E. J. R. (2010). Cultural mistrust and mental health help-seeking attitudes among Filipino Americans. *Asian American Journal of Psychology,* 1(1), 57–66.

Nadal, K. L., & Corpus, M. J. H. (2013). "Tomboys" and "baklas": Experiences of lesbian and gay Filipino Americans. *Asian American Journal of Psychology,* 4(3), 166–175.

Schmidt, C. W. (2007). Environmental connections: A deeper look into mental illness. *Environmental Health Perspectives,* 115(8), A404–A410.

Tuliao, A. P. (2014). Mental health help seeking among Filipinos: A review of the literature. *Asia Pacific Journal of Counselling and Psychotherapy,* 5(2), 124–136.

# 6

## TRUST ME, I'M A DOCTOR

### Lynn Breedlove

I'm a visible queer ADD tranz* guy with authority issues, a combo of shy and cocky in a body that has most people confused or pissed, so I spent fifteen years slowly killing myself with drugs. I bought the hype that I didn't belong here.

Never did like the idea of a doctor's office, where your ass is hanging out of a paper dress while he's in the white coat, and guess which one is dressed for success. Whenever I went in with my drug problem, or my queerness, they never held back with the comments or a look of who-did-this-to-you?-You-did-this-to-you.

If I let Them diagnose me, who knows what else They'd find. Paranoid. Anxious. Narcissist. Hot mess. BP, OCD, ADD, ACDC, no ID. The AMA's DSM epithet list is endless.

It's all true. The idea of the DSM is to make enough insanity categories to lock anyone up at any time. Convenient, like laws, to suddenly, selectively enforce a forgotten rule whenever certain people give you trouble. Pissing on a wall in public, if you're rich, not a problem. If you're homeless, or a sex offender. Society edges you out of anything but a jail job. Class war from the inside out.

I always self-medicate. If I need medication, I'd rather go to the corner than a White man in a white coat.

I figure I know more, and these days, care more, about me than they do. So, I study up. Treat myself with therapy and vitamins. Once I had healthcare for a minute, so I went to the local hospital shrink. I felt crazy just filling out the form:

Are you paranoid that people are watching you?

(Yes! I think the government is gonna add this to my files, which already fills a whole extra room somewhere, and lock me up in a strait [straight!] jacket! ain't telling you shit!)

I said,

Hey doc, I think I have ADD. Can you help me?

He says,

What are the symptoms, all leaned back in his chair looking at me like I'm a mouse
in a cage, only he can't tell, girl mouse? boy mouse?

Well, lessee, I forget stuff, lose things, spaz out, say rude shit, say too much, haven't
said enough, get mad, mood swing, impulse shop, fall down and I'm not even
drunk. Famous for chopping up rubber dicks, half naked, which made angry
young feminists happy in the Nineties, but my parents don't get it, so I don't know
whether to be proud or ashamed. Energy issues. Disorganized, late, impatient,
frustrated by technology, math, Judith Butler and any other academic jargon I see
as a special code, like legalese, algebra, or medical terms.

Judith who?

Never mind.

I used to drink, smoke weed, and do speed. Drug dyslexia. Speed calmed me down.
Pot and beer speeded me up. Now I use smokes, java, and sugar in a vain attempt
to focus.

Mm-hmm.

He's looking at me like I'm the mouse that keeps choosing the cocaine button over
food pellets or water until it dies.

So, do I have it?

Probably.

Whaddaya mean, probably?

If you think you do, then you probably do.

So, this is what twenty years of school looks like. . . . What can we do?

Do you want drugs?

Nope. Tried that. Didn't work.

Well, then I can't help you.

OK. It's been lovely.

So, I go back to my previous plan. Twelve-step programs, they say it's a cult but hey
it's a cult that benefits people, so I brainwash myself out of suicidal sabotage, because
like Pink says in the ADD national anthem, I'm a hazard to myself.

Amino acids, gingko, vitamins, green superfoods. Switch bike messenger job for
dog walker, social worker, cabbie. From punk frontman to comic, to writer, to fool
who shares ideas on getting through hard shit, translated into layman's terms for the
cultphobic, back to frontman.

Slow down. Age, gracefully—or not. Dharma talks brainwash me to sleep, because
things do fall apart, and when they do, I channel my impulsivity into faith, as I step
off cliffs with intention.

Wake up more patient. Pray and meditate because if I'm gonna be fanatical why not be fanatical about sanity. Ride my bike in less traffic, run my pit bull at 3 AM down the middle of deserted suburban streets, quit smoking, smell flowers, hear crickets, mourn, celebrate, sing.

After thirty-five years of nonstop no-plot action, a babe break is in order. I may be all I can handle right now. You can only handle three projects at a time and a babe is a project. Boundaries are limits on one's own behavior. Oh. Thought it was about controlling other people.

Life coaches and therapists listen without judgement or at least keep it to themselves, collaborate on solutions.

Walking meditation, Tonglen, ever outward expanding compassion visualization, while walking, because sitting is impossible. Tai chi while watching action movies at 4 AM. Late night. Quiet. Focus. Feng shui bachelor pad. When things look orderly, I feel sane. Still call my cell phone and run around the house until I find it under my car. But not every day.

Could I have done that with Adderall? Maybe. But when my pals start chopping that shit up and snorting it, vitamin B looks like a good option.

Sometimes I do too much, talk on the phone while slipping in a puddle I made while steam cleaning carpets to show the apartment, which I better sublet in the next five days because I do not have rent, while I am booking a tour that I am leaving for in a week, and right when asking the guy at the bike store about cheap wheels to replace the ones that got stolen when I forgot several times to pick up a bike my friend loaned me, which, when I finally went to get it, I forgot the key to the lock, and right when the bike parts guy picks up the phone, I slip in the puddle left by the steam cleaner and fly, throwing the phone and the computer through the air and sprain my ankle a week before I am supposed to drive around the country on a solo tour.

And then I'm mad I can't control anything and have to ask for help, which I hate. Call a pal. Give thanks for what I have, hugs, acceptance, gratitude, a body and a brain that mostly work. Then halfway through the tour, when the never expected happens, I get evicted and mom has a stroke all at the same time, I'm able to deal with legalese, lawyers, doctors, in two languages on two continents, in between crying, because compartmentalizing feelings, multi-tasking and switching gears at high speeds with an open heart is the exact combo of talents needed right now, which doctors would like to tamp down.

I turn my risk-taker entrepreneurial gene into a nonprofit that provides safety for my people, with an international trademark and a crew that helps me implement my dreams and at the same time shows up for my ailing mom, and my community, while making art out of it. My community shows up for me, because I've shown up for them with my whole self, not some made-up chemical self. And everything works out perfect, just putting one foot in front of the other, right off the edge of the cliff, no net. I'm either gonna walk on air or sprout a squirrel suit or get caught on a branch or land in the river like Butch Cassidy.

So, if a doctor wants to fix what books call crazy, thanks, but that's what makes me think of the one line that's gonna explain everything, just as I walk onstage.

Pressure, sparks, dots connect to translate gender politics into simplicity and make it funny or deep or whatever is needed to get through to humans.

Because I don't need to fix or medicate. I'm not a problem. I'm a comic, a punk, an evolutionary, a tranzlater, a pal, a writer, a person who creates systems that help.

# 7

## LGBTQ SUBSTANCE ABUSE AND MENTAL HEALTH ISSUES
## A PROVIDER'S JOURNEY

*Joseph Ruggiero*

I have been providing addiction-related services and educating professionals on LGBTQ-sensitive substance use treatment for over twenty years, and I have learned more than I can possibly sum up in one article. But I hope that this will serve as an introduction to what effective programming can look like and how I have gone about growing on personal and professional levels.

Like most psychologists of my generation, I was not trained in LGBTQ-affirmative care. The university I attended was a religious and conservative institution in the otherwise liberal bastion of NYC, and it forbade the formation of an LGBTQ student group. Its diversity courses lacked content regarding sexual orientation and gender identity, and while fortunately I did not encounter any blatantly homophobic incidents, our textbooks and classroom discussions took a pathologizing view of lesbian, gay, and bisexual clients. Microaggressions were not recognized at the time, and the existence of transgender clients was not even acknowledged.

My personal development took a while to unfold; earlier in my career, I was not capable of the work I currently perform. This was due in no small part to my ongoing struggle to be comfortable as a gay man. The deeply conservative Catholic environment in which I was raised entailed very few conversations about sex—and when the subject was touched upon, it was described as something fear-inducing that should be avoided. I came out as AIDS was just beginning to be understood and discussed, which heightened this fear of sex for both me and my peers. As a young man, I experienced anxiety around other gay men and had no idea where or how I might fit into the LGBTQ world. This is not at all uncommon, and this sense of isolation and confusion can inform addiction—it is easy to understand how alienated LGBTQ folks can end up feeling connected to a community of users.

It is well-known that LGBTQ communities and mental health providers have historically maintained a strained relationship and that clinicians being ill-prepared to treat LGBTQ clients has done damage. There are mental health clinic environments hostile to LGBTQ people—but there are also LGBTQ-naive clinics (SAMSHA, 2001). Reparative therapy should be, and yet is not, entirely a thing of the past. Staff at some clinics refuse to address transgender clients by their proper (i.e., chosen) names; some organizations have no LGBTQ staff; and some clinics fail to even inquire about, let alone recognize, LGBTQ status.

Many studies indicate that LGBTQ communities are at higher risk than heterosexuals for substance use disorders—e.g., 27.6% compared to 10.5% (McCabe et al., 2010). One study of LGB adolescents found sexual orientation to be a greater predictor of the use of "hard drugs," such as cocaine and injected drugs, than substances more commonly associated with adolescents, such as marijuana and excessive alcohol use (Marshal et al., 2008). This same study found bisexuals to be at highest risk for substance use.

Also well-documented is our community's history of meeting up in bars and clubs—and, more recently, on the Internet. These situations can entail risk—and unfortunately, in non-urban areas that offer fewer settings such as community centers and other LGBTQ-specific venues aside from bars, there may be few alternatives for socialization. LGBTQ community members sometimes use alcohol and drugs to decrease shame and anxiety associated with sexual or intimate contact. Furthermore, many LGBTQ individuals continue to deal with the loss of friends and significant others to HIV and may self-medicate to alleviate depression and avoid other unwanted feelings. Some of my clients say they use drugs to help them manage the anxieties of negotiating HIV when having sex. Others have lost their entire social networks to AIDS and find themselves navigating complicated grief processes related to these losses.

In my early work in addiction, I ran an HIV support group comprising mostly gay men. One client stated that since he was gay, he assumed he would eventually become HIV-positive and develop a drug problem. I was both speechless and heartbroken. That this man had no examples of healthy gay male life was distressing, to put it mildly. It's a fact that gay men of my generation have had few role models, but fortunately, this is changing. The Internet and social media, problematic as they may be, have greatly expanded avenues for information, connection, and affirmation at the same time that changes to the social environment are moving the concept of a tragic, doomed gay life toward obsolescence.

In 2000, I worked with a gay male client who began using methamphetamine in addition to cocaine. Eventually he became sober, and he began referring people to me. My practice soon comprised 75% gay and bisexual men who had been using methamphetamine. In 2005, the NYC Department of Health and Mental Hygiene visited the Addiction Institute of New York because we were seeing more methamphetamine-using clients than any other project. The Department of Health and Mental Hygiene (DOHMH) funded us for three years, enabling me to co-found a program I continue to supervise to this day, the Crystal Clear Project. Crystal Clear has found effective methods of addressing the methamphetamine problem in NYC among gay and bisexual men. I have done a good amount of work with HIV-positive clients since the beginning of the AIDS epidemic and have always been interested in working with LGBTQ clients who struggle with substances. But developing a specialty in working with methamphetamine users was unexpected. Fortunately, my interest and expertise has progressed as the program has grown.

The larger outpatient program I oversee has always attracted community members via an openly gay-affirmative stance, the existence of LGB staff, and a commitment to LGBTQ clients. I began trying to understand what it meant for *all* staff to provide LGBTQ-sensitive care and to nurture them as they work hard to navigate barriers in providing competent treatment.

I strive to provide an open and supportive environment in which gay and bisexual men can discuss sensitive topics including illegal drug use, sex, identity, race, and intimacy. This takes a lot of courage on the part of our clients, who continually amaze me. It is incredibly stigmatizing to be a substance user in our world, particularly when you are additionally marginalized for being LGBTQ. Because of the ways in which psychiatric providers have mistreated some LGBTQ clients, many have well-founded fears around treatment. When I started the Crystal Clear program, I was surprised by how often LGB clients called me to ask about my sexual orientation right after I introduced myself. These clients were attempting to understand whether our program was a safe space for them. Would they be judged?

I could relate to this: I remember my own fears in seeking out therapy as a young man. I remember listening to practitioners' outgoing voicemails and hanging up because I thought they sounded too conservative. I relate to that fear of stepping into treatment.

Recently a transgender client was verbally abusive toward several staff members at the outpatient clinic. When we met, she eloquently described her struggle with being in treatment. She was triggered early on in the program after having been addressed by the legal name she did not use, and although an apology was made and a resolution presumably reached, she continued to verbally abuse staff. In trying to repair our relationship, she described having been mistreated by so many past providers that her current behavior felt inevitable. She had too often been silenced and needed to raise her voice to get her needs met, even though her approach rarely yielded the results she desired. Ours was a moving discussion. I had encountered a client able to access her voice in such a touching, powerful way, and I reflected that back to her. She gave voice to the struggles of many LGBTQ clients entering treatment.

There is no question that treating LGBTQ clients can arouse providers' own anxieties about sex, sexual orientation and identity, and the nature of intimacy. Transference can arise, and it can be threatening for some clinicians to question their orientations and identities. When clinicians claim to be entirely comfortable talking about all of these issues, I find cause to worry. Providers must be aware and practice introspection when we are uncomfortable rather than disregarding the potential impact of difficult subjects. Clients need to feel that they can discuss sex with a therapist who is open and nonjudgmental and who can help clients define and clarify the choices they wish to make. It's important to know if and when these discussions induce too much anxiety for a therapist to provide objective guidance. As therapists, we must examine our own value systems, our personal backgrounds, and the way these impact how we think about sex and gender. What messages do we give our clients when it comes to these issues?

When I first started the Crystal Clear program, the groups were frequently riddled with conflict (which should happen in group psychotherapy), and I realized how disappointed I felt. I came to think that this was really about my need to create a totally supportive gay-affirmative environment to heal my own wounds. But my own growth required that I learn to embrace conflict among LGBTQ clients; treating people will inevitably involve negative encounters both among clients in group settings and between client and therapist in individual settings.

An ideal therapeutic environment would, of course, be entirely free of prejudices and microaggressions among clients. But realistically, the most important thing I can do is acknowledge these transgressions. So many times have LGBTQ individuals and communities remained invisible. LGBTQ-affirmative addiction care can start a healing process. I feel honored that our clients allow me into their lives so they can grow—and maybe I can as well.

## REFERENCES

Marshal, M., Friedman, M. S., Stall, R., King, K., Miles, J., Gold, M. A., et al. (2008). Sexual orientation and adolescent substance use: A metanalysis and methodological review. *Addiction, 103*(4), 546–556.

McCabe, S. E., Bostwick, W. B., Hughes, T. L., et al. (2010). Victimization and substance use disorders in a national sample of heterosexual and sexual minority women and men. *American Journal of Public Health, 100*, 1946–1952.

SAMSHA. (2001). *A provider's introduction to substance abuse treatment for lesbian, gay, bisexual, and transgender individuals.* Retrieved from: https://store.samhsa.gov/shin/content/SMA12-4104/SMA12-4104.pdf

# 8

## THE BONE CRUSHING

*Bill Konigsberg*

When I was a baby, I used to wake up singing.

That's what my parents tell me. Whereas other babies might cry upon waking up, I'd be crooning in my crib, and that's how they'd know I was awake.

Other things that were true about me as a baby: I ate jalapeño peppers. In fact, my parents couldn't find anything I wouldn't eat. I was just raring to go, to experience, to taste. Everything.

That was before.

Immediately after my dad left our Greenwich Village brownstone when I was four years old, I sat on the floor in the living room and felt nothing. My sister sobbed and screamed. That, I think now, was normal behavior. I didn't know how to do that, or maybe I thought I couldn't. I don't remember. All I know is that I sat and stared at the living room wall and wondered whether the dingy yellow color would always look like that and whether that was acceptable. I wasn't sure that it was. Acceptable.

I stopped singing.

I stopped feeling.

A few weeks later, overwhelmed by not being able to see his kids, my dad broke into our house. He broke down the door to get in, and he picked up my sister and twirled her around. And then he picked me up and twirled me, and he sobbed and he kept saying "My son, my son, my son," over and over and over. And though he made me high and the room spun like an amusement park ride, I still felt nothing. I was numb deep inside, where it mattered. Whatever feeling I was supposed to feel was inaccessible, perhaps. I waited for my dad to put me down. I did not sob or scream.

This was, as I see it, the start of a lifelong struggle with depression.

I don't know what came first: the chicken of depression or the egg of my parents' divorce. It's easier to blame my problems on my parents, though in reality by the time you're forty-four, it's hard to continue doing that. I think that my depressive chemistry ignited when I was faced with my first trauma. And I've been battling it ever since.

There's so much I don't know.

I do know, however, that in ninth grade, I'd spend my free periods sitting in a corner of the hallway, hugging my knees into my chest, scribbling random lines on a pad because I felt that if I stopped scribbling, I might walk off campus and jump off the George Washington Bridge.

I know that in the evenings I'd sit on the radiator next to the window in my room, looking out across the airshaft, trying to see into other people's apartments, trying to figure out what it was that made them want to live. Hoping against hope that someone would do something, something outside my own reach, that would make me feel like a full person, that would bring me up to zero. I felt so far below.

I used to call this desire to have someone else be the catalyst that would make me feel human "electronic." I felt like my life was electric—I wound it up, and like one of those bathtub boats, my life went until I'd run out of energy, and then it was time to wind myself up again. I felt as though everyone out there was in the digital age, and I was a wind-up toy. I wanted something or someone or someplace that would make me electronic.

I fantasized of running away to a magical place where I'd be able to leave my brain behind. My brain was so filled with monsters real and imagined that I felt literally buried every day and that there was an emptiness in my chest that pushed against my ribcage so hard that I could imagine my ribs cracking. The emptiness actually hurt. It felt like it could swallow my whole being if I let it.

What I didn't know was that there was a name for this. Depression. Severe depression. I just figured that my feelings were normal, or at least normal for me. And they were, though it's amazing to think that something that was normal for me could also come so close to killing me. That doesn't make sense.

Writing was one thing I had to help me survive. I didn't write about being sad. I wrote about other people and their huge emotions. Ascribing them to me felt too dangerous. So I wrote about a man dying of AIDS and living out the final months of his life on a Pacific Ocean beach, watching the waves flow in and out and thinking about what came after. Or I wrote about an African-American girl who felt that there was nothing and no one in the world that could get through her thick skin and make her feel new.

Coming to terms with the fact that I was gay was certainly not made easier by the depression. It's another chicken and egg situation. Did being gay—being different from my family of origin in such an elemental way—exacerbate my depression? Or did my depression make it that much harder to accept being different? It's certainly true that when I feel depressed, I cannot see the glass as anything beyond half empty. Objectively I can now see the benefits of being different, but I surely didn't see them as a teenager.

Depression followed me to college. Twice I either left school or needed to take a medical leave because I couldn't function. The first time—when I was in the spring of my freshman year at Oberlin College—I found myself feeling so isolated that one night I sat outside under a tree in the rain and stared into space for four or five hours. I simply couldn't move because I was so afraid of what I'd do if I did move. I finally moved inside and stared at my wall the rest of the night, and had I not called my friend Brigit the next day, had I not reached out for help and then gone home the following day, I truly don't know that I'd be here.

My nemesis has three times caused me to take a medical leave from a job. It's horrifying to not be able to function and have to tell people that you can't work because you're depressed; people simply don't get that it's an illness. And each time I walked around feeling like a weak fraud, like stronger people were out doing their thing while I frittered my time away in therapists' offices and napped away afternoons because I felt unable to do anything else.

As I've gotten older, it's gotten somewhat easier. Longer periods have elapsed between depressive episodes, and, of course, medicine has played a role in that. A few times I've decided I've outgrown depression, and I've stopped taking medicine. None of those episodes has ended happily. Each time, my foe comes back and beats me to the ground. It might take a year to happen, but invariably it does.

These days, I live in a precarious state. When I am well, I am very well. I have love and a writing career that fulfills me deeply. I have two great dogs and a wonderful home and, perhaps most importantly, I have a power greater than myself that keeps me out of my head so much. But I say this state is precarious because it is; a few months ago, out of nowhere, my medicines stopped working for me. The medicines that create a web through which I am not supposed to be able to fall failed, and I woke up one day and the monsters were back, and despite everything going so beautifully in my life, I fell through the cracks and suddenly I was underground again. I have all these tools, but none of them was stronger than the feeling in my chest, the bone-crushing despair and the associated voices that told me that things felt this way always, that they always had, and they always would, and my life as I knew it was a fallacy and this dreadful feeling was the reality.

That's the best I can describe it. Depression crushes the bones in my chest.

The bone-crush told me that perhaps the world would be a better place without Bill Konigsberg, and I began to think about buying a gun. I didn't want my family to suffer, so thinking about them became a bad idea. The only thing to think about was ending my own pain, which felt like it was suffocating me.

It didn't make sense, but of course depression doesn't make sense. It doesn't follow that the boy who used to sing and eat jalapeños became the boy who sat and stared at walls. No one can make a coherent story about that, because it's inherently incoherent. People with everything don't shoot themselves in the temple, and, had it not been for a split-second decision to call a doctor and make an appointment, I would not have been put on the medicine—Abilify—that has so far effectively saved my life.

So it feels precarious because I don't know if that medicine will always work or if, like the other ones, it will stop. And people tell stories about not needing medicines anymore because they found this or that—spirituality or cognitive therapy or what have you—that gave them the tools to deal with the feelings.

I have lots of knowledge and I believe in a higher power and yet nothing has ever been strong enough to help me through that gut-wrenching pain, the thing that I fear more than anything. I feel entirely powerless over it, and it scares me to my core.

A few years back, I went on a tour to help LGBTQ at-risk youth, to spread the word about The Trevor Project and other tools that exist so that they stay alive when it feels like they want to just end it all. It was part of the tour to promote my current novel, *The Porcupine of Truth*. I love the idea of helping other kids who are struggling the way I did. I felt like the only person in the world who knew what it was like to be different and alone. I had no idea that others were struggling, too, and I know now that it's the most helpless of feelings. And some of those kids are suffering from depression, and for others it's just an experience. And yet as I spoke on the tour, I wondered also if I was the man for the job. After all, how can I tell kids that "it gets better" when just three months earlier my life nearly ended? I mean, it does get better. But for those of us suffering from depression, it's better with an asterisk. It's petrifying to me to be writing this not fully knowing how the story ends. I don't know how to remove that asterisk, how to make it so that I control my moods and my emotions, and make it so that if and when the demons return, I know what to do and how to vanquish them.

I truly have no idea.

PART II

# Stories of Survival

# 9

## IN CHIRON'S FOOTSTEPS

*Paula J. Williams*

I have always been drawn to the concept of the wounded healer, an idea going back to Greek mythology and developed as an archetype by Jung. It centers around Chiron, a centaur who is wounded in battle by an arrow dipped in Hydra's blood. He embarks upon a journey to try to find a way to heal the terrible pain of his injury; as he travels, seeking his cure, he teaches others the art of healing. In so doing, he finds his own healing, learning to understand others' pain from his own experience of pain. This idea is comforting to me as it removes the pressure to have healed myself before I can help others to heal, and it helps me make sense of my own path.

### ON BECOMING A THERAPIST

I chose to train as a psychotherapist because of my experience supporting people with a history of trauma, especially around sexual violence. In the late 1990s, I became a volunteer for a website offering peer support groups via email—a fairly new concept at the time. I was asked to take over the administration of the groups while the founder was in the hospital, and she asked me upon her return, and alongside the growth of the site, to be the main administrator for specific groups for survivors of childhood sexual abuse (CSA). People in those groups turned to me for support and understanding, which I found I was able to give, and I learned an enormous amount about the effects of CSA on people from simply listening. I heard stories of the worst things that people can do to one another and the worst things that people consequently do to themselves. I developed the ability to hear those things with compassion and without needing to protect myself from what I heard. I had met my partner through that website; a survivor of CSA as well as rape as an adult, she struggled greatly with mental illness. I was used to supporting her in times of relapse. She would disappear for hours at a time, returning home with a hand dripping with blood where she had cut herself, but no memory of where she had been or what she had done.

My experience running those groups taught me that survivors often experienced similar difficulties. Common effects of CSA and rape include self-injury, dissociation (on a continuum from spacing out a little, to fugue states like my partner's, to Dissociative Identity Disorder), alcoholism, drug misuse, eating disorders, panic attacks—the list goes on. I cared about these survivors; I saw firsthand the lack of therapeutic support available to many of them, I found I had a knack for this work, and I knew that I would benefit from proper training. Even during my studies, I was the person to whom my fellow trainees chose to disclose experiences of sexual violence; they "knew I would understand." And I did, usually. I went on to train as a therapist supervisor and studied for a master's degree with a focus on Vicarious Trauma in therapists, and I now teach in a therapy training program.

I have become an experienced therapist with an extensive background in trauma work. My job is to support other people as they work through the issues impacting negatively on their lives so that they can tap into their full potential. I have read repeatedly that the therapist, as someone who has worked through her own issues and by virtue of some kind of unnamed psychological superiority, is in a position to help the clients who are (to paraphrase) somehow less competent than she is. We therapists, up here, are occasionally troubled by the rigors of normal life, but mentally healthy—helping them, down there, struggling with mental illness to varying degrees. I am a bona fide member of this club, accepted into this world. One of "us."

## THERAPIST AS HUMAN BEING

The problem is that I don't really like that formulation of the world of therapy—because I don't often feel like one of "us." In this formulation, I feel much more like "them." And that's because I *am*. After all, nobody ever asks me this question: What brought me to a peer support website for survivors in the first place? Once the question is asked, the answer must be obvious: I have a history of trauma.

That history is long and full; I experienced a childhood of violence, cruelty, and neglect. I was raised in a single-parent family by an alcoholic mother who chose to buy booze rather than feed and clothe me. Her absence throughout my childhood—work all day, pub all night—left me vulnerable to significant abuse for more than ten years. My abuser was sadistic, subjecting me to systematic abuse, almost daily, from the time I was roughly three until I was thirteen, when he finally left the family home. In addition to the beatings and sexual abuse, his actions amounted to psychological torture. Every morning I doubted I would make it to the end of the day alive, as I would wake in bed to find a pillow held over my face or I would find myself held under the bath water until I believed I would drown. My abuser was a master of gaslighting, leaving me in a permanent state of confusion and distrust, and he made me believe that if I told the truth about what was happening to me, I would be cast out on the streets or taken into care where, he convinced me, things would be even worse. I learned to be silent, and I learned to be invisible.

When I was thirteen, my mum lost her job and things came to a head between her and this man, whose verbal abuse had for some time been directed at her as well as at me. She told him to leave. While we still lived in desperate poverty and she still drank every night, things improved once he left, though the aftermath of what I had been through was harrowing. My vulnerability was obvious, and I experienced sexual harassment and, at times, assault in the street. I became anorexic; I wanted to become even less visible, to stop attracting the attention of men, to punish my body, and to feel in control of it. I suspect I also was testing out whether anybody would notice if I faded away. Nobody did.

Eventually I got my act together academically, as I (correctly) believed that education would be my route out of the small and desperate life I could see rolling out before me, and I regained some precarious control over my relationship with food. I had been known to self-injure at times, but I had that mostly under control, too, expressing my then-volatile temper through punching and kicking walls. I went from one bad relationship to another, never having had any model of what a healthy relationship might look like, but each one did seem an improvement over the last.

At university, I had to study abroad for a year; first I went to Ecuador. While I was there alone, having found a room to rent in someone's house, my landlord violently raped me, threatening to kill me if I carried on fighting, and then threw me out on the streets with nowhere to go. All of my experiences of sexual harassment and assaults were suddenly relegated to minor inconveniences. For three years, I told no one of this. Deeply shocked and traumatized, I then had to leave for Spain, where I experienced more harassment—but I kept surviving. I returned home, got my degree, got married, and had my first child. My husband's behavior toward me amounted to emotional abuse, but compared to the other things that had happened to me, it barely registered. Looking back at that time now, with the knowledge and understanding I have gained, I realize that I was operating throughout from a place of trauma.

After the birth of my son I began to struggle with what had happened in Ecuador, and I sought help from my doctor, a therapist, and the peer support groups, which helped me to understand my experiences and normalized my feelings. I began to grow an understanding then of my desire to become a therapist. It will be obvious by now that my decision to take this path was in no small part due to my own experiences of deep trauma.

## THERAPIST HISTORIES

As someone who teaches people to become therapists, I know that the majority of our trainees have had some mental health difficulties of their own. Often this led them into therapy, which in turn helped them realize that they could help other people. I know about the struggles of most of the therapists I have met from conducting supervision groups and supporting trainees and through conversations with colleagues. Along with the depression and anxiety that are becoming endemic to our society, I hear about substance use, eating disorders, self-injury, bipolar disorder, what some people still refer to as "nervous breakdowns," suicidal thoughts, and more. And, of course, these struggles are often rooted in past traumas. Students must examine their own experiences and increase their self-awareness and ability to reflect. They need to learn the ethical principle of monitoring their fitness to practice and make sure they have sufficiently worked through their own issues. Trainee therapists seem to, for whatever reason, start from the position of *being* clients first, and what brought them to therapy often influences their decision to train. As Rothschild (2006) writes, "For most of us, our own personal history impacts greatly on our choice of career. This is a huge benefit, but can also be a deficit" (p. 207).

## THE PRICE OF MEMBERSHIP

What happens, then, to all these histories once a trainee qualifies to begin practicing? Where, I ask myself, have all the traumatized therapists gone? It is as though the issues leading to the therapy training have all been erased and a silence descends. As though people are no longer willing to acknowledge that they have been "them" as well as "us." While some colleagues sometimes speak in private about their past experiences, these discussions are largely hidden from view. In looking through my library of therapy textbooks, I found references over and over again to the "person" of the therapist and its centrality to the therapeutic process. Per Natiello (2001), "The quality of the relationship goes far beyond what we know, what we do, and how we do it. It is really about who we are—the spiritual, emotional, attitudinal characteristics that we embody as persons, our ability to make a deep connection, to tolerate intimacy, and to offer a climate of safety" (p. 25). Kahn (1997) states that "When all is said and done, nothing in our work may be more important than our willingness to bring as much of ourselves as possible to the therapeutic session" (p. 163). Almost every book I own says the same—and I agree. This does not mean that we disclose our past experiences to clients, of course; to burden clients with our own pain is not only inappropriate but anti-therapeutic and, I would argue, potentially abusive. However, that self we bring to each encounter is inevitably made up in part of our own experiences, so why must we pretend among ourselves that we have no major psychological issues? Why is there an unspoken rule against authenticity? Where are the books that mention therapist experiences of trauma? It seems there is barely an acknowledgment that people like me exist.

It makes sense, of course, that nobody would want a therapist so troubled by their own mental health issues that they are unable to support clients. They might use their therapeutic relationships for their own therapy or lose sight of safe boundaries. Nobody wants a therapist who breaks down in tears, unable to contain their own suffering. The development of therapy itself has its roots in psychoanalysis, in which the therapist is meant to be a blank screen onto which the client can project their own thoughts, feelings, and fears. This aligns with a medical model of psychological distress that locates mental illness firmly in the person of the patient, as a pathology requiring treatment or cure. Viewed through these lenses, the psychologically superior therapist has to be healthy, dispensing help to the inferior sufferer. The line between "us" and "them" is very clear and cannot be crossed. Natiello (2001), in discussing the attempt to create "an egalitarian therapeutic relationship," reminds us that therapy "occurs in a culture of authoritarianism, where some have power and some do not, and in a professional field in which clients are often viewed as sick, helpless, or too disturbed to find their way" (p. 43). With historical labeling of people with mental illness as mad, bad, or sad, how can therapists safely admit to having similar experiences to clients?

In my journey to becoming a therapist, having gained extensive experience from self-help groups, I began training as a volunteer with a rape crisis center. Halfway through the training, the program kicked me out, thereby reenacting all the dynamics of abuse they were meant to be challenging. I was given some spurious excuse, which I rejected, and I moved forward with a formal complaint. During the complaint process I voiced my belief that I was asked to leave simply because I had openly identified—among staff and trainees, but of course not with clients—as a rape survivor myself. Management confirmed this was the case. This was a rape crisis center, playing a public role in challenging stigma against women who have been raped and abused, throwing me out for challenging that stigma by acknowledging my experience! During my therapy training, a fellow student told me that she had been horrified that I had gained a place on the course because she felt I was "far too damaged to be able to help other people." Her view had changed significantly by the time we were training together; regardless, this represented what I was most afraid of.

There are only a handful of therapists who have spoken openly about surviving abuse. Annie Rogers wrote two books about her experience of working as a therapist, of a breakdown brought on by working with a traumatized child, and of her history of serious mental illness and the recovery of traumatic memories. Books about abuse include, in the odd chapter here and there, histories and testimonies from people who went on to become therapists. Bear's 1998 compendium on best practice, which claims to give equal value to the voices of survivors and the voices of clinicians, has only three contributors who openly acknowledge they are survivors. This, in a book about abuse!

These factors, coupled with difficult reactions from many whenever I did take the risk of disclosing, contributed to my confirmed experience of an "us and them" dynamic and how membership in one group precludes membership in the other. It reinforced my tendency toward silence and invisibility, which had been deeply ingrained in me since childhood. But now I found rules to which I attached my behavior. It was easy enough to observe the rule about not disclosing to clients and extend it to colleagues and peers within my profession. I found that this fed the "impostor syndrome" I used to experience, reinforcing my sense that I was not really meant to be in this particular profession and that if people learned the truth about me, I would somehow be cast out.

This evokes my description of my childhood fears and how I believed the story I'd been told that if I broke my silence, I would be cast out on the streets to die. In this world of apparently mentally healthy therapists, demonstrated by the dearth of stories about people with a history of mental illness or trauma-related issues, there did not seem to be room for my story. I did what I have always done: by and large I silenced myself, feeling like this nearly profession-wide silence about mental illness within the profession was rather like the Emperor's new clothes—an illusion through which I could see, but which the majority of people simply accepted as truth.

## THE PERSONAL AND THE PROFESSIONAL

As a survivor of repeated and significant trauma suffering from complex posttraumatic stress disorder (PTSD) and with a tendency toward mild dissociation—withdrawing into myself under conditions reminiscent of the trauma—I continued to work through these issues while going about my daily life and my work. Recognizing how I cling to invisibility and fear of speaking my truth helped me to begin to challenge my behaviors. I began to open up more about my experiences with some colleagues, in supervision groups and encounter groups, and with trusted friends within the profession. I began to see that perhaps some—though certainly not all—of my belief in that "us and them" dynamic came from me, and I began to challenge it by giving myself a voice. This was not easy, as it triggered both my fears about my professional standing and my deeper, younger fears about annihilation. As one therapist who has spoken out about this (in a book of survivor stories rather than one about therapy practice) stated, "I am both a survivor working on my own pain in therapy and a counsellor undertaking therapeutic work with survivors. The assumptions of my colleagues and clients; the collective myths and fears of our society and my own feelings and fears of shame fuse together to make this a most uncomfortable and uneasy combination" (1996, p. 245).

She states further that "Until recently I have unconsciously believed that these two groups are mutually exclusive and that I am guilty of some form of transgression by secretly belonging to both" (ibid., p. 244). She thinks that survivors are guilty of the same "us and them split," and I found that recognizing my own part in this belief was terrifying at times. I was fortunate enough, however, to find the support from supervisors and caring colleagues that helped me become less rigid and more open. I am still guarded, but I can now choose to speak out where once I felt there was no choice. I can really own the journey that brought me to this career at last, and I have made inroads into this element of my struggle. I was learning to question whether there had been actual rules in place, or if I had appropriated and instituted my own rules to reinforce my defense strategies. I began to think that perhaps there is not such a divide after all and began moving from "us and them" to "we."

## PAST AND PRESENT COLLIDE

And then my thinking, my progress, and even my identity, were challenged.

I experienced the kind of trauma that comes pre-loaded with shame and a huge dose of invisibility. The kind of trauma that my critical inner voice says "shouldn't happen to a therapist," as though my job somehow makes me special, immune, "better" than other people—part of "us," not "them." While I wanted to do away entirely with the "them and us" paradigm, instead I found myself buying right into it.

Each of my relationships had seemed to improve on the one before. Leaving my husband and entering into a relationship with a woman wasn't easy, especially since I was a practicing Catholic with a small child at the time. This move didn't present much of a challenge to my sexual self-identity, but it certainly challenged *others'* view of my identity. But I found this worth it—at first. My partner shared my understanding of trauma, shared the same struggles. She was less clandestine about this than I was. Once, just after we arrived home to relieve our babysitter friends, she dissociated and cut herself so badly she severed a tendon in her hand. But even so, we initially related well to each other. We were the poster girls for same-gender relationships, regularly interviewed for LGBTQ newspaper stories, taking on the legal system to become the first same-gender couple in Scotland to gain equal legal rights for our children, interviewed and photographed for an LGBTQ history project and gallery exhibition. From the outside, we looked like the perfect couple.

However, our relationship had rapidly become one-sided. Following the birth of our younger son, my partner's mental health deteriorated rapidly. She was treated at a trauma clinic, but our lives were ruled by her mental illness, which left no room for my own struggles. That early mutual understanding was, by then, long gone. I stood by her for a long time, but the final years of our relationship were awful; the way she treated it was becoming intolerable. Finally, a close friend of mine said, "You *do* know, don't you, that this is an abusive relationship? And that, if she were a man, everyone would be seeing it?" I hadn't seen it myself, but when faced with it directly, I could no longer deny it. I left my partner.

Unfortunately, leaving tipped the scale, and the previously emotionally abusive relationship became physically abusive. The three years after I left were horrendous. Even worse than the violence she inflicted upon me was her screaming that what induced all my trauma never happened, that I had made it all up. She named those experiences in front of my twelve-year-old son. Her use of my trauma against me came up in the courtroom and exposed it to the public eye. I view her taking away my control of choosing when, where, and with whom I share that information as the most abusive thing she did to me.

My "us and them" anxieties returned in full force. I had become relatively comfortable with the idea of disclosing past trauma and acknowledging my present-day struggles that resulted from it, but acknowledging trauma happening in the present was a very different matter. I felt deeply ashamed to find myself in this position, ashamed that it took a friend to point out what was happening as I never once applied what I knew about abusive relationships to myself. I found myself saying, as if somehow the abuse reflected a personal failing, "This is not supposed to happen! Therapists are not supposed to need support workers, let alone the same ones as their clients!" As though, somehow, I should be superior to clients in managing my life. Suddenly, it seemed, I was admiring the emperor's new clothes myself.

I struggled with many levels of invisibility and shame. I frequently experience bi invisibility, and domestic abuse (DA) is often invisible as well, as mine, even to me, had been. DA in same-gender relationships is all the less visible, as it contradicts popular stereotypes of our relationships. DA by women adds another layer. All the elements of abuse that lie outside of the criminalized aspects—such as emotional and psychological violence—are invisible, and it is hard to show concrete examples when a pattern of behavior is at hand. On top of all that, I am considered assertive and strong, and my ex-partner is considered fun and caring. Then there is also our history as LGBTQ poster girls; there's even a short documentary about our happy family unit. To come out about DA felt somehow like disloyalty to the LGBTQ community, as it challenged the very thing we had striven to have recognized: the ordinariness of our relationships. But, of course, DA is not exactly uncommon, so that very ordinariness must by its nature include such phenomena. Still, it felt like giving ammunition to opponents of equality—dispelling the myth that our partnership was "a good example" of a mentally healthy LGBTQ relationship.

Our experience of the legal system further added to the invisibility, focusing purely and simply on whether we had been physically assaulted; nothing else of the trauma mattered. My son and I were treated as though we, not my ex, were criminals. I began to feel like one, and that carried over into my professional identity, bringing a resurgence of impostor syndrome. I struggled with the conviction that colleagues would judge me and think I should not be a therapist, given the mess my life was in. Which, of course, was probably what I thought myself. I struggled with telling any colleagues who hadn't already been aware of my difficulties trying to extricate myself from the relationship. But I had to because I needed to seek support for my client work, and have other eyes around to make sure I was steady enough to work. I took time off from working with DA cases, but on my return to that work, I learned that my client had the same support worker that I did. This took me right back to being "them" not "us" and the belief that somehow, this time, I was lesser.

## INTEGRATION

One goal of therapy is integration, and I strive constantly to better integrate my own experiences. I had come a long way on my journey before my experience of domestic abuse created a road block. That road block taught me that silence in the therapy literature suggests to me a hierarchy of mental health whereby it's okay to have had some issues, as long as they are in the past, worked through, and fairly ordinary. But apparently, "big ones" like trauma or serious mental illness are not okay. I have developed resistance to that hierarchy as I've traveled my road; I maintain my own hierarchy of mental health issues filtered through a lens of acceptability. I had reached a place where my past trauma was acceptable enough to sometimes be made visible, but experiencing trauma in the present felt like a very different, and unacceptable, thing. My ongoing struggle will always concern my visibility and I realize that I can easily be thrown back into that place of fear of being seen. Even writing this is a struggle against my childhood terror of being visible.

But I have also realized that these experiences contribute to my ability to deeply understand my clients and to accept them in all their complexities. For all that the voice in my head may try to shame me, this is not my fault, the shame is not my shame. And if, as a therapist, I continue to stay quiet about the realities of my existence—many of which are dark and frightening and horrific, just like those of the clients I seek to accompany on their healing journeys—then I am contributing more bricks to that wall between therapists and clients. Silencing myself would add to the barrier that hides therapists' own struggles to be mentally healthy from the clients who struggle as well. I would reinforce the "us and them" paradigm I have always loathed. I am no better than my clients. I am not special in the way that being a mental health professional implies. I am an ordinary person, struggling my way through a life fraught with difficulties, trying to become the best version of myself I can be. I try to uncover all the hidden behaviors and patterns that stem from the trauma of my childhood in order to live a better life now; I try to reduce my dissociation in order to become much more present in this life I have. I hold onto the knowledge that it is never too late to change, and, above all else, I am learning that which I encourage in my clients: self-acceptance. I strive to treat myself no worse than I would treat a friend, to offer the frightened person inside me kindness and compassion. We are always becoming. We all have our own journeys to take. I would like mine, like Chiron's, to be of service to others along the way. I leave you with the words of Rabbi Kushner:

We may not ever understand why we suffer or be able to control the forces that cause our suffering, but we have a lot to say about what the suffering does to us, and what sort of people we become because of it. Pain makes some people bitter and envious. It makes others sensitive and compassionate. It is the result, not the cause, of pain that makes some experiences of pain meaningful. (in Sanford, 1991, p. 175)

## REFERENCES

Bear, Zetta (Ed.). (1998). *Good practice in counselling people who have been abused*. London: Jessica Kingsley.

Kahn, Michael. (1997). *Between therapist and client: The new relationship* (revised edition). New York: Henry Holt & Company.

Malone, C., Farthing, L., & Marce, L. (Eds.). (1996). *The memory bird*. London: Virago.

Natiello, Peggy. (2001). *The person-centred approach: A passionate presence*. Ross-on-Wye, UK: PCCS.

Rothschild, Babette. (2006). *Help for the helper*. New York: Norton.

Sanford, Linda T. (1991). *Strong at the broken places*. London: Virago.

# 10

## NOT OUR FAULT

### *Chana Wilson*

My mother and Marian first became friends watching the Army-McCarthy hearings on my parents' television. It was April, 1954, a month before my third birthday. I imagine myself toddling around the small wooden cottage in University Heights, oblivious to the sound of Senator Joseph McCarthy's voice ranting about Communists and dripping with queer-baiting innuendo, "Will [the opposing] counsel for my benefit define—I think he might be an expert on that—what a *pixie* is?" (Oshinsky, 2005, p. 427). None of us could have guessed what McCarthy's hateful voice portended: that eventually the brutal homophobia of that era would fracture all our lives.

Like us, Marian and her husband lived in the cluster of cottages with a shared lawn used by Rutgers University for its married student housing. Dad was getting his PhD in chemistry on the GI Bill. It was a community of sorts. In the evenings, the couples would gather to dip cubes of French bread into pots of fondue and get smashed on alcohol my father distilled on the sly in the school's chemistry lab.

Marian had a particular interest in the Army hearings because she had served in the WACS, the Women's Army Corps, during World War II. With their husbands off at the university, the two women sat in front of the small black-and-white TV screen watching intently, each compelled by a hidden, secret aspect of themselves. Marian had had women lovers in the WACS. My mother, Gloria, though not a card-carrying Communist, was a leftist quietly sympathetic to the cause in those chilling years of the House Un-American Activities Committee blacklisting. The three months of hearings bonded them. They became close friends and spent their days together, talking, laughing, going fishing at the nearby river. Then, one day, Marian told my mother how beautiful love could be between women.

My mother did not love my father. When they met in 1949, she was twenty-seven and living with her parents, having moved back home after a brief, failed marriage to her college boyfriend. Age pressed against her with its looming horror of spinster-hood. Her sister introduced her to Abe. They had quite a bit in common: both were children of Jewish immigrants, both were the first in their families to go to college, both were science majors and lovers of music and art.

Abe was a virgin. Short, terribly shy with girls, and cerebral, his experiences with women consisted of a few disastrous interludes during his military service in World War II. After their dates evolved from awkward to companionable, Gloria pondered: here was a nice guy, a decent, educated guy. As someone to marry, he seemed her best bet. She invited him over to her room when her parents were out, lit candles, and put Frank Sinatra on the portable record player. She took his hand, and they rolled onto her twin bed. The act was simple and quick, without delighted explo-ration. A few days later, Gloria demanded, "So, what are your intentions?"

Abe stammered, "Well . . . um . . . I guess I'll ask you to marry me."

"Okay," she said. It was done.

After they married, Gloria realized that Abe's insecurity, the thing that had made him so reachable, now repelled her. She felt no spark and she withdrew, becoming remote and at times hostile to my father. The congeniality of their community did nothing to warm my parents' private life.

Marian's sexual overture came several months into their spending time together. My mother swooned. She fell deeply, madly in love with Marian. She longed to take me and go off with Marian and have a life together. But in that era where people routinely lost their jobs or were arrested for being gay, this was not in the realm of possibility.

Gloria and Marian were lovers in secret for close to two years, together during the day when their husbands were at the university. When the men returned home in the evening, sometimes the two couples would have dinner or play cards. Then one day, Marian did not show up and was not home. Days went by with no sign of her. Gloria had to go to Marian's husband and ask about her. He said his wife had had a nervous breakdown and was in a mental hospital.

Marian returned several weeks later and told my mother, "Gloria, I'm cured. We can't do this anymore. We just have to be good wives, spread our legs, and be faithful to our husbands." Gloria begged her, but Marian mocked her, calling her a dyke and a sicko.

In her grief and despair, my mother started therapy sessions with a psychiatrist. His whole goal was to treat her for her "perversion," to restore her to heterosexu-ality and preserve her marriage. My mother went along with it because, by then, the culture's profound revulsion of homosexuality had seeped into her psyche, and she believed that something was wrong with her. With therapy, her despair deepened.

One day when I was off at my second grade class, my mother went into the bath-room and held my father's rifle to her head. She pulled the trigger. By some fluke, the rifle jammed. As a child, of course, I knew none of this. All I knew was that my mother was gone, taken to a place my father told me was called a mental hospital. He explained it was her head, not her body, that was sick, but the doctors would be fixing her. The doctors were using electricity to fix her head, and then she would be okay.

Before our first visit to Carrier Clinic, Dad sat me down at the dining room table. "Do you remember what I told you about Mom's treatments at the hospital? How the doctors are helping Mom with electricity?"

I nodded, fidgeting. My hands picked at the woven place mat.

My father paused, looked at me, and then away. He looked back and cleared his throat. "Sometimes after the electricity, people don't remember things too well. It probably won't happen, but when we go to see Mom today, she may not know who you are."

I stared at my father while what he'd said seeped into my body. Then I leaped up and ran. He called after me, but I didn't stop. I raced down the hall to my parents' bedroom. I flung open their closet door and stood facing myself in their full-length mirror. Yes, there was my reflection. I looked into my eyes, amazed and puzzled: *how could I still be here if Mom doesn't know who I am?*

Mom did always remember me during the four months of her electroshock treatments. But after each time she was tied down against her will and her brain was jolted with powerful current, when she had recovered enough to move her stiff and sore body down the hall to the pay phone, once she wasn't so disoriented that she couldn't remember the names of friends and the phone numbers of relatives, my mother would call anyone she could think of and beg, "Please, my God, they're killing me—help me get out of here!" No one could or did.

Once she called my father. "Abe, Abe get me out of here," she pleaded. "I can't bear this, please!"

He tried to placate her. "Gloria, only the doctor can do that. But it will be all right, you'll see." Somewhere in the midst of speaking, he found he was talking to an empty phone. "Gloria . . . GLORIA . . . ?"

"Mr. Wilson?" The voice of a male orderly came on the phone. "Your wife has climbed out the window of her room onto the roof. She says she will jump unless we agree not to give her any more treatments, but don't worry. We'll get her in. We'll call you back."

With each electro-convulsive therapy treatment, more memories were lost; names and faces slipped from her mind; she lost languages: her fluency in French, her on-going study of Latin, her comprehension of German she'd used to read scientific papers, Yiddish phrases from childhood. After eighteen shock treatments, rather than being restored to health, my mother was more severely depressed than ever, and she was transferred to a private mental hospital in upstate New York, about two hours from our New Jersey home.

My situation was taboo in so many ways: a mother gone, and what had happened to her. I talked about it at first. Once, standing next to the metal jungle gym at recess, I repeated to a girl what Dad had told me. I told her matter-of-factly, "My mom's in a hospital, but it's not her body that's sick—it's her head. The doctors are fixing her." She stared at me, her eyes wide, mouth open. I felt I'd made some terrible mistake. A chill of shame overcame me: Mom's condition was not like having a broken leg; something bad was wrong with her.

Over time, I would learn other words to describe my mother's condition. No one shouted them at me. Instead, like radio waves, the words hung in the air, unseen and ever-present: crazy, nutcase, loony, mad, mental, wacko, bonkers. There was no end to the names.

At the mental hospital my mother was transferred to, they brought in a specialist for her—a psychiatrist whose focus was the treatment of homosexuals with the goal of converting them to heterosexuality. He met with my father. By then, my father knew that my mother had been with a woman, although he did not know that it had been Marian. The doctor told my father to have faith, that there was hope for her. He said he'd helped other homosexual patients and gave my father an article about a gay man he'd successfully treated to become straight. Dad had been thinking of leaving her, but realized that if she had tuberculosis, he would stay with her while she was being treated, so he'd stay with her through this disease, too.

My father and I visited the hospital each weekend, but the mother who greeted me seemed vacant, her face puffy and sallow. Often, the hospital gave my mother a pass, and we would go into town to the movie theater. In that dark cinema, I could enter another world and forget the bloated stranger called Mother who sat beside me.

One day while Mom was in the New York hospital, Marian's husband Leslie came to visit my dad. We had moved twenty minutes from University Heights a couple years prior when my father graduated and got a job as a research chemist. It was winter, and Dad offered him coffee and made a fire in the fireplace. The two men sat there, sipping from their mugs. After a long pause, Leslie said that Marian had been lying in bed in their darkened bedroom for most of the past six months. They commiserated about their wives' depression and then fell silent. If either of them suspected that the two women had been lovers, they said nothing of that to each other.

When the insurance money ran out and she was no better, Mom was transferred to a state hospital. Dad and I were buzzed through locked doors to visit her in the common room that reeked of cigarette smoke and urine. Finally, after more than two years away, my mother returned home, heavily medicated, her eyes dark with desolation.

She returned with a regimen of psychiatric medications that sedated her day and night: barbiturates, tranquilizers, and sleeping pills. During the day, the pills made her slur her words. In the evenings, my father knew it was time to put my mother to bed—that her sleeping pills had kicked in—when she could no longer coordinate bringing her cigarette to her mouth, hitting her cheek or chin with the unlit end. Six months later, I would take over the job of putting my mother to bed. It was the summer before I started fifth grade, and Dad left for London because he had a year's research grant. We were all supposed to go, but Mom's psychiatrist said she was too weak to travel, so Dad fled and left me alone with her.

In my bed at night, my body became a tuning fork, my ears alert for the stagger and thud of Mom falling on the floor in her midnight forays to the toilet. I'd jolt up in response to haul Mom up off the floor, grabbing her under the armpits. With one of her arms over my shoulder, we'd lurch to the bathroom and then back to her bed.

In the year my father was gone, my mother attempted suicide twice. In midwinter, one night after dark she jumped in the icy river behind our house. A neighbor brought her back, dripping and shivering, knocking on our back door to wake me. He gave her to me and left. Alone, I wrangled her into a hot bath and into bed. How he found her remained a mystery because neither he nor my mother ever spoke of it again. I never brought it up to Mom, never told a teacher or friend, and I never wrote my father about it.

That spring, one day after school I walked in our front door, calling out, "Hi, Mom! I'm home!" Dead silence. I called again. Nothing. I found Mom in the living room, lying on the couch on her side. Something was wrong; I shook her. Her arms flopped heavily; her eyes fluttered open briefly. Drugged, watery eyes. "Mom, how many pills did you take? How many?"

She slurred the words. "Dooo . . . don't let them take me. Not again!" Her eyelids closed.

*Oh, God, what to do? I didn't want her to go, either, but if I didn't call, she might die.* I ran next door to the nice neighbor lady. She opened the front door, and I sputtered, "Mom took sleeping pills, don't know how many. . . ." She put her arms around me, pulled me into the hall as she patted my back. *Didn't she understand? I didn't want comfort; I wanted her to decide what to do.*

Then, the town siren began to wail. In our small town, that meant it was alerting the volunteer ambulance squad. I pulled away and ran back down the driveway. Our front door, always left unlocked, was ajar, and I encountered our other neighbor. Her sad eyes met mine. "I came by to see your mother, found her, and called the ambulance." The crunching of wheels in our gravel driveway, the slamming of doors. When I followed the two men carrying Mom on a stretcher outside, I found that townspeople had gathered in the driveway, watching Mom get loaded into the ambulance. My body burned with the shame of having a crazy mother and how our whole town knew. My mother would be gone for the next two months, and I would live at my best friend Barbara's house two doors down, but Barbara and I would never speak of my mother or what had happened.

When my father returned from England, he stayed with us for a year and a half, but bitterness only grew between my parents, so they agreed to divorce. I was in seventh grade when he moved out. After Dad left, Mom began rumbling back to life. Her recovery came in fits and starts. She heard about a doctor who practiced alternative medicine. He diagnosed her with low thyroid and gave her armloads of vitamins, thyroid medication, and a regimen for reducing some of her psychiatric drugs. Although still addicted to sleeping pills at night, she became less groggy in the daytime.

Oddly, the Vietnam War helped my mother reclaim something of her spirit. In the spring of 1965, as the war escalated, she joined Women Strike for Peace. She began protesting, marching weekly in front of the Army induction center with a handful of Women Strike for Peace housewives. Mom had found kindred spirits, passionate women, committed to a cause. Not long afterward, I joined the protests, the only eighth-grader among those women, their picket signs held aloft with one arm, huge pocketbooks crooked on the other.

At meals, Mom and I now discussed politics, history, and current events. I discovered something about my mother, something that had been buried by drugs and depression, lost to electroshocks and sorrow: her sharp, passionate intelligence. Mom and I had a new bond. As the peace movement grew, we boarded buses and trains to antiwar marches in Newark, New York City, and Washington, D.C. Chanting slogans with the throngs of marchers, many now arrayed in hippie garb, gave us a focus for our discontent and a place to feel some commonality with others after so much stigma and isolation.

Despite Mom's antiwar activism and new friendships, love was missing—any possibility of love—and she stayed depressed. During my high school years, we moved to a different New Jersey town and into a shabby, two-bedroom apartment that was so close to a hospital that ambulance sirens blared past our windows day and night. My mother and I were deeply enmeshed companions, and we hung out in the apartment, depressed together.

By the end of high school, some part of me knew that I had to get far away from my mother, so I chose the farthest college that gave me a scholarship: Grinnell, off in the Midwest cornfields of Iowa. When I left, I worried about how she would do. Would she overdose again? Something in her rallied, and soon after I left, she admitted herself to a hospital to detox from all her psychiatric drugs. That withdrawal was as intense as getting off heroin. Nurses had to shoot her with muscle relaxants to keep her convulsions at bay. I came home during winter break to a new mother: clean of all drugs.

What is despised by a culture often remains in the dark like a tulip bulb over a long Dutch winter. My own lesbian desire was buried deep throughout my childhood. In high school, as I lost my childhood girlfriends to their dates, I found myself playing Beethoven's "Moonlight Sonata" over and over again on the piano, filled with melancholy. My justification for my lack of interest in the boys of my small New Jersey town was that they were bumpkins and idiots. I believed that once I got to college I would meet some boys at my own intellectual level, and this meeting of the minds would initiate the explosion of my passion.

As I'd predicted, I did have a couple boyfriends in my freshman year of college, but little passion ensued. What did explode was the Women's Liberation Movement, with its feminist analysis of the cultural myths we'd all been raised with. I joined a women's consciousness-raising group where our stories poured fourth: experiences with men, sexuality, abortions, what it meant to be oppressed as women. Our anger shone in us, a light that overcame depression and shame. I had never before felt such a sense of belonging.

In May 1970, the spring of my freshman year, students at Kent State were shot and killed by National Guard troops while protesting Nixon's ordering the bombing of Cambodia, Grinnell College shut down amid student protests, and I decided to drop out and head to San Francisco. I moved into a collective household of feminist activists and leftists. Gay Women's Liberation met in our living room every Friday. I was nervous and scared before my first meeting, but after I entered the room with fifty or so lively women laughing great belly laughs as they listened to an ex-nun tell her story of leaving the convent, I heaved a sigh of relief and joy: *these are my people!* Three months later, I came out with my first woman lover.

When I told my mother over the phone about my lover Kate, she launched into a rant that began, "I don't agree with this!" I'd never heard her so fierce and sharp, at least not directed at me. When I said how incredible it felt to love a woman, Mom's voice only rose in pitch and urgency. "Darling, I'm worried that this is a bad choice! That it's a lonely and alienating life." Something in my mother's voice caught me; she sounded in a panic. Since I didn't yet know her history, I didn't understand her fear. Later, she would tell me how the woman psychiatrist she was seeing warned her that she should get me back to men because if I stayed a lesbian, I was likely to commit suicide. That threw her into terror.

But we were both fortunate, because it was no longer the Fifties. In those ebullient post-Stonewall days of the Women's and Gay Liberation Movements, Mom was about to take an astonishing leap. Within weeks of her initial negative reaction, she sent me a series of mind-blowing letters. In the first, she wrote: *I have quit therapy. Women's liberation is going to be my therapy from now on. I have joined an Older Women's Liberation consciousness-raising group. It's wonderful—we talk about everything.* I sent her back a jubilant letter of encouragement.

Soon afterward, she wrote that she accepted me being gay. Then, a month or so later, came this: *I have told my Older Women's Liberation group that I am bisexual. Several*

*of the women had negative reactions. I know over time they will come to better under-*
*standing. Myself, I wake up in the morning, look in the mirror, and feel so happy to be alive.*

Astounding! But what did she mean? As far as I knew, my mother had been cel-
ibate for years, at least since my parents divorced. I called her. Her voice had a lilt
in it I couldn't remember ever hearing. She explained that she'd read about the gay
women's organization Daughters of Bilitis in the anthology I'd sent her, *Sisterhood is
Powerful*. She had searched out their meetings in New York City.

"So Mom, does that mean you're having a relationship with a woman?"

"Yes, sweetheart. Well, with several. I usually go home after DOB meetings with
a new woman every weekend. But I tell all the women how it is with me, how long
it's been. That I'm into pleasure and being close to a woman, but I'm not serious right
now. It's sex, and it's fun, and it's *good*."

"Wow, Mom!" It was a lot to digest, but I pushed on. "You said you're bisexual. Are
you having relationships with men or planning to?"

"No."

"Well, Mom, I hate to tell you, but you're not bisexual, then, you're a lesbian. You're
just scared of the word."

She was pretty damn nonchalant. "Guess so, honey."

Six months later, in the summer of 1971, my mother came to visit. At the air-
port, she arrived in newly adopted hippie garb, bell-bottom jeans and the orange
and purple tie-dyed T-shirt I'd made and sent her. She grabbed me in a hug and then
hugged Kate, beaming at us both. "I'm so glad you two are together!"

This new mother was game for anything. Kate and I were spending a month at a
rustic cabin on the Russian River, an hour north of San Francisco. We had no car, so
Mom hitchhiked with us and our puppy, climbing into the back of pickup trucks and
VW vans. She skinny-dipped with us in the river and was uncomplaining that we had
no outhouse, but had to squat in the backyard over a hole.

One afternoon, Mom and I were alone at the kitchen table. She reached across the
table and took my hand. "I want to ask you something. Do you remember Marian,
my friend at University Heights?" Mom was staring at me with the most intense
expression.

The question startled me. I reached back with my mind. I remember a big-boned
woman, tall, with long black hair. "Sure, Mom."

Mom went on, "You and she and I spent every day together for almost two years
from the time you were two." My mother hesitated. "We were lovers," she said.

A memory flashed: *I am standing with my mother in the doorway to Marian's bedroom. Marian has her back to us, and she is sitting at a white dressing table facing a
mirror. Her head is bent slightly to the right, and her long black hair cascades down her
neck and over her shoulder as she brushes her hair. Mom leans against the doorsill, and*

*I am pressed against Mom's thigh. We are both spellbound, mesmerized by Marian as she strokes with the hairbrush over and over again. There is some feeling in the room I am too young to name. The room shimmers with it.*

My mother went on to tell me her story, kept secret for so long: her deep love for Marian and my mother's impossible longing to live together, Marian's breakdown and rejection of her, Mom's therapy focused on converting her that led to her suicide attempt. Everything that had happened was now given a new context. As my mother talked, a fury built in me. All those years that Mom and I suffered, all those suicide attempts, all the times when I found her half-dead, all those pills tranquilizing her into droopy-eyed sedation . . . all that was now made clear as the aftermath of her love for a woman, forbidden and punished by society. Then, another thought came, and a wave of relief mixed with my rage. My God, there was a reason! It wasn't our fault!

Later that year, my mother moved from the New Jersey suburbs into Manhattan's Greenwich Village, where she became part of a vibrant lesbian community. She began volunteering as a peer counselor at Identity House, an institution founded on the radical idea of gay people offering support and affirmative counseling to other gay people. Even though she'd quit traditional therapy, she was finding her own healing in Gestalt therapy. At Identity House, she began training as a Gestalt therapist. Several years later, she would open a private practice as a feminist psychotherapist.

In 1973, I became a member of the newly formed radio collective producing one of the country's earliest lesbian programs on Berkeley's listener-sponsored KPFA. The stories of our lives reverberated over the airwaves, breaking years of silence and invisibility.

My mother agreed to let me interview her for the show. At the radio station, we faced each other across a metal folding table, microphones pointed at each of us. After so many years of secrecy and unexplained grief, my mother now went on the air to share her story without shame, giving voice publicly to how cultural prejudice and homophobic psychiatry had nearly decimated her and what it was like to reclaim her woman-loving self.

Toward the interview's end, our eyes met across the table. My now joyful mother had elf eyes, twinkling, irrepressible. She declared, "The Women's Liberation Movement did more for me than all the damn hospitals and psychiatrists, and all the damn medication, ever did. It's given me a whole new life."

## REFERENCE

Oshinsky, David M. (2005). *A conspiracy so immense: The world of Joe McCarthy.* New York: Oxford University Press.

# 11

## FIGURING IT OUT TOGETHER
## MENTAL HEALTH SURVIVAL STRATEGIES
## FROM DETROIT'S QUEER AND TRANS YOUTH
## OF COLOR

*Lance Hicks*

I realized two years ago there was no such thing as mental healthcare for someone like me. It was 7 AM, and I was standing alone in the ice-glazed parking lot behind glowing red emergency room doors. I don't remember if I was crying, but I doubt it. Really, I doubt if I was breathing either. Sunrise was still thirty minutes away, and I had no idea where I was.

Fumbling in my pockets, my fingers searched absently for spare change, a wallet, a bus card, a cell phone—anything, really. If I'd stopped to think about it, I would have remembered not to bother. I had nothing.

Twenty-four hours before, I'd admitted myself to a massive psychiatric facility. After a week-long episode of increasingly terrifying flashbacks, constantly mounting anxiety, and pain I guessed was psychosomatic, my posttraumatic stress disorder (PTSD) felt out of control. I decided to look for a therapist. I knew that most therapists where I lived were expensive and that most of them wouldn't know the first thing about how to treat me as a mixed-race trans youth. After calling the handful of providers I could find online who seemed potentially capable of helping me, I was getting discouraged. Almost none accepted my insurance, and those who did had long waiting lists. My situation was starting to feel urgent. Calling friends and a couple of supremely unhelpful crisis hotlines for advice, everyone told me I should go to a hospital, so I did.

Mental illness can be scary for anyone. In turns, it can leave a person feeling isolated, confused, threatened, and worthless. During extreme states, you choose between asking for help, knowing you're being judged, or suffering alone. This is the reality of even the most privileged person with a mental disability. For people like me—young queer people of color, trauma survivors, trans people—it's only the beginning.

I'm from Detroit: a sprawling city filled with mostly Black and brown communities. My hometown is bigger than Manhattan, Boston, and San Francisco combined. It's been called a "food desert," nicknamed The Murder City, fetishized by White saviors, bought by gentrifiers, and simultaneously pitied and scorned by the national and international communities. We're one of the most segregated cities in the country, and depending on the study you reference, our population is 80–90% Black. The surrounding suburbs, which make up an expansive metropolis, are home to a majority-White population. Services for queer youth—and queer people in general—are limited. Those that do exist tend to cater to White suburbanites, with a few underfunded exceptions. This is where I grew up.

Coming out as trans at fifteen was tough for me, but I don't pretend my experience was as harsh as that of so many of the youth who became my chosen family. I transitioned early, and while I did lose a few friends, I found a chosen family bigger than any support system I'd ever had. My parents—especially my dad and stepmom—struggled to understand my newfound identity. They still don't really get it. For a while, I kept my distance and avoided coming home, and that was hard—but I never found myself kicked out. My mom helped me access therapy, and while it took two years to get my hormone letter, the day eventually came. When it did, she was there to help me find (and pay for) one of the few affirming doctors in the area.

All this made me really lucky. It gave me the opportunity to move forward with life in a gender that fit. But even so, I was still trans, still mixed, still struggling. I went to school every day, affirmed by teachers and peers, but facing regular threats of gun violence. I found a drop-in center full of youth who could relate to my story, but that experience also introduced me to serious abuse and violence at the hands of people I thought I could trust. The youth workers I bonded with were there for me in a way few mentors ever are, but the organization that brought us together ultimately tokenized and exploited me for several years. These juxtapositions are important because, while my story is one of privilege in so many ways, the fact that my experience was one of the better ones is unacceptable. Despite the love and community I was able to access growing up, there were times I truly believed I would kill myself, and times I truly believed I would be murdered. The fact that so many of my friends had it worse is simply not okay.

I'm not sure when I first became depressed, but I think I was about twelve years old. It's hard to say, exactly, because of the way it happened. It was gradual, so I didn't completely realize what was going on until after the fact. It was kind of like falling asleep in class. One minute, you're steely-eyed and focused on some lecture at the front of the room, and then somehow, everyone is staring at you, and there's drool on your desk. How did I get here?

Reflecting on the path my life has taken since high school, I realize that it makes sense that I now live not only with depression but anxiety and PTSD. I could go into detail about each of the struggles I experienced in my teens and early twenties, but I don't know if I'm ready for that. Let's just say things got worse before they got better. I fell out of touch with my chosen community for a couple years, which made growing up that much harder. When I finally did reconnect with the people who helped me survive high school, I realized how much all of us had struggled.

Already, when I was in high school, my newfound queer family was in crisis. Youth I cared about were living homeless, dealing with addiction, and getting attacked on the street regularly. The Black youth and other youth of color who attended programs in the suburbs were constantly getting harassed by cops, but those who stayed within city boundaries often didn't feel safe, either. While the programs we accessed did their best to help us all find housing, access medical care, connect with legal advocates, combat bullying in school, and find jobs, there wasn't much space given for us to process the real trauma that defined our lives. We had to cope on our own.

Detroit has always been noted for its grit. When outsiders reflect on our city's past days of wealth and prosperity, compared to its modern-day struggles, "grit" is always one of the words that comes up. A lot of Detroiters take pride in this concept. It's the idea that, no matter what we're faced with, we're tough enough to rise to the challenge. When new friends come to visit me in Detroit, I love to take them to see parts of the city I believe are beautiful. If we can, we'll spend a day driving up and down all my favorite streets—in a place this big, with limited public transportation, it's the most practical way to get around. On our way to explore all the neighborhood-led art exhibits, the teeming community gardens, the maker spaces in church basements, and the riverside view of Canada, people notice things. The kinds of things you see in documentaries and exposés filled with run porn, fetishizing our struggles.

If you've ever seen Detroit covered in any type of national media, you know exactly what I'm talking about. Abandoned homes, empty lots turned into what we call "urban prairies," shut-down schools with boarded windows and rusted playgrounds, spaces that look empty. I never point any of this out when I show visitors around. Partly, I make this choice because I assume they've already heard stories of abandonment in Detroit. It's nothing new to them, so why spend their precious time in the city rehashing it? More important, though, I skip over these details because they are a lie.

When I was fifteen years old, I was told being trans made me an anomaly. Not by any one specific person, but by the world I lived in. News media was just beginning its voyeuristic fascination with transgender children, painting kids who came out young as spectacles. Books about trans people discussed isolation, the unlikelihood that those of us who identified as trans at a young age were "true transsexuals." I believed all of it. After all, I'd never met another transgender teen myself. A quick Internet search confirmed my fear: that I was one of a tiny minority. That I might never meet another transgender person as long as I lived. Like the media that painted Detroit as an empty wasteland, stories that claimed trans youth were few and far between permeated my world, and I believed them.

Of course, within a few months, I'd done away with this worry. I became one of a crew of trans and queer youth who spent every possible moment together, talking on the phone, or chatting online. The fact that we had each other meant each of us was real. That our existence wasn't strange or unlikely—we normalized our presence by being consistent in one another's lives. That's kind of how things are in Detroit, too. Newcomers see an empty wasteland because our streets don't bustle like New York City, our buses are broken down and unreliable, and we draw the shades on our homes and businesses. At the same time, Detroiters exist. We congregate in community hubs, form block clubs, sponsor street festivals, create art, form after-school revolutions, and tell stories on porches until late at night. We're here, I promise you.

Trans people as a whole, and Detroiters as a community, aren't the only ones facing erasure in the dominant culture. As a mixed-race queer kid, I experienced firsthand a lot of the ways in which queer and trans youth of color are erased. White queers started boasting that "gay is the new Black," as if Black people and gay people were two separate groups. Proposition 8 passed, and the nation blamed the Black church, as if homophobia was perpetuated so much more by Black Christians than any of the ultra-conservative mostly White communities of faith. Maybe even worse, when the media decided to expend some tiny fragment of resources in the exposure of violence toward trans and queer youth of color, family rejection took center stage, even in cases where we were truly accepted at home but still needed to hustle for money or drop out of school because of institutional racism as well as queer and trans oppression. The racism wasn't spoken about because, of course, that wasn't supposed to be the same issue.

Erasing queer and trans youth of color hurts us in countless ways, but maybe one of the biggest blows is to our mental health. Because of what my friends and I went through growing up, almost everyone in my chosen family has dealt with mental illness, emotional crises, and heavy trauma. Of those I keep in touch with today, I know my people have been addicted to alcohol, tobacco, heroin, and crack. We've been sexually harassed, raped, and caught in domestic violence relationships. Some of the youth I grew up with have been physically attacked, and, of those, some didn't survive. With realities like these, how could our mental health be unaffected?

Mental health systems aren't built for youth like us. At least they're not built that way in Detroit, which is the community I know. Here there are a handful of therapists who will treat us, but most aren't competent in any way. Of the few who have a basic understanding of "trans 101," most are White providers raised in White communities. The few who simultaneously understand trans identities, embrace queerness, and integrate racial justice into their practice typically cost more money than any of us can afford. Each of the three counties in our region offers a Community Mental Health network; however, it's been my experience that most of the programs included within these umbrellas of service have little accountability and less investment in providing quality care. After all, they're made for poor people.

Two years ago, when I checked myself into the only psychiatric hospital within Detroit city boundaries, I did so with an understanding that this was my final option. Before this particular incident, I'd been through my community mental health system, which referred me to a therapist at an unknown address that turned out to be a police station. I'd also scraped together enough money to pay "sliding scale" fees that still amounted to more than my weekly food budget, visiting private therapists who insisted on quizzing me about my gender for our entire hour together. The handful of crisis lines I'd used were no help either. For the most part, they suggested that I "see a therapist." When I explained that I'd already tried, the operators would insist on referring me to resources I was already well aware of, then abruptly ending the call. I guess I shouldn't have been surprised.

As a disclaimer, I want to explain that I not only struggle with mental illness in my own life; I've also worked on and off within mental health systems for a number of years. At the same time that I was searching out mental healthcare for myself, I was working bottom-tier direct care jobs within psychiatric systems designed to fail. I think this definitely contributed to my desperation. Over the few years I spent working these jobs, I'd learned a lot about exactly where providers' priorities were (money) and seen a lot of ugly things go down. I carried all of this with me, and expected any care I received in a hospital setting would be baseline at best. I was okay with that, though, as long as I was able to see a therapist, get some medication, or access any support that could help. Even with all my awareness of mental health systems as both a provider and a recipient of services, however, I never expected what actually happened to me.

Queer and trans youth of color usually don't do well in mental health settings. We carry historic trauma, as people who have been and continue to be pathologized for simply existing, so willfully accepting a diagnosis of mental illness often goes against our most basic survival instincts. Of the youth I connected with growing up, few felt supported by the mental health systems they had access to. But being

Detroiters—queer and trans youth of color with grit and creativity and love for each other—we've developed strategies for coping outside the system.

I wanted to interview my friends for this piece, to ask them about all the creative and unconventional ways they get by—but they were all too busy surviving. I reached out to the youth I mention in this article and asked them what they had to share. Most of them were excited—they really wanted to participate. A chance to spotlight their unique strategies for thriving in a hostile world rarely comes along, and they had big plans for collaborative work. Unfortunately, none of this happened. The realities of their struggles meant plans to write articles like this one don't always work out. That said, they are all truly amazing, inspirational people living and growing in a complicated place that's often hard to deal with. For queer and trans youth of color near and far, the providers who serve us, and allies in our struggle, I believe the strategies of my people are too important to go untold. So, with their permission, I've compiled my own observations about how they get by. I hope we can learn from, add to, improve on, and grow from these approaches. That other queer and trans youth will make them their own and that providers and allies will work for a better world, where systems can exist to support us.

## STRATEGIES FOR SURVIVING WITHIN HOSTILE SYSTEMS: LESSONS FROM SOME OF DETROIT'S QTPOC YOUTH

1. *Love yourself first.* Recognize that everyone you love is oppressed. Someone will always need you. If you never learn to set boundaries or say "no," you won't make it.
2. *Stick together.* If you're kicked out of school, homeless, couch surfing, or being abused, do whatever you can to be with your people. Know you deserve to surround yourself with people who don't think being queer or trans is your most interesting quality. Remember that you deserve unconditional love, and don't be afraid to actively pursue it.
3. *Take care of your body.* Do what you have to do to be healthy. For poor and oppressed people, this will be hard. Healthy food is expensive, stress keeps us up at night, exercise takes up time and energy we don't always have. But this stuff is important, so fight for it. Turn your phone off when you can. Try hard to make time for rest. Carve out time in your day to experience worry and stress, in order to avoid those feelings taking over.
4. *Care about something bigger than yourself.* For some of us, this means spirituality. In some cases, this means fighting for social justice. Sometimes

it means taking care of our families. Whatever you care about, believe in, or work toward, remember it. Hold on tight and keep fighting, even when the world is against you.

5. *Set your own standards.* Get comfortable with letting down everyone you ever admired. Remember that you know yourself best, and are better than anyone at knowing what your life should look like. Drop out of school, get fired from jobs, do things you never thought you would, and find reasons to love yourself anyway. Remember that impossible standards are set for us in a world designed for our failure. Rewrite the rules based on your reality.

6. *Make time to be alone.* Sometimes you won't text back for six months. Your Facebook messages will pile up, and you'll no-show to your best friend's birthday party. When you can, remind people you're still here. You're alive, you love them, it's not personal. You're just going through a really hard time right now. The right people will always understand.

7. *Find your creative voice.* Your story is important, and without you, who would tell it? However you do it—in a journal, through painting, in photographs, in late-night phone calls—find your voice. Talk about what has happened to you, who you are, where you are going, and what you need. You deserve to be heard.

8. *It's okay not to love your community all the time.* Sometimes even your chosen family will let you down. You'll be abused, gossiped about, and bad-mouthed. You don't have to take this just because it comes from your community. If you need to cut someone out of your life, do it and don't look back.

9. *Know when it's time to leave home.* Detroit is a hard place for queer and trans youth of color. So are a lot of other places. If you have to run away for a while, don't blame yourself. There's no shame in looking for resources, or seeking out someplace that feels easier.

10. *Know when it's time to come back.* No matter how long it's been, know the community that's worth loving will always be there for you when need you it. Things may not look and feel the same as they did before, but recognize that you leaving in search of whatever you needed wasn't a betrayal. Survival is honorable. If and when you want to come home, never question your right to do that.

Reflecting back on my night at the psych hospital is painful but important. After checking myself in, the nurse who took my blood pressure realized it was extremely high. Not surprising given the fact that I was in the middle of a full-blown panic attack. I assumed this explanation should be satisfactory since one of my major presenting problems was anxiety. Apparently not. The nurse explained I would need to visit a medical hospital in order to ensure I wasn't on drugs. Storing all my belongings in a plastic bag, the staff called an ambulance I couldn't afford, which drove me to a hospital I had never heard of and didn't provide any information about where I was going or when I would be back. After waiting all night to visit a doctor who was very confused about why I had been hospitalized at all, I was discharged. A clean bill of medical health, as expected, and a hospital bill I still get calls about from collections.

After my discharge, I asked how I would get back to the psych hospital. Nobody knew. The doctors and nurses all around me were busy with patients who actually needed their care. I called the psych hospital and was told they would "try to send someone later," if they had enough staff. I was stranded. Not sure exactly where I was, without money or anything else to get home.

That's when I stumbled out into that icy parking lot. Looking around at the pre-dawn sky, my breath iced in front of my face. Of course, it was community that got me out of this crisis, too. I called a mentor of mine—a former youth worker turned mentor, who picked me up, bought me breakfast, then called off work. I heard him tell his boss on the phone he had a "family crisis" to deal with and knew it was true. This was my family. No matter what broken systems had failed me, I knew we'd get through this together.

# 12

## SISYPHUS (OR: ROCKS FALL AND EVERYONE DIES)

*J. R. Sullivan Voss*

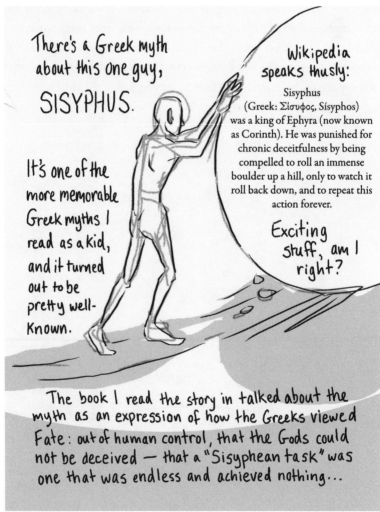

There's a Greek myth about this one guy,

SISYPHUS.

It's one of the more memorable Greek myths I read as a kid, and it turned out to be pretty well-known.

Wikipedia speaks thusly:

Sisyphus (Greek: Σίσυφος, Sísyphos) was a king of Ephyra (now known as Corinth). He was punished for chronic deceitfulness by being compelled to roll an immense boulder up a hill, only to watch it roll back down, and to repeat this action forever.

Exciting stuff, am I right?

The book I read the story in talked about the myth as an expression of how the Greeks viewed Fate: out of human control, that the Gods could not be deceived — that a "Sisyphean task" was one that was endless and achieved nothing...

FIGURES 12.1–12.13 "Sisyphus (or: Rocks Fall and Everyone Dies)," a graphic diary by Sullivan Voss.

FIGURE 12.2

FIGURE 12.3

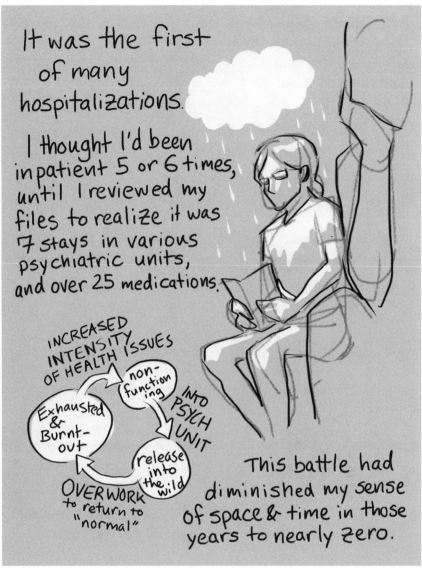

FIGURE 12.4

FIGURE 12.5

FIGURE 12.6

FIGURE 12.7

FIGURE 12.8

FIGURE 12.9

If I'm not visibly depressed or anxious, I am assumed to be mentally healthy & "normal!"

If I'm not dizzy and weak and showing signs of my chronic illness, it becomes "invisible" as well, since I appear "normal" here too.

And this false assumption of "normalcy" is applied to my sexuality and gender identity as well.

As a transman unable to medically pursue transition, my being anything other than male-presenting means my gender is assumed to be female, "normal", cis.

"Normal" is the mountain.

FIGURE 12.10

FIGURE 12.11

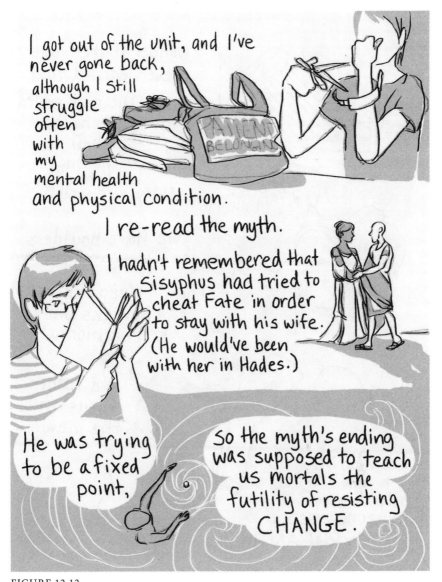

I got out of the unit, and I've never gone back, although I still struggle often with my mental health and physical condition.

I re-read the myth.

I hadn't remembered that Sisyphus had tried to cheat Fate in order to stay with his wife. (He would've been with her in Hades.)

He was trying to be a fixed point,

So the myth's ending was supposed to teach us mortals the futility of resisting CHANGE.

FIGURE 12.12

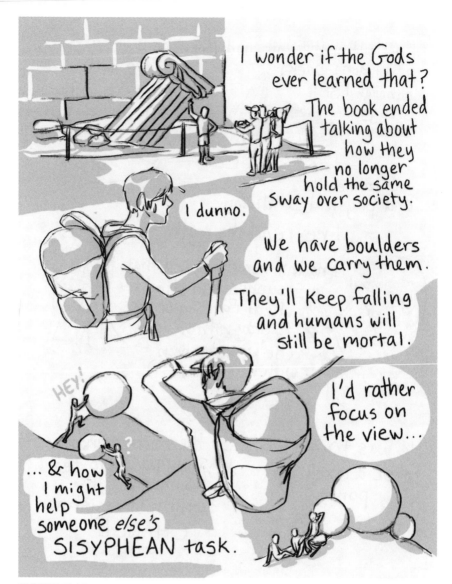

FIGURE 12.13

# 13

## THE FAMILY LEGACY ENDS HERE

### Teresa Theophano

All grief involves feelings of loss, and all loss requires learning how to live in a permanently changed world, where love and memory must replace physical presence . . . Despite their pain, many survivors [of loved ones' suicides] also show great resilience and growth, including discovering unexpected inner strength, reordering priorities, a renewed appreciation of life, and developing compassion for the suffering of others.
—American Foundation for Suicide Prevention's *Facilitating Suicide Bereavement Support Groups* manual

Social support is a biological necessity, not an option, and this reality should be the backbone of all prevention and treatment.
—Bessel van der Kolk, MD, *The Body Keeps the Score* (2015)

I never could have anticipated this: somehow, surviving trauma has freed me. My troubles had been unnamable and largely inscrutable—just persistently malicious whispers in the back of my head. When external circumstances forced me to grieve more tangible losses, something cracked wide open and never closed back up.

The terrible shit my brain did to me for so long! I experienced a constant dysfunctional mutter exacerbated by a dreadful deep sinking sensation in my gut. I had irrational, intrusive thoughts about being unworthy of everything. That whisper was so loud sometimes that I found myself completely distracted from whatever might be happening around me in real time. My focus was compromised enough that my graduation from college came as a pleasant surprise; I didn't think I'd end up finishing. I knew my perceptions were not to be trusted, and I knew my fatalistic thoughts didn't make sense. The terrifying thing was that I couldn't stop thinking them anyway.

I felt like I was being held hostage by my own brain, but in my youth I did not know how to verbalize that feeling. At sixteen or seventeen, I tried to tell my father about the noise in my head, and he thought maybe I meant I heard voices. That wasn't exactly what I meant. While I never experienced auditory hallucinations, my brain simply would not shut off. No diagnosis over the decades resonated. Was it major depression? Dysthymia? Bipolar II? Generalized Anxiety Disorder? OCD? I was even told ADHD could be to blame.

For years I puzzled over why, in spite of my privilege as a middle-class white girl from the suburbs with access to resources like seemingly adequate mental healthcare that maybe could have made my attempts to keep myself emotionally afloat at least a little bit easier, I continually thought, "If I were to die right now, I probably wouldn't mind." My brain kept up a steady stream of irrational nonsense. Ashamed to take up space, I made myself as small as I could, wallowing in self-hatred and alienating my peers.

As a teenager I had no idea how to articulate what was happening, the rush of nonstop thoughts crowding my head at the same time I slogged through major depression or to describe how awful I felt. "Ah, but what's 'normal' anyway? I don't know anyone who's 'normal!'" well-meaning friends and family members would sometimes tell me when I would say that something was wrong, that I didn't feel "normal." But I know what *my* normal is; it's when I can move through life without my mind's constant, painful interruptions causing anguish unseen by and seemingly incomprehensible to others.

In his classic memoir of surviving depression, *Darkness Visible*, William Styron (1990) wrote, "If the pain were readily describable most of the countless sufferers from this ancient affliction would have been able to confidently depict for their friends and loved ones . . . some of the actual dimensions of their torment, and perhaps elicit a comprehension that has been generally lacking." He quotes William James: "It is a positive and active anguish, a sort of psychical neuralgia wholly unknown to normal life." Normal life. I felt validated upon reading those words.

In the darkest days I prayed for a clear and accurate diagnosis, an *a-ha* moment that would tidily pave the way for an effective remedy. "So that's what's wrong," a kindly doctor would say, "and now we know how to treat it! We can fix you!" And I would be okay. This never happened, but I would learn later that despite the overall great many flaws with the medical model and current systems of mental healthcare. I'd find it tremendously empowering to be recognized as having a disorder that is treatable. I found dignity in acting with self-determination and pursuing a course of treatment.

That process took some time. Meanwhile, the only counselor with whom I spoke while in high school was a therapist at the local VA, where my Vietnam vet dad received services. She met with me individually just once following a not-particularly-helpful family counseling session when I was fifteen, and she didn't take me seriously. Surely she meant well, but she thought I was just experiencing growing pains and suggested with a straight face that I "join some clubs at school to make new friends."

It was like a scene from some John Hughes movie from the Eighties—I was dealing with the quintessential clueless grownup at whom the kids all roll their eyes.

Suffice it to say that, as the resident high school weirdo after my best friend moved away, I didn't try joining more clubs or figure out how to fit in with the jocks, preps, and future Stepford Wives. Instead I did what many smart, artistic, miserable girls my age did: I read Sylvia Plath, painted my nails and lips black, holed up in my room to listen to the Cure's "Disintegration" album while scrawling god-awful poetry into my journal, and hid out in the school library during lunchtime to avoid the clique-filled cafeteria.

Unpopular from a young age, teased because of childhood strabismus that caused one of my eyes to drift—doing nothing to counteract the pariah status I had already begun acquiring thanks to my bookishness and socially awkward behavior—I started to embrace Goth and punk music and culture. If I was going to be given a hard time by the other kids, it may as well be for something I consciously chose. Going to all-ages punk shows, wearing thrifted dresses, and reading zines made by peers in other cities made me feel less alone—and also like I might be even a tiny bit cool.

When a miraculous opportunity to leave home after my junior year of high school and begin college early in another state presented itself, I jumped on it. At age sixteen, I was thrilled with the idea of getting a head start on "real life" outside of the small-minded NJ 'burb in which I grew up. I was relieved also to escape the familial strife that had long been a part of my life; the often-painful dynamics with my family, loving though my parents had been, were hardly conducive to improving my mental health.

I thought everything would get better once I escaped. Instead, I sank to new lows on the tiny campus, which I found elitist and suffocating, in small-town western Massachusetts. My textbook for Freshman Composition held a poem, written from the point of view of a teenager's parent, with which I became obsessed. The compassionate parent answered the teenage daughter's question of "Will it ever get better?" with the realistic answer of "Yes, but it will take a long time."

I read that poem countless times, wondering how long it would take *me* to feel that things were getting better. As the semester progressed and the temperatures began dropping in that drastic, bone-chilling New England way, I sank further and further down. I was so obviously depressed, crying so often, gaining weight so rapidly, and moping so dramatically that I alarmed my roommate, who encouraged me to seek help as November rolled around.

I listened to her advice and soon began meeting with a campus psychotherapist who didn't really seem to understand me and spent much time in our sessions just gazing at me silently, which made me feel all the more self-conscious and ashamed. Depression: that was what she termed it. I knew that was accurate to some degree, though I felt there was more to it because of what I could later identify as racing, obsessive thoughts. Trying to talk about my terrible ruminations didn't get me far, especially since I lacked language to accurately communicate just what was going on; I was mystified by the workings of my brain and deeply embarrassed about whatever was wrong with me.

That therapist did do something helpful: she got me a psychiatric evaluation that yielded my very first prescription for antidepressants. The selective serotonin reuptake inhibitor (SSRI) I was prescribed was not a miracle drug. It did not and could not change my life the way I'd hoped it would, and the intrusive thoughts did not magically subside. But things felt a little more tolerable. Until they didn't, when I switched to another SSRI, then another, then yet another.

In retrospect, I marvel that I did not begin self-medicating, but I think that something in me has always been hopelessly idealistic—the part of me that got involved with a Quaker youth organization in high school and began identifying as a feminist and then an LGBTQ rights organizer. Feeling like a part of a progressive community, being among like-minded youth—punks, artists, social justice activists, geeks— saved my life, even if I didn't realize it at the time. I am grateful for the hope imbued in me by this sense of community and being part of something much larger and more important than me. Because if I had known that it would take a solid twenty years to start feeling truly well, I don't know that I would have stuck around long enough to wait it out.

But I did. I'm still here, and I am finding the blessings in having waded through my madness. Sometimes being a headcase isn't really so bad. For all of the suffering through which my brain has put me, I have learned coping skills galore, advocacy and self-care tools, and authentic ways in which to connect with peers that make me feel, at last, like I have grown up. I have stopped believing that I have a personality defect, that I am unworthy of happiness, or that there is something fundamentally wrong with me. There is a biological underpinning to my difficulties, exacerbated by familial dysfunction in my formative years, and I have learned to manage it. I understand that others may disagree with my theory, but this resonates as my own truth. I wish that I had had access to more proactive forms of treatment and the different therapeutic modalities about which I have learned in my clinical social work studies. Maybe CBT, DBT, or EMDR would have helped, but I didn't know about any of them when I was suffering the most.

Until I reached a level of profound wellness, a combination of ongoing talk therapy and adherence to my medication regimen along with acupuncture, self-help books, homeopathic treatments, yoga, and journaling, kept me going. Calling or emailing my mother in a panic—even though I knew she didn't quite understand what was going on in my brain, she understood that it wasn't good, and she responded without fear—helped also.

Together, all of this *almost* worked.

Twice I thought I could manage to titrate down from my meds, and twice I found myself ready to die, feeling utterly desperate because of my incessant agitation and inability to sleep, hold a meal down, work, or stop crying long after withdrawal symptoms ended (or should have). I wore people out and scared friends away—although, thank god, the ones who truly loved me have stuck around to this day. In any case, I'm not trying it again because I've got important things to do in this lifetime, and I don't have time for a relapse.

Since the onset of symptoms in my early teen years I have struggled with the idea of being a burden, with guilt and shame. Long terrified that I would end up defeated by my madness, a lost cause, I resent what I think of as the wasted years—the ones I spent deeply mired in the self-destructive thoughts that were truly my only barrier to meaningful participation in life. I grew up in the shadow of mentally ill family members and was dispirited, to put it mildly, when I discovered a family legacy of suicide—which apparently puts one at higher risk of attempting suicide oneself.[1] Though a family member had voiced suicidal ideation to me in the past, I had not known until recent years about a paternal uncle who threw himself off a bridge before my dad was born. And I could not have suspected that Dad's only sibling, with whom I was not close, would choose to end his battle with bipolar disorder and alcoholism at age seventy-five rather than struggle through another year.

Suicide turned my world upside down in 2010, and it wasn't an ancestor or a barely known relative whose self-induced fatality suddenly and drastically changed the course of my life. It was my then-partner Julian, who killed himself in my presence at my home, despite my pleas just inches away from his face moments before he took a fatal plunge from my fire escape into my courtyard.

I had survived other, different types of traumas, like bearing reluctant witness to my parents' altercations through the years and enduring severe bullying in school. Later, there were hugely traumatic events including a campus shooting at that tiny college where I spent my freshman year and seeing the twin towers burn from the Manhattan bridge while I was en route to work, from which I was immediately evacuated, on 9/11.

But this was different. This was up close and personal. This was literally losing my loved one before my eyes as I reached out and grabbed only a fistful of air.

Suffering from a chronic, degenerative illness that resulted in permanent disability status in his mid-thirties, in denial of his alcoholism, and struggling to believe that he could be truly loved and accepted as a person of transgender experience, Julian lost hope. I could not save him, and I grew to realize and accept that although I can do my best to help people in my life who are floundering, I cannot save *anyone*.

Writer and survivor Carla Fine, who rebuilt her life in the wake of her husband's suicide, says that this kind of event can make you feel like your life is over—and really, it is. When someone you love dies by suicide, your life as you knew it has ended. Now you are a survivor, like it or not; immutably and unfathomably, everything has changed, and suddenly you are navigating a new life. It is going to be an incredibly long and difficult path, and you are going to need a *lot* of support as you find your way.

I lucked out: I got that support. A great many people helped me—my parents, with whom my relationships improved exponentially following their divorce in my early adulthood and the subsequent formation of a genuine friendship between them. A few other cherished members of both my blood and chosen families were instrumental in my healing, as was my community of friends: those same kinds of queers, artists, activists, and fellow former high school outcasts with whom I had allied myself in my younger years. Several old friends had kept in touch from our Quaker youth group days. Together, they were, quite literally, lifesaving in the aftermath of Julian's death, stepping up to stay with me during the interminable nights in the heavily subsidized co-op apartment I was jubilant to have recently landed but now loathed. They helped me find support groups, kept me fed and feeling loved, and fielded my teary late-night phone calls.

I maintain a critique of the "bright-sided" approach that can be too easy to take toward survivors of trauma and mental illness; I think encouraging survivors to find a silver lining is often insensitive and sometimes downright damaging. But I did find that coping with the sudden, debilitating change in my world ended up bringing out a strength I had no idea I possessed and that no one in my life could have foreseen. Through the years-long process of learning to live in this new world, one without Julian in it, my perspective and priorities shifted. I saw this even in the wake of a mistake I made: too soon, I threw myself into what quickly became an emotionally abusive relationship with someone jealous, demanding, and unwilling to give me the space to grieve. Extricating myself from that situation, which I managed to do in less than a year despite feeling terrified of being alone again, furthered my self-confidence, understanding of self-preservation, and sense of resilience.

It has been a very long path to recovery—and I'm not done yet, nor do I believe I ever will be. I can't deny being fearful of the world that late 2016 began presenting to us. But my life took a turn for the better years ago, and I remain grateful. My former therapist said some time ago that sometimes you just need *one* thing to go right in your life for everything to change. I found truth in this: I had experienced a series of failed dating situations and struggled for a couple of years to find stable full-time employment while feeling caged in my cramped, grief-filled apartment. And then, just when I figured I was only ever going to keep dating the wrong people even though I'd stopped hating myself at last, I met a kind, smart butch who became a loving partner to me for several years.

Later that year, after dogged pursuit, I was at last offered my dream social work job at an LGBTQ nonprofit; I began thriving professionally in a way I'd never experienced. Within two years I was promoted to a managerial position, and I have found my work extraordinarily rewarding.

Once I was able to stop struggling financially, I began a long and challenging hunt for a new and better apartment—no easy feat in NYC, but I found what I wanted. Less than a year after I began that dream job, I finally moved into a wonderful home with a couple of friends of mine; I love the sense of community my shared living situation in a vibrant neighborhood has granted, and I soon formed familial bonds with a couple living down the hall from us. Every single day during those couple of dream years, I felt relief and I basked in gratitude for this trifecta of good fortune. Even when my relationship ended abruptly, leaving me feeling bereft again, I became able to accept that experience as temporary, knowing that mourning does not last forever and that I've survived worse. I was left with the gratifying assurance that I was indeed capable of keeping my heart open and forming a healthy partnership. I had feared that I did not know how to be happy and never would. The novelty has yet to wear off.

Emerging from those years of darkness has enabled me to participate more fully and with much more confidence in the organizing and community-building work that is my passion—especially now, in the face of such tremendous risks to so many. It's not possible for me to engage effectively with others to critique and challenge oppressive and unjust systems if I am not well—so I plan to stay well. Once I recovered enough to get out of my head, I could better learn to tame feelings of guilt and concentrate instead on organizing alongside my peers and colleagues to address gaps in care for marginalized communities and to advocate for change. I also began to develop a better understanding of intersectionality in my approach to social (justice) work, to hold myself more accountable, and to improve my ability to communicate kindly but directly in the face of conflict.

Last but not least, with my newfound clarity—which I attribute to my brain's development of new neural pathways thanks to the work I put into emotional healing— I discovered an ability to actually enjoy myself, laugh frequently, revel in silliness, and start having big ideas and making future plans. Surviving seems to have made me both brighter and far more hopeful than I had ever been.

Not all of what I affectionately dub my hare-brained schemes have worked—I never did complete that yoga teacher training and suddenly turn into this incredibly disciplined person who enjoys activities like going to the gym and drinking tea instead of beer—but I became excited to try new things. My increased energy made it possible for me to organize a benefit talent show in 2014 for a small nonprofit serving undocumented queer folks. I made my burlesque debut (which doubled as my burlesque finale) at the show, and that same year I coordinated an online fundraiser, which quickly met its goal, for a transgender services organization. With the momentum I had built, I helped launch an LGBTQ peer support network here in NYC that summer. We named ourselves the Queer Mental Health Initiative and began holding twice-monthly free support groups in Brooklyn, as well as maintaining an online presence and a publicly accessible resource guide.

This anthology was something of which I conceived and began to compile in 2009, but after Julian's death I felt unable to devote myself to the exploration of such intense subject matter. Years later, when I finally became ready, my then-acquaintance Stephanie emerged as the perfect co-editor and partner in crime, and our friendship and working relationship have flourished.

In 2016, I joined the board of directors at the queer homeless youth shelter where I once worked, and I began pursuing further clinical training. I have relished both being back in a classroom setting and gaining yet more insight into my own experiences and behaviors. One critical phrase from a trauma course I took stands out in my mind: don't ask the client "What is wrong with you?" Ask the client "What happened to you?" and go from there. Maybe I am at last whole enough to become someone else's therapist—and maybe we are all works in progress anyway.

These days I refuse to harbor shame about any part of myself: everything about the way I am—my unabashed extroversion, my difficult past, my aging punk aesthetic, my identity as an out queer femme, even my still-drifting eye—is just right. I'm proud of who I've become, the decisions I have made, and the work I have done. While little makes me angrier than the ableism of people who have never lived with mental illness advising others to "pull themselves up by their bootstraps" or dismissing psych meds as a "crutch," I feel good about my proactive and tireless pursuit of a happier life, about my innate idealism that others have at times mocked. I refused to stop believing that this was possible, that my brain could do better, that *I* could do better.

Managing to build a fulfilling life in spite of being born a headcase (or maybe with the secret gift of it within me this whole time) was deliberate. It has taken tremendous perseverance; it has taken a village. It was fucking *hard* to become this fierce lady. I am never going back. I will do whatever it takes to stay well, to keep on living, and to show up for the resistance.

# NOTE

1. According to the National Institute of Mental Health, family history of suicide and mental or substance abuse disorder are among the most prevalent risk factors for suicide in the United States.

# REFERENCES

Styron, W. (1990). *Darkness visible: A memoir of madness*. New York: Vintage Books.

van der Kolk, B. A. (2015). *The body keeps the score: Brain, mind and body in the healing of trauma*. New York: Penguin.

# 14

## ROLL THE DICE

*Michael Brown*


Let's play hangman
our names will be revealed
do you know how overwhelmed we feel?
Call the Doctor
read us our last rites
this is the end of our lives
tell the boys never to cry
cover up male suicide

"Roll the Dice" and "The Wall" by Michael Brown were previously published in *The Exhibit* (2014, SilverWood Books) and *Mercurial* (2016, SilverWood Books). Reprint permission given by the author Michael Brown and his publisher SilverWood Books.

The Wall
Michael Brown


Sitting five feet tall
between East and West

Written in blood on the wall
Madness

Holes in my hands
match cuts in the blocks

Watching guards count my steps
history regrets regrets regrets

Decorate this wall so tall
with barbed wire, torn clothes and flesh

Street art graffiti kiss
no man's land, death strip
Now boys play with water pistols
to soak up summer sun and freedom

Walls of the most dangerous kind
are the ones we put up inside our minds

# 15

## JESUS AND THE CLOSETS

*Sara Zaanti*

I was born in a quaint Midwestern town to what would seem like a typical Midwestern family. I was born a sister to three boys and grew up in the same 1970s ranch house where my parents still live. There are guns in the basement—in a hand made decorative rack, of course—and pegboards full of tools in the garage and basement. When we get together, it's a blur of nieces and nephews, multiple generations and time-honored traditions like "driveway sitting," which, to the uninitiated, means literally that the whole family sits in lawn chairs in the driveway, talking, drinking beer, and eating barbecue. Pork is serious business for us Midwesterners—almost as serious as Jesus.

In eighth grade, when all my friends were busy securing awkward, open-mouth kisses from boys, I committed my life to Jesus Christ. I became a devout and loyal born-again evangelical Christian. I was serious about my love for Jesus. Very serious. I loved Jesus. Until the day I didn't. Ironically, my love for Jesus and my experiences with born-again Christian communities would inform my entire life and create a throughline of honesty, straightforwardness, and an ability to be an "out role model" in my lesbianism, as a queer parent, and, eventually, as a genderqueer person. But I'm getting ahead of myself.

In the early 1990s, I was living an active and devout Christian life attending an evangelical church in Long Island. I was born again, attended church three to five times a week, studied the Bible, and attended numerous church-sponsored meetings and social events. I loved Jesus with all my heart.

Concurrently, I was working at a local hospital, where I started becoming preoccupied with thoughts about my new boss. She was New York-born and -bred, a runner, and so kind and caring with the patients. I was trying to find my way in New York and I thought about her a lot. I wanted to know her. I wanted to spend time with her. I didn't understand what was happening. I couldn't explain what was happening. I was confused.

I did what any confused person would do: I called one of my best friends to seek advice. Not surprisingly, this best friend was one of my church friends. I explained everything to her, including my questions, my uncertainties, and everything I didn't understand. I told her how I thought about this woman all the time, how I only wanted to work if she was working the same shift, and how *very much* I wanted to know her better. My church friend, in all her beautiful wisdom and without any judgment, told me that it sounded like I had a crush on my boss. While I was shocked to hear this, she was right. I certainly did have a crush on my boss.

Once the realization of my feelings for my boss sunk in, there instantly wasn't enough room for loving Jesus anymore. My evangelical faith didn't allow me to love women, and I also knew I had to be true to myself. I had finally figured out what was happening to me—why when my friends were pursuing boys, I devoted myself to Jesus, for example—and I decided the very same night of that phone call that I couldn't live in the closet. As a result, I lost all of my evangelical friends, and my social circle instantly evaporated. But I have never, not for one single day, regretted my decision to leave Jesus or to love women. The day I realized that I loved a woman was the exact same day I stopped loving Jesus.

This love, which turned out to be mutual (with my supervisor-turned-girlfriend), was exciting and new and felt so good. It felt perfect in every way, except that she didn't want to be out. Not for nothing, but if I was going to give up Jesus and lose all my friends for choosing to love a woman, it was certainly *not* to live a closeted life. We could not find a middle ground and soon gave up on our relationship due to our differing investments in the closet. I was without Jesus and now without a girlfriend, but quickly became interested in an African-American woman in my new job. She was dating a guy, but what did I care? I thought Lori was cute.

Lori and I soon had our first date, which of course led to her moving in with me in nothing short of three weeks—ever heard that lesbian U-Haul joke? We stayed together for more than eighteen years and had two children together. Giving birth and lovingly, if loudly, pushing two beautiful biracial babies into this world tops the list of favorite days in my adult life. My now ex-wife (the children's sometimes present and many times absent other mother) always lived as an out couple. Living in the closet or denying we were a gay family was never up for discussion. We were out at work—at a Catholic organization, nonetheless—went to the NYC Dyke Marches and Pride parades and lived openly as a couple in Brooklyn in the early 1990s.

As a divorced and now remarried family, we have also remained out. There have been no secrets with doctors, teachers and educators, service providers, insurance companies, or any other people who came into our lives. The roots of the decision to live an out life—with my biracial kids having two White stepmothers, one Black mother, and one White genderqueer parent—serving as positive role models for our community can be attributed to a Jesus camp I attended circa 1988.

A week-long getaway in the woods somewhere deep in the Midwestern plains led to my commitment to live my life with no regrets. All good Jesus camps have a theme. The theme of the 1988 week-long Jesus camp I attended was (aptly) "No Regrets." Living without regrets has been a driving force throughout my life. Embracing this mantra has driven me to attend college for a bachelor's degree, move from the Midwest to New York, obtain a master's degree despite scoring miserably low on the GRE, accept increasingly challenging employment opportunities, and connect and love, despite my fears. I have felt so much pain in love and yet I have no regrets. I have never, not for one day, felt shame about the fact that I love women.

While living this out and proud life, I have also remained deeply closeted as a person and a parent with a mental illness. The shame and fear of being a parent struggling with depression, posttraumatic stress disorder (PTSD), anxiety, and Dissociative Identity Disorder (DID, formerly called Multiple Personality Disorder) meant that I never once disclosed my mental illness to anyone outside of my three closest friends and one brother. It has felt too risky to come out as a person with a mental illness. I fear being judged about my ability to love and parent my children. I fear, most of all, false assumptions and allegations against me and anyone trying to take my children away from me. While I've survived a great deal and have much about which to be vocal and proud, I'm also still in the closet as a person living with mental illness.

I am a survivor whose father would come to my bed more nights than not and excuse my mother to her kitchen duties; a survivor who had a mother who pretended not to know or notice. I am a survivor of the same two parents who would leave me alone with troubled teenage boys who would insert loaded shotguns into my vagina as a joke. I am a survivor of the same parents who failed to recognize or acknowledge a female third-grade teacher who regularly sexually violated me with sharp objects, leaving me bleeding and scarred for life. I am a survivor who has scars. Scars that you can see and scars that you would never be able to find, buried deep in my soul.

I am a survivor who endured such horrific and sadistic sexual abuse at the hands of multiple perpetrators that my mind literally splintered into pieces. Despite years and years of daily, hourly, or minute-by-minute thoughts of ending my life, cutting and burning myself all over my body, and out of control drinking, I have crawled toward recovery. I have inched my way forward. I have refused to give up, refused to quit.

I first tried therapy when I was in college. I was raped my freshman year during homecoming weekend, and while I had no recollection of my earlier abuse, I thought I should get "help" for the rape. Like most acquaintance rape victims, I blamed myself and felt depressed and guilty for what I presumed I had allowed to happen to me. I liked my new friends in the support group and felt deep sorrow for their painful childhoods and campus rapes, but I could not tolerate or hold the stories of childhood abuse told by my new friends. I quickly dropped out of that support group to seek individual therapy, where I thought I would be better able to steer clear of talk of childhood sexual abuse. Exactly one session into my new therapy, I began to experience unrelenting flashbacks to my childhood abuse. I was tormented by these memories and could not contain them. They flooded my days and nights and intruded as unwelcome visitors in my dreams. My entire life was consumed by these memories, none entirely new to me, but now filled with details I had managed to keep at bay for so many years.

Somehow, I continued to live my life, go to classes, and graduate successfully with a degree in social work. I don't know, looking back, exactly how I managed to do this, given the sheer amount of energy it took to battle against my flashbacks and painful memories. I somehow, in a moderately disassociated state, managed to put one foot in front of the other, until I could move out of state. Once I was in New York City, far away from all my abusers and my early traumas, my life began to unravel.

Soon after moving in with Lori, I began to arrive home much later than either she or I expected. I had a sense I was getting lost on the subway ride home, but I couldn't actually account for my whereabouts. Some nights I would go to therapy after work, but many others I would just be lost somewhere with no recollection of how to get home or how I got home. I was twenty-one or twenty-two at this time and realized that there was something terribly wrong with me. My realizations came when I was working with a new therapist. I could not describe my feelings to her and was so terrified of them that I wanted to keep them a secret. I needed for her to think I was okay. More importantly, I needed to think that I was okay.

It was likely two or three months into therapy that my first alters emerged. I didn't recollect it at the time of my session. I only knew that I somehow ended up lost (again), bleeding from razor blade cuts on my arms, and on a pay phone with my girlfriend telling her I was lost. I would often lose time during therapy, as if I had been asleep for the hour-long session. It was frightening, but not nearly as disconcerting as "waking up" on a street in a strange neighborhood, sometimes drunk, sometimes sober, having no idea what day it was, where I was, or how on earth I had gotten there. I was terrified I was going crazy. I was terrified I was losing my mind. In fact, I was sure it was gone. I could not have predicted the next ten years.

It was a solid decade of complete insanity. Alters coming and going, new alters emerging. There were young alters that loved to play and those that held the pain and fear of the abuse, adult protector alters that attempted to keep me safe (though not always exhibiting the best coping skills), angry alters that battled with my therapist for control. There were appointments with psychiatrists, numerous hour-long appointments with my therapist each week, and lots of pretending that I was okay, my life was okay, and I was fine. There were days I could not get out of bed and nights I could not sleep from the terror that still lived in my body and mind. I never told my friends, my colleagues, or my family. Through it all, I went to graduate school and obtained my master's degree in social work; continued professional success was the only way I knew to win against the perpetrators.

And I was determined to win this battle, no matter how long and hard I had to fight, as long as I didn't have to disclose my mental illness. I worked in the mental health field but didn't feel I could share my own struggles with depression, anxiety, PTSD, or DID. I just kept going, driven to keep my mental illness in the closet, driven to keep it all a secret. I didn't want anyone to know.

I don't recall ever walking into a therapy session and saying I wanted to stop cutting myself because it was unhealthy. It was the only relief I could find from my overwhelming memories. I did, however, often say that I didn't want to be cutting myself when I had children. I never told my therapist I didn't want to have DID because it was a burden, hard to hide from others, and disruptive to my life. Instead, I told my therapist I wanted to be integrated so that I could be present for my future children. I didn't want to stop drinking because it was causing problems in my relationships and my bank account. I did say I wanted to be physically well and model healthy coping skills for my children one day.

I struggled for years and years and crawled toward a better life, driven to be a good mother. I skipped therapy sessions, forgot therapy sessions, took too much medication, didn't take enough medication, cried, and dissociated for more hours and days of my life than any human being should ever have to count. I lost time and eventually, I lost the safety of my alters, lost the security of my cutting, drinking, and benzos, and I faced those ugly memories. I fought, day after fucking day, to find myself so that I could be a mother. Not just any mother, but a mother who could lovingly guide my children into a life that was full of love, security, and hope. I fought to change the course of my history and that of my lineage. I am not perfect, but I am a present and mindful parent.

My desire to have children and not fuck them up beyond repair was a driving force in my therapy. I desperately wanted to birth, breast feed, and raise children, and I battled to find a way to become whole so that I could parent them in a loving way. Medication, years and years of therapy, and keeping my mental illness as my one and only deep, dark secret have been the pillars of my recovery. My choice to remain deeply closeted as a person with a mental illness has been both a pillar of safety and a painful burden.

The shame that I feel for remaining closeted is significant. My work, for more than twenty-five years, has been to support individuals with mental illness to live full lives in the community. Yet, to this day, I live a secret. Every day I am a secret statistic. Secrets often keep us sick and inhibit our recovery. My remaining secret is painful. Not acknowledging that I have a mental illness or a disability feels dishonest. Dishonest to my recovery, dishonest to my survival, dishonest to survivors everywhere who have fought to stay alive—and most importantly, dishonest to myself. However, the safety and well-being of my children is more important, and that's why I remain closeted.

My story is one of a life lived openly and secretly, proudly and shamefully, straightforward and bent. It's a life broken and healed. My story is one that I hope will bring hope and light to many people who are living in darkness. There are triumphs and struggles in my past and every single day of my present. You cannot experience the level of trauma and abuse I experienced and find an end to the pain. I don't believe it's possible. But I do believe it's possible for days to be filled with more light than pain and more hope than despair.

# 16

## THE LIVED EXPERIENCE OF LGBT VETERANS FINDING SUPPORT WITHIN THE VA HEALTHCARE SYSTEM

*Kathryn Wagner*

### INTRODUCTION

The Tuesday following the Orlando shooting I walked into my psychotherapy group and was greeted with tears and silence. This was the LGBT Group for Veterans, run by myself and another co-leader at a VA hospital on the East Coast. Most members didn't know what to say and many were openly crying. "Shocked," "sad," and "fear" were just a few words these veterans used to describe their feelings. Throughout the hour, my patients expressed strong reactions to Orlando, remembering their own experiences of being stigmatized and even assaulted within the military for being lesbian, gay, bisexual, or transgender. Our discussion also touched on racial dynamics, both within Orlando and the group itself. A few of the older veterans in my group, who had come out later in life, were not aware about safe spaces for LGBT people of color, such as the dance club where the shooting took place; these men appreciated learning from other members in the group about why such spaces were important. This particular group was populated with four gay men, two lesbians, a transgender man, and two transgender women. While not a veteran, I am queer, gender-nonconforming, and disabled—identities about which I talk openly in the interest of educating and learning from my patients.

Since 2015, when I began working in the VA Healthcare System, I have come to a better understanding of how mainstream society—specifically, those who have not served in the military—tends to perceive veterans, especially those who are marginalized due to sexual orientation or gender identity. Broadly speaking, if a veteran has overcome a mental or physical disability to obtain a job, a partner, or a house, they are often treated with respect and frequently thanked for their service by non-veterans. If they were not one of the lucky ones—that is, if they became one of the many veterans seen on the streets asking for support—their service to the country frequently becomes invisible or ignored. Thus, veterans are often glorified or vilified for events outside of their control. Moreover, those veterans who were not allowed to come out as LGBT while in the service, for fear of backlash, abuse, or discharge, often have higher rates of mental illness than heterosexual veterans, making it more difficult for them to join the ranks of the "lucky." Wishing to expand awareness of the unique issues the participants in my group and others like them face, I explore in this chapter some of the insights I have gained as a queer-identified psychologist working with veterans who identify as LGBT.

## A BRIEF BACKGROUND ON LGBT VETERAN HISTORY

As my clients know, and to their cost, there is little public awareness or understanding of the experiences of LGBT people in military service. The first mention of LGBT military personnel was recorded as early as the Revolutionary War, at which time there were no LGBT-related laws in place and members continued to serve. In 1943, during World War II, LGBT veterans were banned regardless of evidence of sexual acts (Williams, 2015), and two of my elderly group members were found "guilty" of "sexual misconduct" while serving in Vietnam. This was the period in which same-gender attractions, behaviors, and identities were viewed as mental disorders and/ or sexual deviations in the *Diagnostic and Statistical Manual of Mental Disorders* (*DSM*), though military anti-LGBT policies continued long after the reclassification of homosexuality by the APA in 1973 (Eaklor, 2011). In 1993, Don't Ask, Don't Tell (DADT) was created with the aim of "protecting" LGBT veterans by rendering them invisible—yet this policy resulted in more than 16,386 service members being discharged between 1993 and 2011, when DADT was repealed.

After DADT's repeal, LGBT veterans began writing books and appearing on national TV (see Beck & Speckhard's *Warrior Princess* and the CNN documentary of Navy Seal Kristin Beck). But the repeal of DADT did not mean the end of discrimination for all veterans. Up until June 30, 2016, transgender veterans could not serve openly, unlike gay or lesbian veterans (Transgender Legal Defense & Education Fund, 2016). Today, about one million veterans identify as LGBT; transgender veterans represent 30% of this number (Williams, 2015). The Transgender American Veterans Association currently has more than 2,200 members (Chumley, 2016). Yet many of these members, while out and proud, continue to suffer from mental disorders, often resulting from having had to conceal their sexual orientation or gender identity while in the service. Research has suggested that concealing identity during service results in an increase in stress, psychopathology, self-harm, and suicidality (Alford & Lee,

2016). LGBT veterans are more likely than heterosexual and cisgender veterans to experience negative mental health effects related to discrimination and stigmatization, including higher rates of anxiety, depression, alcohol use disorders, tobacco use disorders, and obesity (Blosnich, Foynes, & Shipherd, 2013; Blosnich et al., 2013; Mattocks et al., 2013). In addition, they face lower overall health status, higher rates of sexual trauma, and higher rates of sexually transmitted diseases (Sherman, Kauth, Shipherd, et al., 2014).

## LGBT EXPERIENCES IN THE VA HEALTHCARE SYSTEM

Given the high rates of mental illness among LGBT veterans, especially those identifying as transgender, it may seem surprising that many struggle to seek treatment from their local VA, preferring instead to seek outside care even though this is more costly. As I learned from my own patients, this is largely because many LGBT veterans do not experience the VA as an accepting place, even after the repeal of DADT. Research shows that 24% of transgender veterans have reported being refused medical treatment due to transgender status, 43% of LGBT veterans have postponed or neglected to seek medical care because of perceived discrimination, and only 33% of LGBT veterans speak openly with providers about their sexual orientation or gender identity (Sherman, Kauth, Shipherd, et al., 2014). This last fact is especially problematic because when providers assume veterans are heterosexual and do not ask about sexual orientation or gender identity, not only do the stress levels of LGBT veterans increase, compounding already existing physical and mental health issues, but conversations about sexual health and safety often go unaddressed (Pelts, Rolbiecki, Albright, 2014).

Through my individual work, and in the LGBT group, many of my veterans shared stories of being discriminated against due to LGBT status, including experiencing their primary care doctor or psychologist as being insensitive or ignorant to LGBT issues, as well as lack of institution-wide support for LGBT veterans. For example, a few members of my group described providers who asked inappropriate questions about gender identity and sexual orientation—and one person reported, "My doctor asked why it even mattered!" Moreover, many transgender veterans have been forced to resign from VA-related jobs due to their gender identity. One of my patients described leaving her job at the VA after she came out as transgender. She had received so many negative comments and microaggressions from coworkers that she no longer felt safe. Yet she continued to attend our LGBT group as she experienced the behavioral health department as a safe and accepting environment, unlike the rest of the VA. This example speaks to institution-wide discrepancies among acceptance and care of LGBT veterans often not experienced outside of the VA. A few of the veterans in my group also frequented the community LGBT Pride Center, a space where the focus is not on their veteran status but on celebrating their stated gender identity and offering support. Such spaces also have gender-neutral restrooms for nonconforming or transgender veterans, unlike many VA hospitals.

As a psychology trainee specializing in LGBT healthcare, I was somewhat surprised to hear these stories. I had assumed that because the mental health department had worked to develop a space that was open and accepting, the entire VA had received the same LGBT Safe Zone training. I was also surprised to learn that not all psychologists within my department were educated on issues related to LGBT veterans. In presenting a case about a transgender patient to a group of psychologists, I was astonished at how few of them were fluent in the issues facing LGBTQ veterans. My presentation was as much about educating my fellow colleagues on transgender identity and terminology such as "queer" and "genderqueer" as it was about my patient's clinical concerns. Giving this presentation provided me with an inside look at the lack of education within the VA in terms of informing providers about the mental and medical conditions to which LGBT veterans are especially susceptible.

## BEING AN OUT PSYCHOLOGIST AT THE VA

I have been out as queer since the age of fifteen. My experience as an employee at this particular VA has been one of acceptance, and I feel lucky to have the opportunity to work with LGBT veterans. I also learned that being part of the same minority group does not make me immune to issues of transference and countertransference. For instance, I had the opportunity to work with a veteran who came out in his sixties as gay. After witnessing what happened in Orlando, my patient felt he could no longer stay in the closet. "It was my duty to come out," he said, and described how he had hidden this part of himself for many decades out of fear that he would be ostracized by his family and by other veterans. While he found support through the LGBT group and in therapy with me, this was not without internal struggle and growth. My patient was quick to project onto me his own internalized prejudice about being gay and coming out late in life. For example, he frequently assumed that I did not see him as the "right kind of gay person" because he did not want to participate in online dating or explore a social community; he had assumed I engaged in such activities because I was younger and out. In our individual work, he would frequently bring up things that I had shared about myself in an LGBT group meeting as evidence that he was not living up to a particular image. Throughout our therapy, he came to realize that these projections stemmed from his own fear that he would not find a partner if he did not look or act a certain way. He also came to understand that he needed to spend some time discovering who he was as a gay man, to explore this part of his identity, and to discover what it meant to be attracted to men later in life.

As one of the few out staff at a VA in a small town that was not known for its LGBT culture, I also found myself occasionally over-identifying with my gender-queer patients, wondering sometimes about their lives outside the VA. Early on in my internship training, I noticed that I was often more excited to see these patients than my non-LGBT patients, something I was able to address through supervision and by slowly building up a network of friends over the course of the year in which I worked at this location. The issue of boundaries is one that all therapists encounter with patients, especially in small towns where paths are likely to overlap or in an inpatient hospital setting where the therapist may wear multiple hats. Not as often discussed is when the therapist and patient identify as being part of the same cultural or social community, such as LGBT. In these situations, the therapist and patient may run into each other at the same events or social settings. Unlike at the grocery store or local coffee shop, these encounters can often be fraught with tension and anxiety, as being a part of a shared identity is often self-affirming for individuals. In such instances, one or both members of the therapeutic dyad may feel uncomfortable.

I still vividly remember the moment a patient told me she was planning to attend the "queer family dinner" that night in the small town in which we both lived. My patient had recently come out as poly and lesbian and was looking to build a community. QFD, as it was known, was populated with about thirty queer folks in both monogamous and polyamorous relationships. She knew I identified as lesbian but I had not self-disclosed my relationship status or that, in fact, I was not polyamorous. Being a fairly new member of the QFD, I made the quick decision in that moment to no longer attend as I often saw my closest friends in that group on an individual basis. I could see that my patient needed this outlet more than I did and that my presence would not only disrupt the therapeutic boundary but would likely also be uncomfortable for us both. Therapists who identify as being part of the same minority group as their patients often make similar decisions, as it is not uncommon to be a part of the same circles.

## INTEGRATING BETTER CARE FOR LGBTQ VETERANS

As demonstrated earlier, institutional discrimination persists despite the existence of LGBT-inclusive non-discrimination policies appearing at VAs across the United States. Psychologists and psychology trainees are integral to the care of trans-gender veterans, including the work of diagnosing and treating gender dysphoria; making referrals for gender confirmation surgeries, voice modification therapy, and cross-sex hormone therapy; serving as LGBT experts within healthcare systems; and advocating for addressing barriers in systems in which transgender individuals live and work (Johnson, Shipherd, & Walton, 2015). They are also integral to the training and education of other medical healthcare providers who may not be as skilled in LGBT issues. For example, I strongly believe that training for VA security and/or police officers should be implemented during the initial orientation period such that officers can learn sensitivity when interacting with transgender veterans. Staff education should also include training in specific skills for initiating conversations with patients about LGBT status and safe sex practices. In addition, psychologists and medical providers should use inclusive terminology and be willing to modify history forms and intake documents to reflect the name and gender pronoun with which the veteran identifies.

After I created the very first LGBT group at my VA and advertised it widely, my LGBT veterans reported that they felt safer simply coming into the building. This speaks to the necessity of having a safe space across all VA hospitals nationwide for LGBT veterans, such as a support group co-led by facilitators who identify as LGBT and/or who have received formal training in LGBT issues. (Since beginning this chapter, I have become part of the LGBTQ VA Fellows program, which aims to do just that across the VA system.) Finally, staff should speak up when they witness a microaggression against an LGBT veteran. They can begin by stating that the hospital has policies that prohibit anti-LGBT behavior and treatment. For example, if someone overhears "That's so gay," they can say, "That statement is hurtful to people who identify as gay, and it is offensive to me." As VA providers, the burden is on us to demonstrate allyship among LGBT veterans and to establish ourselves as trustworthy, accepting, and nurturing of LGBT people and identities.

## REFERENCES

Alford, B., & Lee, S. (2016). Toward complete inclusion: Lesbian, gay, bisexual, and transgender military service members after the repeal of Don't Ask, Don't Tell. *Social Work, 61*(3), 257–265.

Beck, K., & Speckhard, A. (2013). *Warrior princess: A U.S. Navy Seal's journey to coming out as transgender.* Villa Park, IL: Advances Press.

Blosnich, J., Bossarte, R., Silver, E., & Silenzio, V. (2013). Health care utilization and health indicators among a national sample of U.S. veterans in same-sex partnerships. *Military Medicine, 178,* 207–212.

Blosnich, J., Foynes, N. M., & Shipherd, J. C. (2013). Health disparities among sexual minority women veterans. *Journal of Women's Health, 22*(7), 631–636.

Chumley, C. (2016). Transgenders press VA to cover operations. *World Net Daily.* Retrieved from: www.wnd.com/2016/05/transgenders-press-va-to-cover-operations/#!

Eaklor, V. (2011). *Queer America: A people's GLBT history of the United States.* New York: The New Press.

Johnson, L., Shipherd, J., & Walton, H. M. (2015, May 11). The psychologist's role in transgender-specific care with U.S. veterans. *Psychological Services.* Advance online publication. Retrieved from http://dx.doi.org/10.1037/ser0000030

Mattocks, K., Sadler, A., Yano, E., Krebs, E., Zephrin, L., Brandt, C., & Haskell, S. (2013). Sexual victimization, health status, and VA healthcare utilization among lesbian and bisexual OEF/OIF veterans. *Journal of General Internal Medicine, 28,* 604–608.

Sherman, M., Kauth, M., Shipherd, J., & Street, R. (2014). Communication between VA providers and sexual and gender minority veterans: A pilot study. *Psychological Services, 11*(2), 235–242.

Transgender Legal Defense and Education Fund. (2016, 30th June). *Pentagon ends discriminatory ban on open transgender military service.* Retrieved from http://www. transgenderlegal.org/headline_show.php?id=813

Williams, C. (2015, June). *Providing safe access to VA care for LGBT veterans: Safe zone ally training.* Presentation at the Bedford, VA Healthcare System.

## PART III

# Encounters of the Mad Kind

# 17

## PSYCHIATRY

*Kate Millett*

FIGURE 17.1 *Madhouse, Madhouse . . . Memories of Incarceration*, Flux Sculpture Exhibition, NOHO Gallery New York, 1995.
Photo: Kate Millett

# 18

## SURVIVING SCIENCE, OR
## HOW I LEARNED TO STOP WORRYING AND
## LOVE BEING MAD AND QUEER

*Calvin Rey Moen*

My mom can't use my pronouns because of science.

She's been struggling with them for a while and asking for alternatives to *he* and *him* and asking don't I want both of us to be comfortable, and I finally pinned her down and asked, "What about my pronouns makes you so uncomfortable?" She said it's that she doesn't believe it's medically possible to change genders, that being transgender is pretend and medical transition is purely cosmetic. Therefore, nothing I can do will change my gender and using any pronouns for me other than *she* and *her* would be a lie, and she just has too damn much integrity for that. I asked, trying to keep the smirk out of my voice, "So, this is not any kind of moral or spiritual judgment? This is you objecting to my pronouns as a *scientist*?"

This is a new argument for her. In the past, she has told me that homosexuality is a sin, that gay people are possessed by demons. She's told me that, as a trans person, I'm delusional, I'm wrong, and I'm broken. So now, by changing her argument to this purely scientific one, she thinks that she's avoiding controversy, retreating into the rational and the unemotional. The thing is, science has been employed to make moral and spiritual judgments throughout (mostly European) history, wielded by those who claim to be impartial, rational, and correct. Often, though, those scientists are straight, white, and male. Their studies tend to look for and reinforce their own biases and beliefs.

There is a liberal movement to gain acceptance for our differences on the basis of biology. After a conservative Christian culture had said for so long that queers were an abomination in the eyes of God, medical science and psychiatry changed the nature of the blame and where it was assigned: They put it in chromosomes and brain chemistry. So now, I'm okay because I was "born this way." Some people are just born in the wrong bodies, but thankfully, modern medicine and a gradually more tolerant society (catching up to science) are helping people like me (represented mostly by rich, white trans celebrities) to live normal, happy lives.

If I don't buy into the biology hype, it's largely because I've been through all this before, having been medicalized around another supposed genetic difference and found it not at all empowering.

## SWALLOWING THE MEDICAL MODEL

A campus doctor at the university where I was a student gave me my first psychiatric diagnosis and a prescription for a selective serotonin reuptake inhibitor (SSRI). To his credit, he didn't tell me to take the pills for the rest of my life, that they were like "insulin for diabetes" (I'd hear that speech from others plenty of times along the way). No, he told me to take them for six months and then stop, which is potentially even more dangerous. I don't imagine he had any idea. Because drug companies fund and control much of the research, we don't know nearly enough about how psych drugs work or what happens when they are discontinued. What I've learned since that time, from the work of peer activist communities like the Icarus Project and the Freedom Center, is that sudden withdrawal from psychiatric drugs can cause some pretty intense physical and psychological reactions, and that tapering off is, for many, the safest way to stop taking them.

So, I crumbled. I would go from flat and emotionless to sobbing into the carpet to laughing inexplicably. Usually very articulate, I couldn't tell anyone what I was thinking or feeling. I all but stopped eating and barely got out of bed for a week. I somehow managed to make an appointment with my primary care physician, during which I just cried at him. He told me to go to the emergency room. Do not pass go.

The psych ward was as disorienting and nonsensical as a trip down the rabbit hole. Yet I realized pretty quickly that there was nothing for me in this place, figured out what behaviors I needed to exhibit in order to convince them I was stable, and got myself discharged to outpatient treatment with a fresh prescription and my very own psychiatrist and therapist.

As the months turned into years, I learned from the psychiatrist that I likely had a genetic predisposition to depression, a chemical imbalance in my brain, that caused my prolonged periods of distress, my occasional acute desperation, my thoughts of taking my own life, my struggles to keep up with the stress of academic life and supporting myself (and my partner) financially. His theory was supported by my total collapse when I stopped taking the SSRI. This determination was not based on any objective testing, of course, simply on my failure to produce an alternative explanation for what was going on. "My life is great," I had told him. "I have nothing to complain about."

If I failed to properly set the stage for all that I was going through during any of the 15-minute sessions with my doctor, I see that now as a display of the coping skills I developed in order to survive my life, which were no longer serving me but did not know when to quit. So much of the terror, stress, shock, and anger I felt growing up I attributed to the absence of control over my own life. I distanced myself from the pain and betrayal by envisioning a day when I would be grown up and therefore capable of maintaining the control I couldn't have then. The day after I graduated from high school, I threw whatever belongings I could consider mine in the back of my friend's pickup truck and left my mom's trailer home and the town where she lived, intending to start over from scratch. The idea that any of those preceding 18 years could touch me now—that I would continue to feel the reverberations for the next 18 years—did not occur to me.

There's a phenomenon I've heard described as the "let-down effect," in which a person's body holds up under a great deal of stress, and then upon completion of that stressful event, the person becomes ill or has a flare-up of a chronic condition. I've noticed it on a small scale, when I would collapse into bed with flu symptoms after a large family gathering. It's possible that the relief of moving into my own apartment, choosing with whom I lived, and experiencing full autonomy and physical safety at home was the let-down of 18 years' worth of adrenaline overdrive, and my emotional immune system was trashed. I'm not ruling that out.

What I'm sure of, though, is that I lacked a framework for interpreting my big feelings and the extreme states to which they led me. I hadn't learned to listen to despair and loneliness as inner guides who wanted to lead me toward hope and connection. When I heard voices whisper that I should bleed myself to death, saw inner visions of myself drinking the bleach in the laundry room, laughed uncontrollably when overwhelmed with fear or anger, or felt cut off from my emotions, my body, and those around me as though I were floating in an impenetrable bubble, the only reference points I had were those Sunday-morning sermons about demons who possessed the souls of the spiritually weak. In our house when I was growing up, everything was a demon. Poverty was a demon, pride was a demon, and when the man we lived with got drunk and broke things or gave my mom bruises, it wasn't him or the alcohol, it was a demon. And when that man's brother tested positive for HIV, his "gay lifestyle" was a demon that bore the virus. Whenever I was overtaken with a "spirit of rebellion" as a teenager, the remedy was for everyone to lay their hands on me, shouting at the demon to be gone until my attitude improved. At the age of about 13, I decided this belief system didn't work for me and fearfully told my mom—my first "coming out."

As a newly minted adult and a college student, I was committed to rational thought, logical explanations, and anything you could show me using a graph. A doctor drew a straight line across a piece of paper, representing "normal." Then he drew another line below it, parallel to the first line, except with deep valleys. That was me. So I bought into the medical model of mental illness, and it was a huge relief in a lot of ways. I was unburdened from much of the shame I carried for not living up to my own expectations, and I had a reason for the seemingly unprovoked feelings of loneliness, grief, rage, and fear. *Just those silly misfiring neurons again. Good thing I have this bottle of pills to balance out my serotonin or whatever.*

Except that balance didn't really come, and I was suspicious. As I continued down the path paved by prescription pads, no combination of drugs seemed to give complete relief; some seemed to do more harm than good, and I questioned the scientific validity of this guessing game.

Me and Davy Jones Go Down in the Waves
(circa 1998)

This is the sad confession
Of my terrible, terrible double-depression.
"If this line represents a normal mood"—
Why reinvent the wheel?
But this will stop the spinning
Or at least slow it down.
And this big, big bowl of green and white
Is all that I'll eat tonight.
My brain doesn't work
Like traffic signs; my brain—
Excuse me—my brain
Doesn't synchronized swim.
It is taking a piss in my
Lemonade, it do-si-dos
When I say, "Promenade."
Why reinvent the wheel, indeed?
Davy Jones and me are working up speed.

# IT'S THE COERCION

Many years later, I would learn that the "science" behind behaviors like mental distress and supposedly inborn, innate characteristics like gender and sexual orientation is gravely flawed. It has its roots in the biological determinism of 15th century European imperialism and the slave trade. In order to decimate and enslave entire populations in the Americas and Africa, Europeans invented the white race, creating a superior identity to define themselves against those they wanted to subjugate. To these other "races" they assigned attributes that made them less human, relieving Europeans of the duty to treat them as such. Since then, no DNA test has been able to identify anything like different races within the human species.

Current theories about the biological basis for our behaviors may seem relatively refined and reasonable compared with those that rationalized slavery, but they're still a long way from actual science, and they're still doing harm. In his groundbreaking book *Mad in America: Bad Science, Bad Medicine, and the Enduring Mistreatment of the Mentally Ill,* Robert Whitaker details the history of mental health "treatments" in the US, from insulin-shock therapy, lobotomy, and other cures that could only be called torture, through a parade of "breakthrough" drugs starting with Thorazine in the 1950s and continuing to today's top-selling "atypical antipsychotic" medications. It is the story of a branch of medicine grasping desperately at legitimacy with very little to back it up.

Similarly, in the 1960s, Christine Jorgenson and the doctor who treated her, Harry Benjamin, set the standard for medical treatment of transsexuals that still dominates today. Benjamin legitimized transsexuality as a medical phenomenon, displacing psychoanalysis as the cure for what had previously been thought of as a perversion associated with criminal insanity. As a result, hormones and surgery are the standard prescription for a pathologized gender expression, akin to psychiatry's drugging on undesirable feeling and behaviors. Doctors remain the gatekeepers for treatments that allow worthy individuals to undergo the necessary transformations to become acceptable in the eyes of society. A couple years ago, when I finally worked up the nerve to tell my primary care doctor, who had been really cool about helping me get off my psych drugs, that I was thinking about medical gender transition, he started looking up urologists. I had no idea what he was doing, as I had been intending to ask for a referral to an endocrinologist for hormone therapy. Evidently he assumed the first thing I would need was a penis.

Outdated and damaging as they are, why are these messages so pervasive in our culture?

David Cohen, a professor at UCLA and a clinical social worker, argues in "It's the Coercion, Stupid!" on the Mad in America blog that, despite the flimsy theories holding up psychiatry, it persists and thrives as it does because of society's need to coerce. People want someone else to rush in when someone in their family or community is acting strangely or dangerously and take that person away to be dealt with by someone else. Therefore, he tells us:

> After decades of engaging in critical analysis of the psychiatric and other evidence, I conclude that there has *never* been good evidence to support psychiatric theories. Psychiatry has *never ever* needed scientific evidence to spread its ideas and practices, and possibly never will. Indeed, its top experts can state today that they have found no biomarkers of expertly diagnosed mental disorders and falsely promised the American public for decades that biomarkers were just around the corner.
>
> Let's face it: No one cares that psychiatric research of the past 50 years failed to turn up one finding of use for a scientific clinical psychiatry. The business of psychiatry continues with barely a pause.

There is a similar underpinning of coercion in the policing of gender that translates into diagnoses of gender dysphoria and medical "cures" of hormones and surgery. Trans people challenge the gender roles that hold up patriarchy and capitalism, systems that rely on hierarchies and binaries in order to function. Like psychiatry, they might collapse if left to survive on their own merits. But because they create classes of people and privilege some over others, those in power are hugely invested in staying there. Medical transition is often motivated by our culture's demand that we fit into the binary in order to retain jobs, relationships, family, and other supports.

I don't want to be dismissive of my friends who invoke "born this way"-type arguments to defend their gender or sexuality, or those who identify as having a mental illness. I don't mean to suggest they are unenlightened or miseducated, just because I've been there and have since changed my view. People who are seen as having gender and mental differences go through a tremendous amount of suffering; face discrimination in housing, employment, healthcare, public benefits, and parental rights; are victims of institutional and interpersonal violence; and have shorter life expectancies than their cisgender, non-psychiatric-labeled counterparts. A friend who has been experiencing a lot of the discrimination and violence I just mentioned and who has had a particularly rough month recently posted a Facebook status about it, saying, "Fuck you for telling me being trans is a choice." When our lives are literally being threatened, we will grab the nearest available weapon and brandish that thing like we mean it.

The problem is, that weapon is a double-edged sword. When activists, advocates, and individuals claim that queer identities are never chosen, they imply that no one would willingly choose queerness, further implicating those identities as shameful, inherently undesirable, and not worth celebrating. I don't believe I can choose how I feel. I can't decide what makes me comfortable in my body or to whom I will be attracted. But I can choose what I do with those feelings. I can work to be authentic and find ways to love myself and others that are nurturing and don't involve suppressing my desires and inclinations. I can choose that because anything else would be self-annihilation.

Someone I follow on Tumblr recently posted in response to being called "brave," something that trans people hear a lot from cis friends, family, and media. The writer described it as the kind of bravery one might exhibit when running away from a huge monster until they come to a steep, endless cliff. At that point, they can either jump or turn and attack. It's not bravery so much as survival—maybe even instinct—when they turn on the monster and don't stop beating at it until it stops moving.

I wouldn't suggest to anyone that they chose a difficult path or that their differences represented a gift if they believed otherwise. What I want is space for a multitude of truths, for binary-identified transgender folks who have "always known" their gender and for non-binary, gender fluid folks who change their presentation like they change their underwear, for the person who wears their psychiatric diagnosis like a badge of honor and the person who rejects labels faster than doctors can dish them out.

## THE LONG WAY HOME

I got my depression diagnosis and discovered I was trans right around the same time, in my early 20s. The "depression" was something I had felt for many years and for which I had just been given a word. The gender feelings were new, and I wouldn't have words for them for many years, and certainly no diagnosis. This was something I just knew and felt. Some of it came from inside me, from sensations in my body. Some of it came from recognizing myself in others, in seeing their bodies and in the words they used to describe how they felt.

In college, I would have gay friends and friends who had "experimented," but no model for what I was experiencing. I took an introductory women's studies class and was exposed for the first time to ideas about alternatives to the gender binary and reproductive sex roles. I explored my sensations and desires in poetry, writing lines like "I've been turning myself into a boy/Secretly, in my room . . . I light my breasts/ Like lanterns." I ran with a somewhat bohemian crowd, so I could get away with a certain amount of theatricality. I began playing with gender presentation: my skater-boy ponytail, baggy shorts, and combat boots evolved into heavy eye makeup with a penciled-on mustache, or a shaved head and a feather boa, or a cowboy shirt and body glitter.

My partner at the time was extremely supportive of my self-expression and the only person in whom I confided about my secret for years. I simply had no idea how I would explain to anyone else that this tiny girl who had been all ruffles and ringlets, baby dolls and ballet, who was just a little afraid of the outdoors, had grown up to be a femme gay sissy boy. I had no role models for that type of identity in small-town mid-90s Minnesota.

In an attempt to be read as other than female, I have put on the "masculine" uniform. (So much plaid. So much flannel. Occasional neckwear.) Binding my chest was great, until neck and shoulder pain made that no longer realistic. But tucked away in the back of my closet are a bag of dresses and a box of high-heeled shoes. As I become more comfortable in my changing body and am occasionally read as male by strangers, I hear those ruffles calling my name, those hot pink pumps asking when I will take them out dancing.

Performing femininity in my day-to-day while being read as a woman was profoundly uncomfortable and awkward. On stage, however, particularly when I was doing burlesque in my later 20s, where the entire context was performance, I reveled in the curly wigs, fishnets, and bold makeup. With my medical transition, I feel like I'm taking the long way home: I am traversing this physical expression of maleness so I can finally embody my femme-ness again with ease, this time with the added pleasure of transgression.

Coming Off
(October 2013)

My brain shudders.
It is autumn, and the colors
Tap into receptors, unstrung,
Frayed, heads waving like snakes
Held by their tails.
Eyes shift, and zap! the briefest
Static snap between film frames
(Where the ghosts live).

I finally got off all the psych drugs about a year ago. It was a years-long process of slowly, painstakingly lowering doses, splitting pills, cramming myself full of vitamins and supplements, feeling nauseous and dizzy and emotionally raw. Meanwhile, the testosterone made my menstrual cycle stop, and with that, my tears dried up, too. When I told a close, longtime friend I was starting hormone therapy, she was surprised, having seen my struggles with psych drugs and knowing my general distaste where pharmaceuticals are concerned. "Won't you have to be on testosterone for the rest of your life?" I chalked up her worries to overly medicalized portrayals of trans people in the media, similar to the way our culture views "mental illness" as a permanent medical state requiring lifelong intervention. I told my friend, "I don't have to do anything."

I have found myself examining whether I am contradicting my values by seeking medical services to change my body in order to move more comfortably through the world. After all, it is the world in which I live and the toxic culture I inherited, not my body, that ultimately should have to change. I have had the privilege of performing in two productions of *The Naked I: Monologues from Beyond the Binary* by Tobias K. Davis and got chills every time I was in earshot of "The Missing Vagina Monologue" by Esther Morris Leidolf, a powerful piece about a woman who discovers in her early teens that she does not have a vagina and the ensuing medical "treatment" designed to restore her to "normal." In particular, I was struck by the line, "People don't fail to meet the definitions of normal gender, but the definitions fail to meet the people."

## SHE BLINDED ME WITH SCIENCE

When my mom says, "You can't change your gender no matter how many hormones you take," she's confusing gender with sex. Sex is generally understood to be biologically determined by X and Y chromosomes and identifiable at birth by characteristics like genitalia. Gender is socially and individually determined and includes things like learned behavior, roles, and presentation, the rules of which are constantly changing. So, to the idea that being transgender is pretend, I say, "Gender is pretend." Language is pretend. Pronouns are pretend. They're all made up, and they all can change.

In addition, I don't claim to be changing my gender. I am making choices about my appearance that signal my gender to others, the way everyone does every day. Genders do change, and mine may have, but that is an internal process and not something anyone else can determine for me. I do not have gender in a vacuum. This means both that my gender exists within the context of the culture in which I live and that, could I take myself out of that culture, I would not have gender. I feel this freedom from gender most acutely when I'm alone in the woods or on a mountain, with no reflective surfaces or people showing me what I look like or how I am perceived. I just am. But in my daily life, I cannot simply take my ball and go home. I have to play the gender game. At work, at the grocery store, on the phone, with my friends, I have a name and pronouns, I have a body with lumps and bumps and hair, I wear clothes, and I speak with a voice that has pitch, inflections, cadence—all of which signify gender.

Furthermore, sex is less of a fixed binary than we are led to believe. There is more of a range of chromosome combinations, hormone balances, and genitalia than the two check boxes at the doctor's office would suggest. Most of us never know what kind of diverse sexual makeup we carry because chromosomes or hormones are tested only if there are problematic symptoms that suggest some variation or "syndrome." Since the 1950s, babies born with genitals that don't conform to male or female standards have often been given surgery almost immediately to "correct" this "abnormality," sometimes at the cost of later sexual functioning as an adult.

Like gender (and to a certain extent, sex), mental illness is a social construction. Yet the language of mental illness is mechanistic: *symptoms* are *assessed* and *diagnosed; disorders* are *treated*. Someone with whom I was in a support group meeting recently compared his brain to the HAL 9000 computer from *2001: A Space Odyssey*. As a computer, HAL cannot make a mistake; yet it malfunctions and kills most of the ship's crew. The idea of the brain or person as machine relieves us of individual responsibility, shifting it to faulty wiring or bad programming. I have heard many people talk about their mental health inside this dichotomy: as a fault either in their brain or in their character. Of the two, it is kinder to say it's the brain.

However, there is another argument that represents a shift away from this false binary, illustrated by a 1970s experiment with rats by a psychology professor. Bruce Alexander took note of experiments being done with rats that were put in a cage alone with two water bottles: one with plain water, one laced with heroin or cocaine. The rat would ignore the plain water and drink the drug-laced water until it overdosed and died. The conclusion from these tests was that these drugs are hopelessly addictive and lethal. Alexander wondered, though, if the rat would respond differently in another environment, one with other rats around, in which there was something to do other than take drugs all day. So he built Rat Park, a lush cage outfitted with all the best toys and food and plenty of rat friends. The happy rats tried the drugs but did not become dependent, and none of them died.

Although the conservative view of drug addiction as a moral failing was displaced by the softer liberal view of addiction as a disease of a brain helpless against a powerful chemical, the result has nevertheless been a corrupt "drug war" resulting in a prison population explosion and a disproportionate focus on individual treatment for addiction. What if we saw addiction instead as an adaptation to an environment that does not support our human needs? As Johann Hari, author of *Chasing the Scream*—about the war on drugs—says, "It's not you. It's your cage."

Recently my mom proposed writing me a long letter. She wanted to explain to me, through her own history and mine, why I am the way I am, why I'm doing what I'm doing. She wanted to change my mind. She has suggested that my own mistreatment and the violence against her that I witnessed have caused me to reject my femaleness and to seek transition in order to have control over my body. What if there is any validity to what she has to say? What if she could show how my trauma became my dissociation, my dysphoria, my identity? What if?

I don't care. Just like I don't care about a supposed "gay gene" or what a multi-billion-dollar drug company says my dopamine receptors are doing. My gender is not a problem to be solved, and I am not a helpless victim tragically mutilating my life and my body because of the pain and loss I have suffered. My mom says I am broken, or at least severely damaged, from the hurt and chaos inflicted on me by my life, making poor decisions that will further damage me in an endless cycle of unhealed wounds. If she could strip away the many layers of judgment, however, she would see me as I try to see myself: an adaptable, creative person with the resiliency to re-imagine himself in a body and a life that makes it possible to survive and thrive a little longer.

Likewise, I have come to view my depression and anxiety—I prefer descriptors like "sensitivity" and "self-preservation"—as reasonable responses to stress and trauma, states of being that have made me more empathetic and compassionate to suffering, and a deep source of material for creative expression and connection with others.

Medical specialists have spent centuries attempting to "understand" human differences through scientific means, but none of their tests, studies, or theories have brought about our liberation. The most significant progress has been made when the people who actually embodied those differences organized themselves and made their voices heard in grassroots efforts to take back power. Psychiatrists in the late 19th century attempting to establish a medical basis for homosexuality created a mental disorder out of what had been a criminal act. It would take the gay liberation movement of the 1960s and the Stonewall riots for homosexuality to be removed from the *Diagnostic and Statistical Manual of Mental Disorders* (DSM) in 1973. A psychiatric survivors' movement began to build around the same time, which has had considerable influence on mainstream mental health treatment as well as developing alternatives and promoting self-determination.

I believe what it will take for our total liberation is not waiting for people in lab coats to tell us when we're broken or fixed. Writing about undoing racism, patriarchy, and homophobia, poet and activist Audre Lorde said famously, "The master's tools will never dismantle the master's house. They may allow us to temporarily beat him at his own game, but they will never enable us to bring about genuine change." We need to give ourselves permission to adapt and grow, to transform ourselves and the world via all available tools and means. We must have both access to medical care and freedom from medical intervention, each according to our needs as we determine them.

I may not have chosen to be queer or mad, but I've come to view these parts of myself as sacred gifts that require careful tending as long as they are mine. And I intend to hang on for the ride as long as I can.

# 19

## KNOWING REYNOLDS

*Lucy Winer*

It was the summer of 1969 and it was hot, even by Long Island standards. And we were used to the kind of heat and suffocating damp that never quits. In those days heat meant something. It took you over, crushed you, even made you cry. And there was no escape. Air conditioners were still rare, at least in people's homes, and they didn't necessarily work. Just made a lot of noise, promising something they never delivered, leaving us gasping for relief. In my mind's eye, I see clouds of steam coming up from the roadways. But I think I'm making that part up.

I had just been admitted to the state hospital again. Sent for my second time in two years, this time because my mother's insurance had run out at the private hospital. My mother was an English teacher in the rich part of town. Don't misunderstand. Where I grew up, pretty much everyone had money, or at least they pretended they did. You had to or you would die of shame. But where my mother taught was *really rich.*

Back then, public school teachers had health insurance to burn, but I stayed locked up long enough to use it all up. So the fancy hospital in Connecticut with the long and incredibly stupid name where I was staying at the time said they couldn't afford to keep me anymore.

I was scared out of my mind. With good reason. My first time at Queens Park, two years before, branded me for life. My friend Camille put it best: "They could do anything to you there, and no one would ever be the wiser." That was the deal.

But right away I could see that it wasn't going to be as bad this time around. Things had changed a little, and for the better. For starters, when I got there this time they didn't take my fingerprints, and they didn't strip search me, and they actually let me keep my own clothing. They didn't make me wear a state dress and they didn't lock me in a massive "day room" with no way to reach the outside world—no mail, no phones, no visitors—and nobody to explain what was going on, and no one I could turn to for any kind of help. And that was just the beginning.

Don't get me wrong. I still had the same feeling of danger—that this huge hospital could swallow me up without a trace—do anything to me—and no one would know or care. But the feeling wasn't as intense. More than danger, this time around, I felt thrown out. Like the trash. But that was a step up from what I'd known before.

I spotted Reynolds pretty fast. For one thing, she was young like me. I was nineteen. She was maybe twenty-three. For another, she was the only Black patient on the ward. Besides the two of us, there were mostly middle-aged White ladies, and they were everywhere. The ones who could played cards—and they played all day long. That's how I thought of them—the "Card Players." Mostly I liked them, and more to the point, I wanted them to like me, but they really didn't.

They were a unit. Like I couldn't keep them straight as individual people. A cloud of smoke with bleached hair, hunched shoulders, and skinny fingers stained with tobacco. That was them. When they weren't coughing they were muttering snarky comments and, believe me, you didn't want one of those zingers aimed at you.

So Reynolds and I turned to each other. Basically, for the two of us, we were the only game in town. But still we approached with caution. We both knew we had way more to lose than gain. Like most deeply insecure people, I was a snob. I would have died rather than admit it, but that didn't make it less true. And trust was foreign to me.

But from the start she felt like family. Not like *my* family, mind you, but family like they have on television or in books or at other people's houses. I felt at ease a little. Safe. Understood. Blah, blah. It was nice. Why did I feel that way? I don't know. But it wasn't just me. Other people liked her, too. I'd say she inspired respect. Around her, people were on their best behavior.

It was Reynolds who suggested that we go for a walk. *Outside.* Me, I was not so excited. Over two years on different locked wards in different psych hospitals had left me conditioned to confinement and the joy of sitting on my ass 24/7. They call it "institutionalized." That was definitely me. I had no desire to venture out. Zero. Sun and fresh air held no appeal. I liked my breathing stale with a touch of mildew. Still do at times. But Reynolds was different, and she wasn't giving in.

Before I knew it we were standing in the nurses' station where no one who was a nurse ever worked, except once or twice a week for a little while. We were there to apply for a pass. Some part of me must have wanted this because I let myself be coaxed along even though I knew this whole thing would take a lot of effort. Even though I couldn't have cared less about the "grounds" and the physical surroundings outside our ward.

We got the pass and Reynolds was proud. She had pulled something off and she knew it. So there we were. Outside our building in the blazing heat, both of us crammed full of psych meds, which don't do so well with the sun. Reynolds was chipper and light on her feet and she led the way. I was definitely dragging to keep up.

She was a slight woman. Physically, I mean. And in my memory she always wore the same white tee shirt and the same pair of men's jeans that fit her perfectly. Her hair was cut short in an Afro. That's what we called it back then. Her features were so regular that she looked pretty good almost bald. Bottom line, she was at home in her body. You know what I mean? Take me. I am definitely not at home in my body. I leave it at the door like a coat you don't need any more. Not Reynolds. She didn't make it a big deal, but she kept her body *on,* enjoying the sensation of it all. Quiet like. Aware of all her parts, she *communed* with her body, minute by minute, never losing contact. It was something.

Sticking to the tradition of newly forged mental patient friendships, we got to the business at hand and basically spilled the beans, explaining to each other how we we had gotten to where we were and what was "wrong" with us.

I went first. I could tell that Reynolds was a forthright type, and not much impressed with my tale of woe—the overdoses, the cutting, the multiple commitments. She had one simple question, "Why?"

It's not like she judged me, or maybe she did, but either way she expected an answer. Per usual I had none. I was blank, and try as I might to reach inside and find the feelings and memories like other people had that could explain me, I couldn't find them. They were missing. AWOL. Absent without leave. Period.

Reynolds was kind, but she dismissed me. I think she said something like, "You need to quit acting like that."

*No kidding.* I felt ashamed, kind of like dog shit. I nodded obediently and tried not to hate her guts.

The air was heavy and I began to notice that walking around outside like we were made the place more *for real.* Made my situation more *for real.* And that didn't feel good. Not at all.

Then it was Reynold's turn. Even before she started talking, I knew it was going to be a showstopper. I'm kind of a babbler when I talk, once you get me started. Reynolds was the quiet type and there's power in that. She reeked of dignity.

Eyes down, focused on the ground, she explained to me that she had come to the state hospital from the county jail, where she was sent two years before for killing her mother. That's right. You heard me. Killing her *MOTHER!!!!*

Almost like an afterthought she added that she'd done it in self-defense. Shit. Like I said, a showstopper.

We kept on walking and I tried to focus on the world around me. I could see now the place was built on a kind of incline. Like a slope. And looking all the way down I could see a sparkle, like water, beyond all the buildings and trees at the bottom.

I was blown away. So all this time we'd been living on the water! Who knew? Even though this was my second time around, I had no sense of what was going on outside the building I was in. Why would I? If you're never allowed to go out, how would you know the place was right smack on the Long Island Sound?

I wanted to scream it was so hot. I didn't though. In a psychiatric hospital— especially a state psychiatric hospital—screaming was definitely a mark against you and I wanted to get out of there someday.

The two of us kept walking. Quietly. I couldn't help but wonder, was Reynolds going to kill me next? Maybe right there on the edge of the road? And if she did try to kill me, would anybody in this godforsaken place try to help me out?

I saw she was watching me. Weighing my reactions. I didn't know what else to do, so I kept on moving my feet, resigned to the possible end of my life. I smiled inside—I sure could pick 'em.

She went on talking. Her mother was a drunk and when she drank she was mean and she was violent. She showed me the scar where her mother had stuck a fork in her neck during dinner one time. I asked Reynolds if it hurt. She said yes, all the time. Then there were the men. A stream of boyfriends who would come after Reynolds when they got tired of her mother, which only made her mother meaner and more violent.

It happened on Christmas Eve. She went looking for her mother and found her in the basement, messing with the gas controls for their house. Her mother said she was going to kill everyone who was there that night, including herself. That was the last thing Reynolds could remember. The rest was blank. She couldn't remember actually doing it—actually killing her mother.

They carted her off to jail, and they kept her there almost two years until her case finally came to trial and she was let off by reason of temporary insanity. I'm no big believer in the judicial system, but I found this reassuring.

"There's something else." She looked at me.

"You gotta be kidding," I thought to myself. I kept on walking. Everything in me resisted the look of the place. It was so neat. So tidy. It offended me. I felt like I weighed a hundred thousand pounds. "I'm not here, I'm not here, I'm not here . . . "

"I'm gay." *Whoa.* Everything turned. The perfect lawns, the ugly brick buildings, the road, the benches, it all turned upside down.

Reynolds stopped walking. So did I.

"Don't be scared." She was smiling. It was a sweet smile. Generous. But it was too late. I was scared shitless. It was one thing to kill your mother. It was another thing to be a goddamned dyke.

I looked away again. You could see right away how much effort they put into the outside of the place—the grass and the trees and the flowers and all of that. Not like inside the buildings where we lived. But none of this swayed me. No matter how well they cared for this place, in my humble opinion it was still a dump.

Maybe the problem was imagination. As in there wasn't any. Instead there was order and there was duty. Begrudging duty. Even the flowers stood at attention to the point that they weren't really flowers any more. Like their flower souls had been stolen.

We turned back. It was coming on lunchtime and the sun overhead was blazing. Our little walk had definitely confirmed my low opinion of venturing out. Never go anywhere—that was my motto. Whenever possible, stay where the fuck you are.

I don't remember our walk back. What I do remember was the huge relief I felt when we got to the ward and things felt more normal again. And I felt safer.

Reynolds and I found a couple of unclaimed chairs away from each other. I couldn't look at her, and I think that made me feel ashamed.

In the corner, the card players were doing their thing. It was almost lunch and their table was covered with Styrofoam coffee cups and metal ashtrays brimming with lipstick-stained butts smoked down to the filters.

My first day there, a week or two before, I had sidled up to their table. I was trying to make friends. "What are you playing?" Of course I knew better, but I was lonely. Sure enough, no one answered me. So I tried again.

"Can I sit down?"

There was a long pause. "Taken," one of the ladies muttered, nodding at the empty chair.

I played dumb. "'Scuse me?" I waited a minute, then cleared my throat. "What'd you say?"

Another woman looked up, making eye contact for a minute. "*Taken*," she repeated in no uncertain terms. There was no bargaining. No mercy. These women were drained dry and they had no intention of suckling needy newcomers like me. They had earned their seen-it-all disgust with life. Probably they had spotted Reynolds as a big old lezzie from day one. They were smart. I was not.

Someplace a bell rang and the day room began to show signs of life. Women were going through the motions, pulling up stakes, getting their stuff together. We lived like nomads. Wherever we went, we took everything with us that had value. Cigarettes, multiple cups of old coffee, maybe some candy, a leftover dessert, all precious. Those who still cared how they looked carried makeup and toothpaste. Highbrows had old magazines and crosswords.

Cigarettes were the best. No question. They were as good as money. Anything that could be bought, could be bought with cigarettes. If you had a carton you were rich. Simple. If you had nothing to carry around with you, you were poor. But it was a delicate balance, 'cause if you had too much to carry around, you were seen as a little loony. Everything in moderation. See?

Obediently, we headed for what passed as a cafeteria. The food was disgusting. But we went, partly because we had to—it was the rules—and partly because old habits die hard. No matter how many times we gazed down at our plates with no idea what we were looking at, the memory of pleasure brought us back again; another time, we would be fed something worth eating. Something delicious. Someday. That was our hope. And there lay the source of our obedience.

Mind you now, it's not like I'd never met a lesbian before. The private hospitals were filled with them. But I had never felt the kind of fear that I felt that day with Reynolds. Actually, I had never felt any kind of fear at all. Admiration, maybe a touch of hero worship in some cases, but never fear.

Take Dee, for instance. I knew her from the private hospital in Connecticut. And I could have spent the rest of my life hanging on her every word. No lie.

She was a big woman in her thirties, so to me she was old, and she referred to herself openly as a bull dyke—"of the sissy variety"—and you could tell that she loved talking like that, which is saying something, since it was the late 1960s and being queer was still considered a disease by the kind of doctors we saw. Shrinks.

She wore her short black hair slicked back with a streak of silver in the front. And no one knew how she managed it, but her clothing was always perfectly ironed and she made a careful ceremony of fitting her cigarettes into a small black and silver holder that matched her hair. When that was done, she leaned back against the wall and waited for an aide to walk by eventually and provide her with a light. We were on a locked ward and all of us were considered potentially dangerous, so no one was allowed to have matches and we had to ask the staff for our lights if we wanted to smoke. Just about all of us did. Most of us wanted to chain smoke.

Dee was there because of her love of heroin, and she would regale us with stories of her life as a junkie in Coconut Grove. All of her stories were awesome, and like I said, she could have talked all day and I would have wanted more. But the story that stands out was the one about the day she was diapering somebody's baby, and she was so high she mistook the diaper full of shit for skin cream and spread it happily all over the baby's ass. Dee could definitely hold your attention.

So you see, I wasn't scared, more like entranced. But as far as the whole sex thing went, I had pretty much given up. Actually, I had decided it was all basically bullshit. I had tried it. Way more than once. So when people carried on about how good it was, I figured they were full of it. Everyone was just going through the motions and lying their asses off. Sex was a big hoax perpetrated on the rest of us to make us feel bad. So what did it matter about straight or gay? It was all one big made-up deal and people who said otherwise were big fat liars. It was simple really.

Usually in the lunchroom I sat in front by the window near where we stood on line to get handed our food, but I'm not really sure where I sat that day. What I do know is that's when it happened. I was struck. Like out of nowhere. Sitting there, unable to move, I was struck suddenly and hard. Like getting kicked by a bull. It was overwhelming. I wanted her. With all my nineteen-year-old heart and soul I wanted her.

I felt faint. I could hardly walk. I staggered from the day room to the back hall where we slept. In my mind's eye the card players looked up to watch my retreat. No matter, they had already seen it all.

I shared a four-person room with a mean-as-a-snake young woman with a curdled soul who liked to act like she was already going through her "changes" even though she was just a little older than me. I figured she'd been born that way—past middle aged with a bad taste in her mouth.

I can't remember her name and don't really want to. What I do remember about her was the horrible quilted blue bathrobe with the pearl buttons that she wore day and night. Most of the time she stayed in our room, except for meals and meds, and she would shoot me disapproving looks whenever I showed up. Especially if I looked happy.

There was no comfort for me there, so I headed for Reynolds' room—a small single room on the shady side of the hall with its own door and one barred window and a narrow, sagging metal-framed bed. I lay down and before I knew it Reynolds was there. She perched on the side of the bed looking down at me. We didn't say a word; no words were needed. I could tell she knew everything. How did she know? She leaned down, we kissed and that was that—all hell broke loose. We made love like in the movies and nothing could have stopped us. So this was what they were all talking about!

Looking back, two miracles happened that day. Miracle number one was that I let the whole thing happen in the first place. You see, I'm a life-resister. That means I avoid all things connected to being alive—feeling things, being intimate, being vulnerable. So to let a major rush of passion take me over without crushing it dead was out of character to say the least. And the passion—it continued. For days, maybe weeks. At every opportunity.

Miracle number two was connected to miracle number one. Although I didn't know it at the time, I beat myself without mercy over every little thing. That was pretty much how I spent every waking minute. But in this case, with Reynolds, I was spared. Not by *me*. I had no awareness and therefore no control over my thoughts. But I think I was so elated from the joy of the whole thing that all those judgments that were always coming at me—they just stopped for a little while.

Talk about a miracle.

In my thinking, we fell in love across a chasm. There was the obvious stuff: she was Black, I was White. I came from a middle-class, look-good-or-die-trying family; her family drank a lot and got high and made scenes. She was quiet and kind of naturally dignified. I was an emotional train wreck with little or no self-control. It's true.

Reynolds had little patience for all that I felt defined me back then. My complaints with life didn't make sense to her. But I knew in all the ways that really counted, she *got me*. And she felt the same. She knew that I saw her nobility. Her humor. Her kindness. And her patience. She taught me things that mattered. Standing in line for lunch, she explained that the food in the hospital was even worse than the food in "the joint." Information like that was helpful and put things in perspective. She was worldly.

But all was not well. Very fast we noticed that my evil roommate was watching us. Actually, it was more like she was stalking us—we even talked about how we had to be careful. But that was easier said than done.

One afternoon, we slipped into the utility closet on the ward for a quickie. We were deep into things when, out of nowhere, the heavy door was suddenly shoved open and my blue-quilted roommate was standing there, glaring at us. Victory and horror competed for the muscles of her pale ugly face. Vindicated. She had been *right!*

We stared back at her, defiant. But that was it. We were done for. And sure enough, she made a beeline for the office to tell the staff what everyone already knew—we were having sex.

What happened next was amazing. And totally fucked up. The following day, first thing in the morning, I was sent off the ward on some bogus pretext. When I got back, Reynolds was gone. Gone! They had discharged her. In their great wisdom, the hospital administrators had chosen to release the slightly older, convicted Black dyke murderer, and keep her slightly younger, White middle-class mentally ill girlfriend. Total CYA damage control.

But that was just the beginning. For the first time in all my time at the state hospital, I was signed up for therapy. *Therapy!* Nobody got *therapy!* A social worker was assigned to meet with me and help me "understand" everything that had just happened.

We met in a small office that looked like it hadn't seen much action in the past few years. There were two mismatched chairs on either side of a battered metal desk. I was relieved to see that the social worker didn't look mean—just kind of sad and battered by life. Neither one of us wanted to be there, but she dutifully did her job and it went like this. My feelings for Reynolds could be explained by my two and a half years locked away in psych hospitals, mostly with other women. I was experiencing a natural "displacement," and these very natural coping mechanisms would leave me when (and if) I reentered the outside world.

As for my total lack of feeling when I tried to have sex with men, well, unfortunately I was suffering from a condition common among tall women like myself. It seems that for us big gals, the inordinate distance between the vagina and the clitoris could make reaching orgasm during intercourse difficult. Puzzled, I asked her what could be done. She shook her head. She wasn't sure. Her grief seemed to fill the room to capacity. I couldn't breathe. I understood that her pain had little to do with my sex life and, thankfully, that was the beginning and end of my treatment.

Without actually knowing it, from that afternoon I began to feel shame. The wild joy of my time with Reynolds was now linked with the sad social worker peddling crap theories in an airless room, and I withdrew. And went more than a little numb inside. Even though I knew she was handing me a pile of horseshit.

I was bereft. They just took her. They could do that. Reynolds was *gone*. Gone in a moment. To make matters worse, she was the ward-favorite and pretty much everyone blamed me for her sudden absence. The staff, the card ladies, the other patients, they blamed me. Everybody except my roommate who blamed us both. But no one ever said a word. Not one. And with Reynolds gone, it was like someone had stolen the spirit from our ward. We were like air gone out of an inner tube. All of us. And it was my fault.

I was discharged later that summer—a truly anti-climactic event after so many years in so many hospitals—and job number one was to stay out. I knew that. Stay out of the hospital. Did I believe I could do it? Not really. I had nightmares for years that I was back there for reasons I couldn't understand.

Once I was out I called Reynolds and told her over the phone that we were finished. It was a brutal thing to do, that's for sure, but by that point I was all about being normal and a big part of being normal was being heterosexual.

But Reynolds seemed to take my news in stride. In fact, the next day she came to visit me at my mother's house with her new girlfriend, who was pretty and very friendly. The three of us sat in the living room and drank iced tea with fresh mint from my mother's garden. Surrounded by doilies and candy dishes and spotlessness, it was all very civilized.

That was the last time I saw Reynolds. Four years later I called to let her know that I had finally come out. I was all psyched about lesbian liberation and the women's movement and I wanted to tell her. She was less than enthusiastic. In fact, she sounded depressed, not like the person I had known. She wondered out loud what being gay could have to do with liberation. She warned against my newfound freedom. It wouldn't last. For Reynolds being gay was a stroke of terrible luck in a cruel world. We promised to stay in touch, but we didn't.

I think the channel between us was pain. Pain ruled me, but I couldn't feel it. Not really. Reynolds could. She could feel things. But then, she couldn't access the most important moment in her life. It was gone. Tucked away behind a wall no one could get past, including her.

In some ways it was like pain had hollowed her out and made her deeper—and she was deep, let me tell you. The wild thing was, her being like that, being deep like she was, gave me the space I craved. That I needed just to be. Her suffering was my refuge. It was like all my cramped and shut down parts could relax and let go and get a little sun. Until the mindless machine of the hospital went to work and I acquiesced.

Reynolds was my first love. And I know exactly how much it took, over how many years, to circle back to that moment to be able to love again. When I think what might have been, had all this been handled differently, it takes my breath away.

# 20

## ON A SUBWAY PLATFORM, A LIFE
## FLASHES—HERE, GONE

*Antoine B. Craigwell*

Mark stood at the edge of the subway platform, balancing as if on a seesaw's fulcrum point, on the uptown side of the local No. 1 train at the 34th Street/Pennsylvania Station in New York City. Most of the soles of his feet hung over the side into the well where the electrified rails ran below him, precariously perched on the sliver of yellow-warning-painted wood at the edge, demarcating that point of no return. Leaning so far forward, he could see the twin lights of the train illumining the darkness of the tunnel and feel the force of the head wind preceding it as it roared into the station. Balanced as he was, any involuntary reflex action, a sneeze or a sudden shudder, could tip him forward directly into the path of the oncoming train and propel him into nothingness, into cementing the past as a single moment, removing the future. Finely balanced, he debated what he should do: should he allow himself to fall forward or should he pull himself back? The image of his mother flashed in his mind, causing him to lean back ever so slightly. Mark felt his heels connect with the solidness of the platform and, as if willing the past to become one with the present to take him to the future, his right leg involuntarily stepped backward; the left followed. He could feel the wind as the train rushed past. He could see the whites of the train engineer's eyes staring at him through the front and side windows, as if rebuking him for what he thought to do. So close to the edge, if he had worn any loose clothing it could have been caught in any outcropping part of the train: snagged and with a violent, sudden jerk, yanked off his feet and dragged along the platform, likely crashing into passengers waiting for the train or into the steel girders, as pillars.

In an instant, he realized and experienced a sudden rush of adrenaline. All the past came flooding into his mind, as if it all happened yesterday, welling up like a mountain spring runoff capped by a dam and trapped in an artificial lake that was suddenly broken. In his head was a seething cauldron of thoughts, like angry waves riding over and competing with each other for attention, threatening to overwhelm the dam with a force not felt since the glaciers from the Ice Age melted and rushed down through those narrow confines of gorges in his mind.

Athletically built, Mark is tall, slim, with a medium-brown skinned complexion, now a shade lighter—the effect of living in the cold of a northern climate—than that richer and darker color that a summer's sun could restore. By the time of this close encounter with the subway, he had been living in the United States for five years, having arrived from Guyana just as he turned thirty to attend college. Along the way, out of necessity and mostly economics, as someone accustomed to being independent—not to wanting to live off his relatives—he landed one job after another, enrolled in college, and for two years took courses. The experience at the time seemed a blur, but in retrospect, he didn't seem to progress. No one counseled him. At seventeen, he was ejected from the only home he knew and was forced to learn survival. He became accustomed to making decisions and living on his own, his pride as his foremost survival tool, resisting ever asking anyone for help and not looking too kindly on unsolicited advice. Mark had become embittered early by life's experiences and had become hardened far too long—much too long to dwell on memories. He felt as if he was always in survival mode, never reaching the next level to exist or even higher, to live. He had become accustomed to survival and doing whatever was necessary to see himself through to the next moment, living one day at a time. He dared not plan for the future; to him, it was never a guarantee.

Growing up in a heavily Christian household, Mark recalled that he lived a protected life, as if shielded from the vicissitudes and dangers around him. Where he lived, in South Ruimveldt, a residential suburb of the country's capital, Georgetown, he was forbidden to go outside the house without wearing some type of footwear. In the house, in conversation, he was expected to speak proper and formal English and not use any of the slang or colloquialisms of the street, and, if he should mispronounce or misuse any word, he was sent to the dictionary to look up the word. As a teenager, a dictionary, an atlas of the world, a Bible, and a copy of *Roget's Thesaurus* were his literary companions. Often kept indoors, he learned housekeeping and decorating; how to cook, beginning from the first time he fried an egg to cooking elaborate three-course meals; and how to do laundry, even knitting and crocheting, taught by his mother's aunt before she died. These lessons formed the foundation for his survival in later years.

Notwithstanding that these chores were lessons in self-sufficiency, behind them there were lingering feelings that he didn't quite belong, couldn't quite fit in. There were times he recalled when he was kept indoors on orders from his mother and sister—who had governance over him—forbidden to go outside, even to join in a game of cricket, a sport everyone in Guyana and throughout the Caribbean played as a national game or as a pastime, in the neighbor's yard. During those Sunday afternoon cricket games or impromptu weekday afternoon post-workday matches, when he stood at the window, from his privileged spectator box, he marveled at the sight of the players. Often, he would peer through the glass louvre windows, looking out and down on the players' sun-burnished brown and light-brown skins, admiring their muscles rippling and pulsating on sweat-glistened bodies as they hit the ball, ran, and caught it. He watched as they enjoyed the competition and camaraderie of the game played on the open stretch of concrete next door. Many times, when they played cricket, he would stand at the window for hours, even when the sun had retreated from night's advance, and watch them. From a darkened room, no lights on to reveal his presence, he looked on, wishing, hoping, straining to hear what was being said; listening, watching, mentally recording every movement, nuance, and body language to see if there were any signs, any indications that at least one of them exhibited any traits or signs. Often at the end of a game, tired, sweaty, the game allowing for the physical release of pent-up emotions, the guys would repair under the neighbor's house in a tight knot, chatting, teasing, making fun of each other, and recounting tales of exploits. Longing to be among them, he felt left out. While many of the guys knew he was watching, they generally pretended he wasn't there. Sometimes, one or another, with a quick glance up and a short imperceptible nod, would quietly acknowledge his presence. But he had hoped from his vantage point they could not see the desire smoldering in his eyes.

Mark realized early that he was attracted to other guys, but didn't quite understand what it was about, and while he didn't think he was feminine in appearance or behavior, in common language, some would say he was a "touch soft" or "he had a little sugar in his tank." He wasn't as overtly masculine as was expected of any man in a heavily religious and conservative Guyanese society. Any actions or behaviors that seemed to stray out of the norm were not only frowned on, but rebuked: he often heard, "It's a man's world," and "You have to stand up like a man."

He recalled the experiences growing up in New Amsterdam, the main town in the county of Berbice, which lay to the east of the country. Along the East Coast of Berbice are towns and villages predominantly inhabited by descendants from India of that period of indentureship when Guyana was a British colony. He remembered, as a child, attending weddings—especially Indian weddings where he saw men dancing with each other, and funerals—where a man dressed and made up to look like a woman led the procession through the village or town to the cemetery. He remembered other social events, such as corn house (similar to bingo, where instead of using coins, bits of dried corn were used to cover the numbers on a card) and bingo in New Amsterdam's town hall, where he saw and encountered many men who appeared trapped between male and female, often dressed like women, their previously tiny tightly curled hair pressed straight with a hot comb or misaligned wigs, and strutting about unsteadily, their thick feet squeezed in tight-fitting high-heeled shoes that looked uncomfortable and painful. Some of these unclear, questionable genders painted their faces with clownish looking makeup; bright cherry red lipstick daubed on full lips was a central feature, stark, bold, and garish against many dark faces. They went about their appointed or self-imposed tasks, whatever they were, oblivious to their surroundings and with an air of importance. There were those men who sold different local dishes, such as cook-up, black pudding, and souse from street carts late at night for the many men and women revelers who wanted food before returning home after partying. Many of these late-night food sellers were often quietly suspected of being "anti-men" but never openly accused, because of their popularity and the tasty food they sold. To Guyanese, an "anti-man" is the derogatory name hurled at anyone who did not appear to conform to what is expected of a man; he was a man who didn't behave like a man or who displayed feminine traits, behaviors, or mannerisms. At a corn house or bingo, many of the men would make derogatory or lewd comments about these effete men. The women, Mark observed, largely ignored them; it was their actions, such as "cutting their eyes," rolling their eyes, or turning away to signal their disapproval, which communicated clearly how they felt. While the men made fun and called the cross-dresser "anti-man," the women on the other hand whispered among themselves about whose child or son it was who was behaving in this manner. Some suggested that the person's behavior was related to him being just released from the mental asylum, located next to the Canje Creek, which lay on the town's northern boundary.

Mark remembered visiting the homes of family friends as a child, and, on occasion, he would see a young man cleaning, cooking, carrying water, sweeping, or repairing walls or floors made with mud or cow dung "daub." His head would be tied with a headscarf and his body language and mannerisms would be effeminate, yet no one in the family took notice of him; he wasn't accepted as part of the family, and while no one referred to him as an "anti-man," he wasn't mentioned, discussed, or introduced—he was ignored, and he didn't socialize with the family. At night, he was often the last to go to bed, sleeping in a hammock under the house, a thin blanket to cover his body against the dew, rain, and wind, and he had to be the first to rise early in the morning, to begin preparing breakfast for the household. He was seen as an embarrassment to the family and was relegated to the background because of the shame he brought to those who knew him. He was often verbally abused and at times beaten, even raped by male relatives, but could never report it because he would be branded a liar or called evil, having encouraged or made himself unnaturally desirable to his molester.

When Mark was about three or four years old, he and his next-door neighbor, Steve, boys of the same age in that process of discovery, fondled each other's penises.

He remembered the pleasant sensations those moments of touching produced and has since often wondered if the feelings he had then had cursed and doomed him to a life of wanting and desiring that which he could not have and which his family and society instilled in him was wrong. When he was about thirteen years old, as his sexuality awakened, the intense passion and the pleasure he felt with two of his friends, early teenagers, was phenomenal. Mark and Charles, his next-door neighbors, often met in Frank's house on the opposite side of the street, ostensibly to play with racing cars on a magnetized track. Instead, they went into the Frank's bedroom and fondled and masturbated each other. By the time he joined this pastime, he realized that Charles and Frank were already adept and that he was being initiated into a practice, a secret that only they shared. No one could ever know. For the first time, he felt as if he belonged. The pleasure of touching, stroking, and seeing another's penis; the rush of intense sensation as they watched each other achieve orgasm; and the potential danger, the possibility of Frank's parents or sisters returning home unexpectedly and discovering them, only served to heighten the excitement. This mutual masturbation became a daily occurrence among the three teens, and since Frank's parents and sisters were hardly home, it presented the perfect opportunity for them to meet in his bedroom. Their houses were in close proximity to each other, allowing them to use bird-like whistles, in short bursts, to arrange their rendezvous.

Entering into this secret practice was like a newly discovered drug for Mark. The intense pleasure he received from the association with his two friends, the acceptance, the sense that he belonged, which the sexualized bond created, made him feel one of the gang. He was aware that the adults were talking and making references but didn't interpret their remarks as directed at him. Many commented that it was a "phase" that would pass and opined that he would grow out of the attraction to other guys. He hoped and wished that the adults weren't whispering about him and that he had not brought shame on his family. He knew from overhearing conversations among the grown-ups that it always seemed better not to have someone in one's own family who was an "anti-man," but it became a subject for discussion when it was about someone else's family.

One afternoon, Mark heard a whistle; from the direction, he knew it came from Frank's house. He heard another whistle, as if in response, and realized it came from Charles' house. Rushing to the window overlooking the street, he whistled. It was the signal summoning a meeting, only this time Charles and Mark didn't go up to Frank's bedroom, as they were accustomed; he met them at the gate. In a whisper Frank said that his parents were sending him to Canada and he was leaving later that night. A stab of fear pierced the other two teens: were the adults aware? With Frank gone, Mark and Charles grew closer, they were almost inseparable, only apart when they went to their separate schools or went to bed in their own homes; they contrived to spend as much time together as possible. They devised more and more convoluted and intricate ways to continue their sexual liaison, planning elaborate schemes, weighing as many contingencies or methods as possible to slip away. They both had bicycles, and, in the afternoons, when they had returned from school and after finishing their homework, they would whistle, slip out of their homes, and ride off in separate directions only to meet up on another street and together go to a secluded place. Often, because Mark's parents were at work or out and he would be home alone, Charles would come over to his house, into his bedroom where, with one ear cocked to the sound of the gate opening, signaling an adult's return, they reveled in passion-filled sexual encounters. Charles's father liked the outdoors, he liked going camping and hunting, and on weekends both teens often went along and were able to enjoy moments away from the others. Sometimes at night they slept together with the stars as their canopy, wrapped in a blanket and intertwined in each other's arms on the warm volcanic rocks of Rockstone on the Essequibo River. Other times, Charles would pitch a tent on the lawn in the back yard and the two teens would spend the weekend together in it, only going home to shower, change clothes, and eat, sometimes bringing food to the tent.

Mark returned home from school one afternoon in May and saw Charles's mother and sister descending the outside stairs with suitcases. Charles's mother called out, "We're going away." Charles looked out from the back seat of the family's Land Rover to see who his mother was talking to, and, when he saw it was Mark, he beckoned him over and whispered that he was leaving for Canada and wasn't sure if and when he'd return. Mark suddenly felt confused; questions swirled in his head. What was happening, why this was happening, who would be his friend? He was thrown onto his own devices. Suddenly, he was forced to suppress his awakened passion and sexuality, which had flamed and burned with desire, the equivalent of capping a flaming oil well. A few months later, he, too, was sent away. He was enrolled as a recruit and found himself early one morning on a boat, the *MV Kimbia*, sailing out of the Demarara River on route to the Guyana National Service (GNS) training and orientation center at Papaya, in the country's northwest region. The GNS was a paramilitary organization established along socialist principles by the late president, Forbes Burnham, which required the country's young people to perform military service. In the space of less than a month, and in just over twenty-four hours, he found himself thrust into an all-male and extremely homophobic environment of barked orders and regulations. When he asked his parents why he was sent to National Service, they told him that he needed to learn discipline and the only place to teach him any would be in the military. But, in quiet moments, he really wondered if it was the discovery of his relations with Charles that led to him being sent away, or did the adults observe a change in his behavior after Charles left (he had become withdrawn, morose, and gloomy, often thinking the world was against him) and feel he needed the rigors of the military to make him more masculine?

He felt a deep pain, but it wasn't the type where someone could take a pain killer and it would go away; it was as real as life. It wasn't the kind of pain one could put a finger on and identify as this or that; it was there, a constant reminder of many unresolved issues, which separately and together formed a block of complications in his life: each fact of his life interwoven and overlapping the other, each clamoring for its own share of attention. He felt tired. It seemed as if a lethargy had crept into his very being. He was tired of living and saw no point in continuing with the daily struggle to live. Each breath seemed an effort, as if he had some type of lung disorder, except it was in the depths of his mind; it hurt to think.

In the here and now, he was dealing with the recent death of his sister, he was living in an abusive and failing marriage, and seeing no other options for academic advancement, no job prospects—and, if any, in menial positions. He was also dealing with issues relating to his sexuality—his attraction to other men and his inability to process and deal with these feelings because of what he was taught about men and other men and the shame and embarrassment of relationships between two men. Except for occasional transient sexual encounters, which, at the moment, provided a pleasurable salve, those trysts left him feeling empty, cheap, and with a deepening sense of not belonging, not fitting in, or being part of any one family.

Standing on the subway platform, these thoughts, in a flash, came crashing into his consciousness, perhaps in less than a nanosecond, overwhelming him, inundating his mind, and momentarily paralyzing him in one spot. In an instant, his only thought was to end it all. Who would miss him, who would care if he was hit and killed by that fast-approaching subway train? But just as quickly as that thought entered his mind, it was replaced by another that seemed to pull from the depths of his being—a desire to live, if only to avoid visiting the sorrow of his death on his already grief-stricken mother.

# 21

## THIS WORK IS ABOUT DIGESTED SOCKS

*Gabrielle Jordan Stein*

Growing up with a dog whose favorite food was socks meant finding them partially digested and scattered around the house. As the youngest child, I was forced to clean them up. It left long-lasting stains on my memory as well as the oriental carpets. At nineteen, when I was diagnosed with Crohn's disease, it was those partially digested socks that became my only reference for what was happening inside my body. My body digests itself, and, when functioning at its best, it's still unable to survive on its own. Each pill and medical intervention makes me feel more and more removed from my body. And my discomfort in my own body dictates how I explore, experience, and articulate pain. I am a cyborg. Part human, part biologic intervention, and part sock.

FIGURES 21.1–21.5   "This Work Is About Digested Socks," by Gabrielle Jordan Stein.

FIGURE 21.2

FIGURE 21.3

FIGURE 21.4

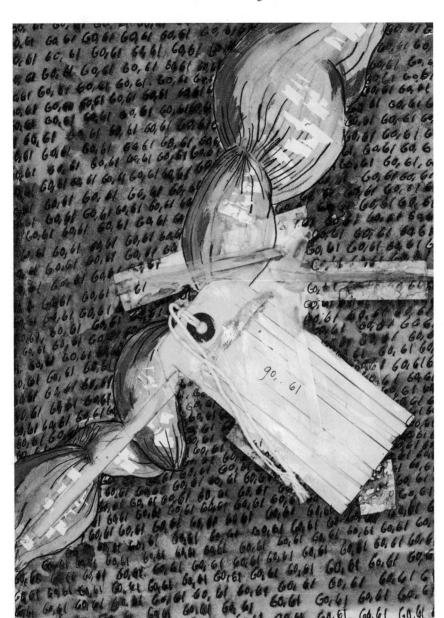

FIGURE 21.5

# 22

## TAMING MY INNER FUNDAMENTALIST

### Kelly Barth

Though I felt more at ease in a progressive church, fundamentalism was, for me, a dormant virus that lurked in my psyche and waited for lowered spiritual resistance. Each outbreak was usually less severe, but nonetheless debilitating. I regularly woke disoriented and discouraged from dreams about Celeste, a British missionary friend, with whom I had fallen privately in love during my Southwest Bible Church Singles Group years. She had come to the states for a year to provide hospice care to her cranky, toothless American grandmother.

A straight-backed young woman smelling of Ivory soap, Celeste railed against any number of things-—Darwin and abortionists and the transgender woman we saw together on a BBC profile. "Rubbish," she said. "How can a person just decide he isn't who God made him to be? All the physical evidence is there." I hadn't been brave enough to say in a voice louder than a whisper, "Not anymore it isn't." The dreams always went badly. Celeste would discover how much I had really been attracted to her because I finally made the play for her that my wakeful, vigilant self had tried not even to fantasize about. She would rise up in all her clanging religious fury to say how inexplicably sick and wrong I was.

My inner fundamentalist used whatever means necessary to air her grievances. If she had to wait until I was asleep, just as my once-closeted lesbian had used to have to do, so be it. Instead of dreaming I was ripping an Asian woman's clothes off behind the woodpile in my childhood backyard or causing my Sunday school teacher's wife to climax, I heard British sermons. I would wake from them feeling surprised at how guilty I could still feel for enjoying how my partner Lisa's skin felt in the nest of our pale green flannel sheets. Like a newly erupted cold sore, such dreams came often enough to remind me that my inner fundamentalist needed reassurance.

"Taming My Inner Fundamentalist", an excerpt from *My Almost Certainly Real Imaginary Jesus*, by Kelly Barth, Red Hen Press, 2012. Reprinted by permission of Red Hen Press.

This inner fundamentalist took advantage of my weakened spiritual immune system two days before Thanksgiving when, still reeling from Momma's sudden death from colon cancer, I took a phone call from Brad, the friend who had introduced me to the clandestine ex-gay ministry that had failed to convert me many years before. I hadn't seen or heard from him in more than a decade. Though the complete lack of context did concern me, Momma had raised me to take telephone calls even when I didn't want to, even when the caller neglected to ask if I had the time. There would never be a good time to talk to Brad, but I naively hoped he had called to tell me he was questioning his beliefs. For a brief while, I even entertained the idea that this troubled, beautiful man had finally allowed himself to be authentic.

For several minutes, I relaxed into a Lord-free conversation. Then he asked me what I'd been doing. As I used to with Momma before I came out, I carefully edited out any mention of Lisa. I'd forgotten how tedious and demoralizing lying could be. I remembered, after all those years, to ask about his schizophrenic brother. And then the conversation took a turn. The brother had died, but only after Brad had the opportunity to "really share the plan of salvation with him." Deep inside me, a gland secreted adrenalin. I did not heed my body's short, simple warning. I stayed on the line pretending all was well and that I could handle whatever came up.

My inner fundamentalist liked to know what was going to happen; she liked to brace herself. She didn't "read the daily horoscope for entertainment purposes only." She was certain Something out there was trying to tell her something and that that Something would use anything—traffic lights, astrology, or sidewalk cracks—to let me know what could happen to me if I didn't heed the warning. My fundamentalist kept me on the line with Brad who said the Lord had told him to share something with me. He wondered if I wanted to hear it.

"I've been hearing from the Lord a lot lately," Brad said. "I've gotten messages for several people. I think it's because I've been so close to the Lord. It's been a really sweet time." He said this to establish himself as one with a reliable connection—cable or DSL, rather than dial-up. The message had come across complete and ungarbled. "Do you want this word?" he asked. Would I want to hear what, in my heart of hearts, I knew Brad had to say? Any ex-fundamentalist worth her salt knows that when someone says they have a word for you, it's never good news.

"I know you've made lifestyle changes," he said. I could hear his throat tightening with fear as he began his speech. Thanks to my inner fundamentalist, rather than wonder *why* Brad would so grossly violate my boundaries, I wondered *how* he had. Probably, like a few billion other people, he knew how to use the Internet. I hadn't made any secret of my relationship. I had even gone so far as to speak on behalf of the Lawrence, Kansas proposed domestic partnership registry and to allow the newspaper to take a picture of me posing next to Lisa on the eve of its initiation. The caption below us expressed my plans to register as one half of an all-but-married partnership as soon as the doors of City Hall opened the next morning. Figuring out where Brad had breached my boundaries was the first of many things I would obsess to a powder in the coming days.

We both knew the rules here. Brad mustn't let me get a word in edgewise. "The Lord told me to tell you that you shouldn't deepen your commitment—I'm getting March pretty clearly here," he said, pausing for a second to adjust his antennae. "So what I get strongly that is that you shouldn't, absolutely should not go through with whatever you'd planned—what do you call them—commitment ceremonies?" To have said the words like he knew what they meant would have lent them credence. "Were you planning something in March?"

I didn't tell him he'd gotten bad information, that Lisa and I had already been deeply committed for the last twelve years and extralegally married for ten. With a last fleeting grain of sanity, I felt sorry for him. "We were planning on maybe getting a couple of kittens," I said. "Does that sound like what you might have heard?" Had I known both of these March arrivals would manifest the first signs of ringworm after we'd already worn them like boas for a week, I might have thought Brad had simply gotten the ceremony part wrong.

"No. This is coming through loud and clear. It isn't about kittens. I distinctly heard ceremony.

"Anyway, I also heard the Lord say that you need to change your life and leave your partner. I know it will be hard, but you need to do this. God says to let him fill the empty place inside you. Let him offer you the love you're seeking because his love is enough after all. I seem to remember you saying a while back that you weren't sure whether God really loved you. And I remember thinking at the time, 'Well, I'm not that sure God loves me either.' " Here, he swallowed involuntarily. "But now I know he loves me beyond what I can even ask or think. And Kelly, he wants to love you that way, too." From what I remembered, Brad had always talked like that. God was always speaking to him and telling him he was loved. Maybe Brad hadn't been exactly lying, but hoping just by repeating that he felt close to God would make it so.

"You need to know we're on very different paths now, Brad," I said. Like a fly bitten by a spider, I tried to fend him off, but my struggles were pointless. His venom knew its mark. It went there and commenced its work. He spun me around, his gossamer words tightening around my brain.

"I know, but this is our Father God we're talking about here. You know He meant men to be with women. It's the way He designed us," he said. Imaginary Jesus, the voice I had heard since childhood that challenged the strident condemnation of the church, called out a contradictory warning to me that already sounded like it was coming from the bottom of a well. "You know that," Brad said, appealing to my common sense.

I had never known that.

"Anyway," I said, a bowel movement urging me onward, "I'll talk to you later," even though I had no such intention. I could be caught, but I didn't have to like it.

"I love you Kelly. I really do," I heard him hollering, frantic and fervent, as I set the phone in its cradle.

* * *

"I hate to sound blunt here," my therapist said when I called her the next day in a panic, "but he's nuts. This is his shit, not yours. He found out you were happy being something he couldn't let himself be, and he had to make you stop. If what you're doing is all right then his whole life ceases to make sense. He's close to fifty, right? Tick. Tock. Do you see what I'm saying?" She sounded like she was calling from the bottom of a well, too.

"Uh-huh," I said.

"This is garden variety religious abuse," she said. "Sometimes you just have to tell yourself 'I have to do what's right for me'. Also, you have to tell yourself the truth. You're in a loving partnership." Lisa and I had fought that morning. "You have a good life. You're happy."

While my therapist talked, my inner fundamentalist strutted about, wagging her finger. She didn't want me to suspect for one moment that the recent collapse of my libido might not be a direct result of God's disapproval. I'd been depressed before, but never when I had the opportunity to have sex. I didn't yet understand that depression and libido don't like each other. It's one of life's natural safeguards, lest someone should conceive a child feeling like I did.

"As soon as this guy said God told him something, he took away your voice," my therapist said. "It's the oldest trick in the book. Are you feeling better now?"

"Much," I lied. I didn't want to disappoint her. I wanted her to like me. I wanted Brad to like me. I wanted everyone to like me.

I tried to make immediate use of the sense she had made, but viruses don't respond well to treatment. You can try to manage symptoms, but ultimately, they have to run their course.

The first week or so after the phone call, the only thing I could do for myself was take to my bed—not to sleep but to hide. Each morning, I put my feet on the floor determined to get something done, but exhaustion and terror would get the better of me and back under the covers I would go. There I lay contemplating the life of misery I would live again once I had the energy to make the required destruction of my current one. God Himself—the mean Big Daddy with the booming voice in which

I had been well on my way to not believing—had sought me out to tell me he wasn't pleased. For my sake, he wanted to take my life as I knew it away from me. If I obeyed this God, the love I felt for Lisa I should try my level best no longer to feel. The home we had made together, every soft and beautiful thing around me must go. No more writing, because without Lisa's emotional and financial support, I would need a full-time job. No more reading or environmentalism or bird feeding or hanging clothes on the line. I wouldn't have a clothesline. They don't let you have them at the ugly apartment I would be able to afford where God would fill me up with television, which is all I would have energy for. I didn't feel loved but imprisoned and punished. Click went the latch, away fled my appetite and my mind.

During a second phone call to my therapist, I said, "I think I might be depressed. It's only 10:00 in the morning and I want to go back to bed."

"I don't think you're depressed exactly," she said. "It's exhausting to tell yourself the truth when you been handed such a sack of religious lies. You may need to write true things down. Keep a pen and paper handy. Write them down and carry them around in your pocket with you."

I didn't know the first thing to write.

"Just go to bed if you need to—watch movies, relax."

I went back to bed, but I didn't relax. I hardly slept at all either, day or night.

When our Mac technician first connected us to the Internet because one of my freelance jobs demanded it, I had scoffed at his warning. "Be careful," he said. "This can be addictive." Addicts can be the most puritanical of people. My parents voted against gambling in Kansas City. They railed against the Catholics for relying on bingo proceeds to fill their coffers. They predicted organized crime, explosions, and blood in the streets. That was before Station Casino started giving away free T-shirts and vouchers for all-you-can-eat breakfasts and before my parents started stashing their winnings in Topsy popcorn tins all over the house.

By the time Brad phoned, I already had great practice cyber-obsessing, usually about my health. Every year, it was something else—breast cancer, colon cancer, a rare neuroendocrine disease. Every year, it was a fresh look into the abyss, and after, great rejoicing.

In seeking electronic reassurance from the Christians who did not believe I was a hapless deviant, I found all of those who did believe this. I found a national "reparative therapy" organization with a picture of its towering ex-gay complex and impressive list of psychiatrists and doctors who said they could, through the use of any number of clandestine procedures, retrieve someone's "normal sexual orientation." I found Exodus International with its gee-whiz website full of shiny faces of hip people who almost don't look gay anymore saying how happy they are now that they've found the "help" they needed. I was vulnerable all over again to the ex-gay gospel. In the few seconds I allowed myself to look at this site—it was like looking at the sun; I knew it wasn't good for me but I couldn't help it—I saw big pulsating letters that said something like, "ARE YOU READY FOR THE JOURNEY?" It's what someone says to you as you stare up at the shiny rails of a five-story roller coaster. It's a dare, really. Once you're strapped in, it feels like the most exciting thing you've ever done. Dropping over that first hill, it feels like your skin might be pulled off and that your bones might come unhinged. Eventually you realize, though, that it doesn't feel good and that you'd like to get off and do something else. The ex-gay journey is one that threatens to drag you over the same track of self-loathing so many times that you'll never feel well again. The website doesn't tell you that. I found numerous other sites with pictures of less hip people with captions about their hideously abusive childhoods and history of sexual abuse that drove them to the unfulfilling wasteland of homosexuality. All of these sites had links to each other.

By the time I'd visited enough of them, I couldn't take in help from the Christian organizations and individuals who had reconciled homosexuality and Christianity. Nor did it matter that the American Psychiatric Association, the American Psychological Association, the American Counseling Association, the National Association of Social Workers, and the World Health Organization all agreed that any mental disorder I might have had nothing to do with my homosexuality. I couldn't take any of it in. My brain was hardpan.

At the suggestion of my beleaguered therapist, who finally said enough times that people with my tendency to obsess could more easily get through a bad patch with a short-term dose of anti-anxiety medication, I got a prescription. The last domino fell. I was caught between a rock and a hard place. I could either take the moral high ground, insist on getting through this "difficult time" on my own—as my family always had—and risk complete mental collapse, or I could contribute to the already measureable level of antidepressants pissed into the waterways. Because I chose the latter, I am still here to write this. With the help of a little pink pill, I gradually returned to my senses.

Among other things, my therapist forbade me to browse the Internet since, she reminded me, my sexuality wasn't a disease for which I needed a treatment plan. Otherwise, she offered me weekly paper cups of hot tea and let me look out the window at a neighboring chip-and-tar roof and try to figure out why I'd been blindsided again. In between sessions, I came home and finished a book I'd been paid to write. I made and ate meals. I slept beside Lisa, and I quit thinking of a future without her. My daily anti-anxiety pill allowed me to tolerate the pain I'd never allowed myself to feel. Unlike most people who find themselves languishing in an ex-gay ministry year after year, I had snuck away after one academic year. I'd sequestered the trauma others continue to feel someplace inside me and pretended to have gotten away unscathed.

Ironically, Brad's awful phone call left me capable of suffering not only *because* of other people but also *with* them. I had finally processed the shame of being an ex-gay graduate, of having anyone know I'd ever hated myself enough to go through it. I felt everything through protective fathoms. I could hear the drilling, the cutting; I could feel the pull of thread through psychic skin. Healing voices took deeper root—Marcus Borg, Elizabeth Stroud, Peter Gomes, Frederick Buechner, Sister Helen Prejean, and Shelby Spong. Their encouragement gave me compassion for Brad who, in his fervor to believe his self-induced deprivation and suffering had meaning, hadn't heard God at all, only his own fear and despair. On bad days, I called him names.

As I healed, I had extremely lucid dreams. In one, I wandered the upstairs of Trinity Presbyterian, the church in which I'd grown up. I walked past the choir rehearsal room, bell tower, and Sunday school classrooms toward the sound of construction. I passed the pastor's study, beautiful woodwork exposed. The sanctuary had been completely gutted. I could see frame and joist. I could see the pulpit, open end out. Everything was exposed. I could see and be seen. People from my past—loving, strong people—strained to pull out rotten floorboards and replaced them with new ones. The whole place was being restored.

If I came to believe the lesbian raw material of me was thoroughly loved, supported, and equipped, I'd have to find something else to worry about. Could it be that, at least in part, I'd clung to a lie that everyone disapproved of me? Believing it kept me ineffective, yes, but it also kept me off the hook. No longer a hapless victim, I would be without excuse.

# 23

## FIX ME PLEASE: I'M GAY!

### *Guy Albert*

He looked as if he was straight out of *One Flew over the Cuckoo's Nest*. Not just one but both of his eyes were lazy. One never knew where he was looking and if indeed he was looking at you. His voice was a slow drawl that took great patience to listen to. And he shuffled along at a turtle's pace, barely able to motor himself, and he was seemingly constantly absorbed in some kind of trance. I was just beginning my career as a psychologist when I encountered him. I eventually learned of the unfortunate circumstances that led, at least partially, to his unusual demeanor. Early in his adulthood, he had been lobotomized, a procedure that involved inserting a sharp tool through the eye sockets to reach into specific areas of the frontal cortex—that is, the front part of the brain. The now-outdated procedure attempted to alter some mental functions to reduce certain mental health symptoms by removing small segments of gray matter.

Unfortunately, this patient's attractions to men were considered a mental illness at the time and a condition that needed treatment. It's unclear whether the lobotomy was specifically meant to address the alleged sexual deviation alone or some other condition as well, but I was left wondering, "Is this really happening?"

When I met him about four decades after his unfortunate procedure, his attraction to men was still present. In other words, the attempt to cure him of his alleged mental illnesses did not have the desired effect on his same-sex attractions. He was otherwise so debilitated that he had become a ward of the state. I was shocked by the brutality of his early treatment; it marked me for life. To this day, I can still easily recall his poor state of affairs. I was also glad to know that lobotomies no longer existed. Nonetheless, as I've grown to understand, attempts to change people's sexual orientation or gender identity or expression still exist. In fact, some reports suggest such practices (commonly called conversion therapy, reparative therapy, or Sexual Orientation Change Efforts [SOCE]) are still fairly common in the United States and around the world.

In early 2010, some twelve years after my encounter with this man, a colleague invited me to participate in initiating legislation that would prevent the practice of SOCE in California. I was immediately drawn to working on this effort, remembering my encounter with my former patient years earlier. SB 1172 became the first bill in the world to protect minors from the harms of SOCE by licensed therapists. But the steps to getting SB 1172 passed were tremendous.

When we first initiated this effort, we contacted a couple of California Assembly members to ask for their support of the bill. A couple of them expressed interest, but we didn't hear back from them for a while. A little under a year later, one Senator— Ted Lieu, D-Torrance—had taken up the bill and decided to be its sponsor. A few LGBTQ advocacy organizations became involved in its support and several other parties also joined the effort. We were thrilled with the sudden appearance of the bill in the legislature and surprised at the interest from several individuals and organizations. We decided to reintroduce ourselves in the process by strategizing different ways to get the backing of other organizations and the general public.

A friend recommended that we start an online petition on the popular petition site Change.org to support the effort. I also contacted an international advocacy organization, AllOut, which has been a champion in gathering grassroots support for issues around the world. AllOut gladly supported our efforts and they introduced their own petition. Equality California, an LGBTQ rights organization, also started a postcard mail-in campaign requesting that the legislature support the measure. By the end of this petition drive, we had collectively gathered more than 55,000 signatures in support of SB 1172.

Meanwhile, the largely Democratic California Assembly and Senate passed the bill with a majority vote in both houses. It was then up to then Governor Jerry Brown to sign the bill into law. The stakes were high: many people had put in hours, if not weeks, of work toward ensuring the bill was worthy of passing and that it would protect both the public and mental health providers from harm. Legislative analysts, professional associations, licensing boards, advocacy organizations, and many individuals had invested time and energy in creating the first such bill in the world. It was a groundbreaking effort and one that my colleagues and I celebrated with relief and exhilaration. The bill was signed into law on September 30, 2011. The bill's language indicated that minors in California were protected from "sexual orientation change efforts" by mental health providers. The bill did not address the protection of adults from these practices nor did it address efforts performed by lay people or religious or secular organizations.

## DOES THIS STILL EXIST?

One of the striking takeaways of the petition drive was the most popular comment from signatories. People wrote various versions of something to the tune of, "I can't believe this still exists!" One person's comment stated in jest, "I'm moving to Canada!" In fact, as I've spoken about this and subsequent efforts in which I've participated, people continually mention the same. They react with shock and dismay that attempts to change sexual orientation and gender identity/expression are still in existence *and* that people still seek these methods to cure themselves of such innate aspects of their being. Nonetheless, as I'm writing this, the Republican Party adopted its most anti-LGBTQ platform in history, including support for conversion therapy, and there are still clinics and programs in support of these efforts throughout the United States and around the world.

SB 1172 was a landmark victory with much more than practical significance. Though it was limited in scope—the law targeted conversion therapy performed by licensed psychotherapists on minors—the new bill propelled a series of similar efforts around the country. Several similar bills were and continue to be proposed, and several states and municipalities have passed legislation denouncing the practice. Lawsuits targeting non–mental-health organizations that promote these practices have either been launched or have succeeded in their claims of consumer fraud. Congressman Ted Lieu, who championed SB 1172 while he was a California state senator, introduced the Therapeutic Fraud Prevention Act (HR 2450) in May 2015, a federal bill that would empower the Federal Trade Commission to prevent individuals and businesses from promoting "sexual orientation and gender identity conversion therapy" on the basis of consumer protections. And in April 2015, in response to a White House petition asking for more legal oversight over these so-called therapeutic practices, President Obama and the Surgeon General published statements to warn against the harms of conversion therapy on minors and encouraged states to adopt similar laws to the California bill.

Little did we know that our efforts to target these practices would have such widespread repercussions. We weren't even sure if a ban of conversion therapy would be possible in California, much less were we thinking that other states might follow suit and that the practices would become much more visible. It was a pleasure and a relief to find that this small legislative effort continues to have such an effect on promoting visibility and awareness around the bogus practices. Still, when I talk about these advocacy efforts to people, the greatest response continues to be, "I can't believe this still exists."

## WHAT IS CONVERSION THERAPY?

This is the $64,000 dollar question that has presented us with the greatest and ongoing challenge in legislating these practices. No one really knows what conversion therapy is. Though proponents of conversion therapy have published manuals outlining their practices, efficacy of conversion therapy is inconclusive at best, and efforts to change one's sexual orientation or gender identity/expression have been known to be harmful in many instances and fatal in some situations. Leelah Alcorn's suicide in December 2014 was likely the most prominent of these fatal endings. Leelah realized in her early teens that she didn't identify with the male gender she had been assigned at birth. Unfortunately, Leelah's parents were not understanding of her gender identity and were unsuspecting victims of the promise of conversion therapy, thinking it would help their child heal her so-called mental illness. Leelah took her life in a moment of despair; just before her suicide, she posted a note on her Tumblr blog stating her hope that her death would become a wakeup call to end these practices. The White House petition I mentioned earlier was started in honor of Leelah and the many others before her who had suffered through similar failed attempts. The petition gathered more than 120,000 signatures, requiring the president to present a formal response to the issue.

In my own efforts to debunk these practices, I realized it might be good to understand what they are. I surmised that I needed to go back in history to uproot the origins of sexual orientation change efforts—at the very least. I learned that with the advent of psychology as a science came the identification of "homosexuality" as a phenomenon, despite the existence of same-sex relations throughout human history. When the term "homosexuality" was invented in the mid-nineteenth century, it was mainly for the purpose of designating it as a deviant expression of human sexuality, a perversion, and a psychiatric disorder. Modern psychotherapy's nascence in psychoanalysis led the way toward addressing people's neuroses and psychological complexes, and homosexuality was the target of some analysts' practices.

Some psychological theorists, in an attempt to explain homosexuality's deviant nature, promoted the notions that same-sex attractions might be caused by the ineffective resolution of a childhood complex or by the skewed relational patterns of parents, such as an overbearing mother and a weak or distant father causing a man to be gay. The goal of analysis was to resolve these issues and return to a "normal" heterosexual life. Because many have suffered from living a closeted life and were subjected to a barrage of heteronormative messages, clients—and psychoanalysts— passionately and intensively sought the ultimate resolution of this inner conflict.

Although no longer used and toward the extreme end of the SOCE spectrum, certain controversial psychological interventions of the mid-twentieth century were aimed at disabling people from the negative symptoms of their mental disorders, including homosexuality. With the latter, the object of treatment was to prevent them from committing immoral acts. Two such interventions were electroconvulsive therapy (ECT) and the lobotomy. ECT was usually administered without anesthesia and with great intensity and frequency, hence the reference to "electroshock therapy" as it was more commonly known. The lobotomy consisted of cutting or scraping the brain tissue—mostly the prefrontal cortex. People subjected to these procedures suffered severe negative effects, including significant personality changes and poor psychological functioning, such as the patient I mentioned earlier. On the extreme end of the spectrum were some medical interventions aimed at curing people of their alleged sexual illnesses. Viennese physiologist Eugen Steinbach transplanted a testicle of a heterosexual man into a gay man, believing it would rebalance the latter's hormones and cure his homosexuality. Similar attempts were made under the belief that homosexuality was hormonally based by subjecting lesbians to hysterectomies or estrogen injections.

SOCE have also included a variety of behavioral interventions. Behaviorism, a branch of psychology that grew in parallel with psychoanalysis, flourished out of the idea that it could change many unwanted behaviors. And since LGB clients were seen as having undesirable—and perhaps undesired—sexual behaviors, behavior modification techniques were seen as a solution. In other words, if one can treat the homosexual behavior, one can treat the homosexual.

Aversive treatments were a common form of behavior modification. Aversive SOCE might have consisted in simultaneously administering homoerotic stimuli and electric shocks to, say, the hands or the genitals of the patient. Another similar method involved the patient ingesting a nausea-inducing substance before viewing the erotic stimulus. The patient was subsequently expected to associate homosexual attractions with the pain-inducing or uncomfortable stimulus. Another form of aversion entailed one's self-administration of a negative stimulus, such as pinching oneself with a rubber band each time one has a homoerotic fantasy. Masturbatory reconditioning was a sensitization technique used to recondition the person to associate pleasurable experiences with the opposite gender. Similarly, visualizations and social skills training were also used as ways to address the behavioral aspects of conversion from a sensitization standpoint. Both sensitization and aversion are purely behavioral techniques used by mental health providers to address a variety of basic behavioral issues.

Many of the preceding methods have been used up until very recently, and some are still currently being used in ongoing attempts to treat homosexuality from a behavioral standpoint. Efforts to treat gender nonconformity have not been as commonly addressed by the media. This could be in part due to the much more recent recognition and prevalence of people who identify with a gender other than the one they were assigned at birth. Transgender identity certainly has been prevalent throughout history. Many indigenous people were accepting of gender identity/expression that differed from biological sex; some individuals were actually revered for their special expression of something unique and necessary within the fabric of society. Psychoanalytic theory also grew interested in transgender identity as a phenomenon and attempted to treat it as well. Some mental health providers have attempted to cure gender dysphoria as a problem related to homosexuality. The term "sexual orientation change efforts" is obviously inaccurate in describing these practices, which might be more accurately described as "gender identity change efforts." In the West, gender minorities are more vulnerable and less protected than sexual minorities, making the issue of addressing and discerning the social and psychological conflicts even more challenging. Nonetheless, the term "sexual orientation change efforts" was coined as a way to distance the practices of "conversion therapy" from what is really therapeutic, which should be respectful of one's fundamental psychological nature and its healthy expressions.

## THE SKELETON OF CONVERSION THERAPY

The same intensity and passion behind some of these change efforts feeds the flames of fear and hatred of same-sex desires and gender identity/expression, persistently turning the blame on the LGBTQ person's subjective dilemma. It consistently points to an inner struggle while turning away from the moral, political, cultural, social, ideological, religious, or other external pressures. These pressures sustain the homophobic and transphobic stronghold on current societies that have broken people's lives and split families apart. For at least the past century, the LGBTQ person has been subjected to many social pressures that can wear down our self-esteem. The internalization of these external pressures brings one to the point of self-loathing. The real inner struggle is the internalization of homophobic or transphobic messages promoted by society, including the promotion of conversion as an effective means of changing unwanted same-sex attractions or gender identity/expression.

Internalized homophobia and transphobia can be linked to the self-destructive behaviors noted in some LGBTQ communities. Interestingly, these behaviors also become fodder for fundamentalist thinking. That is, in order to stop these destructive behaviors, one must cure homosexuality or gender dysphoria. A 2014 headline in the UK edition of the *International Business Times* read, "I Slept with over 200 Men, Now I'm a Happily Married Heterosexual Dad." The headline implies that homosexuality correlates with instability and that happiness comes from living a stable married heterosexual life.

I personally know about these inner struggles because I suffered from internalized homophobia for years. As a late teen and early adult, I spent nights praying to be cured of the illness that was plaguing my psyche. Though I was not fanatically religious and my parents were not overtly homophobic, I had picked up the message that there was something fundamentally wrong with my same-sex attractions. At this point, it was more out of fear of being different and fear of disappointing others—my parents, my siblings, my friends, and the different groups or communities to which I belonged—that I tried desperately to "pray away the gay" in me. For several years, I secretly attempted to change my sexual orientation. I was deeply alone and lonely in this effort. I could not and would not tell anyone about it, knowing that even asking for help meant I would disclose my secret and then jinx my attempts to cure myself.

It was especially through meeting others who had gone through the process of accepting themselves that I learned to accept this part of me as my fate and live in the *yes* of my sexual orientation. Luckily, there has been increasing social tolerance and acceptance of the varieties of sexual orientations and gender identities and expressions. Accordingly, I have experienced personal relief from this increasing openness to sexual and gender diversity, and I have witnessed a collective sigh of relief among peers and patients alike. Social acceptance can only have benefits in reducing the effects of internalized homophobia and transphobia on our psyches. This collective transformation has allowed movements such as marriage equality and legislative protections to become a reality across the United States and abroad.

Subsequently, the ongoing debate over the changeability of and the push to change sexuality and gender has come to the surface. After the passage of SB 1172 and the parallel raising of awareness that has occurred, Exodus International, the largest SOCE in the world, closed its doors and its leader apologized to the gay and lesbian community for years of change efforts. The closing of Exodus engendered another collective sigh of relief: the biggest change machine had run out of steam. Yet the battle was not over.

In my efforts to expose the dangers of conversion therapy, I learned that most change efforts in the Western world of late have been focused on effecting behavioral changes, either through behavioral modifications, psychological conditioning, or prayer, or some combination of the above. The behavioral component addresses only how one expresses sexuality or gender. Sexual orientation and gender identity/expression are much more complex traits that include sexual preference and drive, gender identity, gender expression, romantic attraction, affective leanings, and predilection. When people undergo modern conversion methods, they are intrinsically subjecting themselves to a potential lifetime of inner conflict between the behaviors they are trying to embody and their natural inclinations.

I have also learned that the range of existing SOCE renders efficacy studies nearly impossible. A popular provider of SOCE and one of the plaintiffs in the failed lawsuit against SB 1172 appeared in a CNN interview promoting the efficacy of his method as "authentic reparative therapy." What may have seemed like a brilliant attempt at distinguishing his method from others ironically became his downfall. His method became diluted in a field where many other SOCE providers also claim to have authentic methods.

# THE FUTURE OF CONVERSION METHODS—LET'S HOPE NOT!

Though there have been considerable steps forward in protecting the public from the dangers and harms of these practices, there is always more to do. One of the greatest remaining challenges, and one that might be around for decades, resides in our culture's ongoing debate over individual freedom versus governmental control. People are prone to ask, "Why should we keep someone from seeking to change their sexual orientation or gender identity if they want to?" Governmental and professional organizations usually intervene when there is considerable evidence that a practice or procedure is dangerous and the public is misinformed about these dangers. The widespread use of conversion therapy over decades—and the exploration of other barbaric conversion methods over several centuries—is one such area that has needed our collective attention. This is why I have devoted considerable effort to uncover these practices and denounce people's attempts to coercively change sexual orientation or gender identity/expression.

Our society's diminishing but still prevalent homophobic and transphobic attitudes have had significant influence in allowing these practices to exist and proliferate for many years. LGBTQ activism has also focused on other matters of importance like ending discrimination in marriage, employment, and housing. Nonetheless, the ongoing practice of conversion therapy on *anyone*—not just minors—is of considerable importance in the activism spectrum. As long as people believe same-sex attractions and gender nonconformity are solely behaviorally based and treatable, there will be lack of acceptance of the varieties of LGBTQ identities and expressions.

Since the dawning of modern psychology nearly a century and a half ago, conversion therapy interventions have varied widely. Electroshock treatments, lobotomies, surgical methods, aversive therapies all failed in their intended goal. Time and again, these techniques proved that they might end up psychologically harming patients without "treating" their alleged deviance. Current attempts to treat same-sex attractions and gender nonconformity are more commonly associated with behavioral techniques, at least in the West. Psychological scientists have tried to come up with theoretical constructs that would explain the origins of homosexuality and gender dysphoria in behavioral terms. Though the techniques are less barbaric than, say, surgical methods, the message behind their ongoing use is still the same: same-sex attractions and gender nonconformity are undesirable and they must be treated. Because of this, attempts to change sexual orientation and gender nonconformity keep happening in spite of the damages they cause to the patients who undergo these treatments. These methods at most may lead individuals to avoid certain behaviors, habits, and relationships, but they have never been shown to alter basic sexual attractions or gender identity. Thus, they reinforce a sense of self as damaged or inadequate and can increase psychological distress.

Reliable studies have shown that many people who are subjected to these various methods suffer from increased depression, substance abuse, and suicidal ideation. Because there is a lack of consensus regarding what conversion therapy really is, few studies have been conducted on the actual methods used because of the variations in technique and application. Further complicating the matter, subjecting research participants to methods that could potentially cause harm presents an ethical road block. The remaining conclusion is that conversion therapy is potentially harmful and, as such, could be dangerous.

My wish is that people who are drawn to change their or their loved ones' sexual orientation or gender identity/expression through therapeutic means reconsider their decision. I invite them to seek a therapist who can hold a broad view on the matter, understanding the social, cultural, psychological, and religious dimensions of addressing these personal identity issues. And may all—therapists, patients, and the general public—be rid of the notion that sexual orientation and gender identity can be changed through therapeutic means.

This may be a long time coming, especially if I expand my horizons to include people from all countries. I have been deeply saddened by people's attempts to change something that is so basically fundamental to one's being as sexual attraction and gender. I have been moved to address this suffering through local, state, and national efforts.

My ultimate wish is to never have to encounter another person who suffers from the damages of conversion efforts of any kind.

# 24

## CROWDSOURCING MY ANTIPSYCHOTIC

*Stephanie Schroeder*

I'm in recovery from bipolar disorder. I've tried to live medication free. And failed. It's not a failure of which I'm ashamed. What I am ashamed of is this country's broken healthcare system, and how difficult that system has made it for me to obtain life-saving medication.

Writers generally don't make much money, and I've been really hard-pressed to pay for my psychiatric meds over the past several years while still covering New York City rent and other living expenses. These days, I'm just squeaking by with pieced- together jobs.

The last full-time job I had was at a small midtown Manhattan public relations firm. The job was horrendous and the benefits were terrible—among other problems, I had no health insurance. My colleagues, all heterosexual women, had coverage through their husbands or parents.

I made an okay middle-class salary, but after taxes and expenses it barely covered my quarterly visits to my private psychiatrist and weekly visits with my private therapist in addition to the cost of my four psychiatric medications. Not having health insurance was an enormous drawback of my job.

I take four psychotropic medications to remain sane and stable after three attempted suicides and one stay in the loony bin. I've been on the same four medications—an antidepressant, a mood stabilizer, an anti-anxiety, and an antipsychotic—for well over a decade, and this cocktail works extremely well for me. No flattening of my affect or interference with my creativity. No sleep problems or long-term memory loss. My short-term memory is pretty terrible, and I do not recall if that was always the case or if it's just part of getting older. My concentration is a little wonky, but I now live in a world filled with electronic devices, online sound bites, and messages limited to 140 characters. Most people, myself among them, have the attention span of a fruitfly.

In late 2013, I suddenly came to the end of my supply of the atypical antipsychotic I take every night. This particular medication has a bad reputation in some consumer circles, and I know there are people who actively agitate against even the existence and prescribing of it, but it has saved my life! The antipsychotic I take works by modifying sensitivity to two of the brain's chief chemical messengers, serotonin and dopamine.

\* \* \*

Earlier, in the summer of 2011, I had had to stop taking this medication for several months because I couldn't afford the cost of $624.31 for thirty 10 mg pills. I went through a lot of bad times and felt myself slipping back into a place in which I never wanted to be again, in physical pain and mentally cloudy, feeling out of control, having psychotic symptoms, and nearing a rapid-cycling bipolar hell I had left a decade prior.

My therapist always said she wondered what I was like off meds. I had been doing so well for so long she thought maybe I didn't even need them. Buzz, wrong answer! She saw what I was like without the antipsychotic and said she never wanted to see me like that again.

I was extremely irritable and always annoyed, quick to anger, and, most of all, I could not stop talking and interrupting people, even people about whom I care and wanted to hear out. I was aware of my behavior, and I enlisted both my girlfriend and my therapist to make sure my fleeting suicidal thoughts went nowhere. I also enlisted a young but very sophisticated colleague to read all of my email messages before I sent them out. I was annoyed at all my clients, tired of working on their accounts, and without the antipsychotic medication, I was losing my patience.

I asked my doc at the clinic where I am treated free for asthma to prescribe the antipsychotic for me so I could get it for free in that clinic's prescription program. He readily agreed, saying that his father was a psychiatrist and that he had heard some very distressing tales of what people went through without their meds, including taking their own lives.

My doctor left the clinic after about a year and I had no outlet through which to obtain my antipsychotic medication. I certainly didn't have $624.31 to purchase it at the pharmacy.

\* \* \*

Now, here I was again in a dire situation: I made "too much" money to get this antipsychotic from the Big Pharma manufacturer's patient assistance program, but I didn't make enough to afford $600+ a month for one bottle of thirty pills. I'd already talked to some low-level people over at this drug manufacturer; they were not helpful and never had been. They acted like I was some sort of nut for even asking about help beyond or outside the scope of the formal patient assistance program. I wrote to the "new" CEO, but it didn't help except to make me feel like I at least tried.

Being both a writer and publicist, I decided to write about and publicize my plight to highlight the problem of the lack of decent mental healthcare in these United States, circa 2013. So I wrote a blog post about my situation and also posted it on Facebook, asking folks if I could have their unused antipsychotic medication.

Within minutes several people messaged me with offers of their leftover medication and suggestions about inexpensive ways and places to purchase the antipsychotic I needed to remain stable. They had really innovative suggestions about finding leftover meds from family and friends of recently deceased people, paying low co-pays for others to refill their dormant scripts and give them to me, obtaining samples from docs with whom my Facebook family worked or otherwise knew, and all sorts of other unique schemes.

This was the first time I knew of an antipsychotic being crowdsourced on social media!

I made appointments with various people all over the city. We met for coffee or a sandwich and I listened to their stories, sometimes for several hours. My reward at the end of all of these encounters was a bottle, or several bottles, of pills. One correspondent, who would only speak on the phone and didn't want anything in writing, met me and handed over a paper bag with all kinds of psychiatric meds, most of which I didn't need. He asked me not to mention his name to anyone and also said that I shouldn't be putting calls for meds on Facebook. Soliciting drugs is illegal, didn't I know that? Don't put that shit on Facebook, it's way too dangerous, and go see a doctor to get a prescription! He didn't comprehend that it wasn't an issue with a doctor or script, but with the price of meds.

The incredible variety of medications I received was amazing, and the generosity of people emptying their medicine cabinets for me was moving, especially from those generally in the closet about their own mental illness who were willing to meet me in public anyhow.

After my community of queers, artists, activists, and other kindred spirits provided me with their leftovers, I counted all the individual tablets I had on hand—antipsychotic pills from those who were no longer taking them and were kind enough to pass on their remainders, from both acquaintances and strangers who answered my Facebook call, and from random packets of samples hidden in various heretofore unknown corners of my apartment.

The count done, I had exactly enough of the antipsychotic medication to last until my fiftieth birthday in September 2013, which was forty-five days away. That was not a long time. I didn't have insurance or any additional expendable income. I was not qualified for any fiscal support or discount programs other than my chain pharmacy prescription discount card for the uninsured because my barely middle-class income excluded me from all existing financial assistance.

I have fought many battles with the Big Pharma manufacturer of my atypical anti-psychotic, which has sometimes given me a free ninety-day supply and sometimes not.

Big Pharma doesn't really care whether I live or die. I'm just one individual broke lesbian trying to thrive in the capitalist psychopharmacological wilderness. It's all about profits for them and giving away free drugs doesn't make money.

The script for my antipsychotic that my private psychiatrist wrote me the last time I saw him would have cost $2,226.97 (that was *with* my pharmacy Rx discount). It covered a six-month supply of the drug.

My horrible experience being off my antipsychotic a year earlier was one I didn't care to repeat. I had felt totally crazy—and helpless that I couldn't do anything about it.

I publicized my current situation on social media and wrote a bunch of letters to federal, state, and local officials about not being able to afford my antipsychotic on a long-term basis and the ramifications of that reality for me. Following is the approximate text of the letter I sent (personalized to each recipient):

*I was diagnosed with Bipolar Disorder when I was 37 years old. I had two suicide attempts behind me and one in front of me. When I was 45, I finally found the perfect balance of psychotherapy and a psychiatric medication cocktail mix that works to keep me stable, energetic, creative – and alive!*

*I found an anti-psychotic that works extremely well for me. My current prescription is for thirty 10 mg tablets that cost $624.31 per month, which is completely unaffordable.*

*I work full-time, but I don't have health insurance and I cannot afford my antipsychotic medication. I make a middle-class income, but barely enough for two people to live on, and "too much" to qualify for any assistance programs, subsidies, or other support. I've tried EVERY avenue to get my medication and I've reached a dead end.*

*If I go off of this drug, I will most likely kill myself.*

*I'm asking for help because that is what, through intensive psychotherapy, I have learned to do—reach out and ask for what I need when I need it.*

I received various unhelpful and insulting replies such as this one:

*Your correspondence to the Honorable [City Leader] has been referred to the City Medical Department for a response. We here at the CMD are deeply moved by your story and sympathize with your situation. That is why it gives me a great deal of satisfaction to inform you of our program, the State Medicaid Program.*

The reply, a canned response, was completely inane since I stated in every letter that I made a middle-class income and couldn't qualify for any government assistance, pharma-funded programs, or any sort of prescription subsidies of any sort. WTF? I was not even nearly qualified for Medicaid. If I had been, believe me, I would have already been participating.

These are elected/appointed officials who are supposed to represent me. They don't, of course, I know that, and their form letters sent in response to my plea for assistance was the rebuke I expected, the "proof" I didn't actually need to understand that the President, the Governor, and the Mayor didn't actually care about the mental health of folks in the United States.

Then, I received another very odd, and unexpected, response. I was at my office job and got a phone call from a suicide hotline. The woman on the other end of the phone said she was checking in on me because I had sent a letter to a big-wig at a federal health office that I was going to kill myself.

Bullshit! My letter clearly stated that it was my past history that, when I could not obtain my antipsychotic, I made a suicide attempt. I never threatened suicide; my letter was to find a way to secure my medication, not a suicidal stunt!

So my letter to the person in the US federal government responsible for the health of every single person in this country about not being able to afford my antipsychotic was apparently given to a suicide hotline, and "Linda" from that organization called me while I was in the office. I had only picked up my phone because numbers with 212 area codes are usually welcome calls—leads on better jobs and freelance writing gigs and such.

Linda said the federal health department passed on my letter, and she was calling to make sure I was safe. I told her, well, I didn't mail a damn suicide note but an appeal in which I mentioned that I want to live, but, not having my anti-psychotic may mean I won't. Linda was fairly understanding and had the same list of resources that still weren't helpful—unless I reduced my income by more than half.

I didn't need to be referred to a suicide hotline. I needed someone from the federal health department to call up the CEO of the Big Pharma manufacturer and get a guarantee from him of a lifetime supply of this atypical antipsychotic for me (and everyone else who needs it) and have it motherfucking hand-delivered to my door. An entire lifetime worth of pills!

Instead she (or, more likely, one of her minions) passed off my letter and passed the buck. I mean, I didn't really expect anything at all.

A few days after talking to Linda, I got another call, this one from a blocked number. Some guy who said he was from the Big Pharma patient assistance program left me a message. I had to call him back as I was on the way to a conference for work. When I returned his call, I reached his voicemail at an outsourced company that describes itself as "reimbursement consulting and services practice for pharmaceutical and biotech companies."

The outsourced dude called me back the next day, and we had a conversation in which I mostly listened and remained silent while this grown man in a senior position at this consulting company very nervously and uncomfortably discussed with me the "different possibilities" to try to help me obtain the antipsychotic at no cost. We went back and forth. He was clearly assigned to shut me up and get me off Big Pharma's back. But that didn't happen.

In the end, Outsourced Man signed off on my request for a free ninety-day supply of the antipsychotic. This is an example of what happens when one makes a bit of noise.

I had an appointment with my psychiatrist that same week. He said I should be a mental healthcare consultant because I know every angle, every resource, every avenue, every bargain, every discount, and every scam that exists to get quality healthcare and medication. But who the hell with any dough is going to hire *me* to tell other folks how to beat the system?

\* \* \*

I quit my full-time, no-benefit job in order to qualify for a public healthcare scheme that provides low-income New York City artists with deeply discounted care. In the past five years, I have earned 21.5384615385% (or less) of what I made at my former job and I am now a very low-income New Yorker struggling to survive financially.

In the artist-centered program at a public Brooklyn hospital, participants can barter volunteer work as well as make artistic contributions in exchange for our healthcare services.

This is not insurance, and I was assessed a fine by the IRS for not having purchased insurance in 2015. However, a $95 fine is far less than even a quarter of the cost of a single month's insurance premium.

A plan to cover my needs under the Affordable Care Act would cost me $500+ a month. Added to that monthly premium would be an annual deductible, plus co-pays for doctor visits and a medication that is not in most insurance drug formularies. This expenditure is impossible for me. Plus, my private psychiatrist, whom I saw for more than twelve years, doesn't accept any insurance. The heralded "choice" in healthcare providers under the Affordable Care Act is totally bogus for me (as for so many others) because I wanted to see my own trusted providers ten to fifteen years standing. But, since I had to change doctors anyway, I made certain they are very affordable.

Here's my cost breakdown: I see a psychiatrist in an outpatient psychiatric clinic at the Brooklyn hospital every other month, which costs $15. My four prescriptions are $2 each. For an additional $15, I also visit my psychologist every three months to round out my mental health program.

So, my bimonthly investment in my mental health is around $38. I am stable and have made no attempts to hurt myself in the past fifteen years; I work on a freelance basis and also make enormous progress on my personal artistic projects and activist endeavors.

A wise investment indeed! And one I can afford.

Passing prescription drugs may be illegal, even when no money is exchanged, but being forced into that questionable activity to keep myself alive and well is truly immoral.

The Affordable Care Act is a program making insurance companies ever richer by fleecing consumers. It's clear to me that the story that the ACA enhances, rather than detracts from, people's healthcare choices is fiction for a lot of folks. Health insurance premiums are rising while the number and types of services covered are being reduced or eliminated. Necessary treatments have become much costlier for consumers.

Skyrocketing healthcare coverage driven by corporate interests, and not my pursuit of affordable mental health preservation, is what should be penalized.

When I went to renew my artist healthcare membership in 2016, I was shunted onto Medicaid because I made even less than the previous year. This was actually a blessing—free healthcare and free or, occasionally, fifty-cent meds!

In 2016, I didn't qualify for Medicaid, but instead for an "Essential" healthcare plan, with a monthly $20 premium, $25 doctor visit co-pays, and $6–30 medications. That's more than the artists' healthcare program and certainly more than Medicaid, but it's affordable. However, not all doctors I need to see take my insurance. I've been on the hunt for a psychopharmacologist to consult with me about my medication cocktail, which I have been on for more than twelve years. The psychiatrist I see at the public clinic is just a functionary who spends less than five minutes with me, and his only job is to refill my scripts. And, yes, I know it will only get worse under Trump, but that doesn't obviate the position I am in currently: not being able to consult with a pharmacology expert, that is.

I keep needing an update for the end of this chapter, but that update keeps changing. Life ebbs and flows, but healthcare shouldn't. Healthcare is a right, and this tenuous fix that I and others have on the ability to access and continue to receive life-saving treatments, including medications, shouldn't depend on the whims of politicians or pharmaceutical manufacturers. Anyone with a life-threatening illness knows that is enough to deal with; we shouldn't have to stand on the quicksand of constantly changing healthcare policy in this country. It's far past time for healthcare options that are not attached to an employer or romantic partner.

PART IV

# Pushing Boundaries

# 25

## ON LISTENING TO CLIENTS, OR WHY DO PROVIDERS SOMETIMES HAVE A HARD TIME HEARING WHAT RECIPIENTS OF CARE HAVE TO SAY?

*Christian Huygen*

The literature abounds with statistics about the kinds of discrimination and poor treatment that LGBTQ people often receive. But unless we providers are in the habit of actively looking for people's strengths, virtues, and positive qualities, we may tend to view LGBTQ recipients of care as nothing other than a pile of symptoms and pathologies. We may view them solely as disempowered embodiments of suffering—objects of pity about whom it pains us to think.

This is damaging to clients, and it robs both client and provider of inspiration and hope.

I am a clinical psychologist and a gay man, and, for the past fifteen years, I have served as executive director of Rainbow Heights Club, an agency that offers LGBTQ-affirming peer support and psychosocial rehabilitation services to people who are living with serious mental illness and related challenges. We are located in New York City and have served more than 700 clients over the years. A majority of the people we serve are people of color, and about a third of them are transgender or gender-nonconforming. Each year, 90–95% of our clients tell us they were able to stay out of the hospital and in the community because of the support they receive at Rainbow Heights Club.

I often say to members at Rainbow Heights Club, "If you are LGBTQ and living with a mental illness in our society and you are not dead, then there are a lot of things I already know about you." I look around the room with a little sparkle in my eyes. People usually sit forward a little because an opening like that tends to get people's attention.

"I know," I continue, "that you have a lot of courage. I know that you have resilience because I know you've been knocked down a lot, and I can see that you didn't just lie there, you got up again. I know that you are playful because a lot of times a sense of humor is the only thing that helps us survive. I know that you're creative and persistent. If one way didn't work, you came up with another, and you tried that too."

Then I ask people to add to this list. I ask them to come up with positive qualities that they've seen in themselves or in each other. They usually come up with quite a number of them: strength, for example, and persistence, and creativity. The ability to support each other.

Every obstacle that a person survives and triumphs over mirrors a strength or virtue that the survivor found or developed within themselves. LGBTQ people who are living with mental illness are some of the most disenfranchised, poorly treated, and overlooked people that I know of. They are also, in my experience, some of the most resilient, creative, and brave.

We put this strengths-based perspective into practice every day. Rainbow Heights Club is structured as a collaboration between so-called consumers and so-called providers. Whenever we have to make a decision—to add or delete a group from the schedule, to revise our community guidelines, or to hire a new staff person—we consider as much input as we can from the club members themselves. I've worked with consumers and other stakeholders for many years to support and facilitate their participation in a number of advocacy venues, such as the LGBT Citywide Advisory Committee of the New York City Department of Health and Mental Hygiene and the New York State Office of Mental Health's Statewide Multicultural Advisory Committee. Recipients of care are the experts on what helps and what doesn't, and I am deeply committed to helping ensure their voices are heard and their ideas are utilized in a skillful and effective way.

In my experience, this collaborative approach, in which consumers have input into how decisions are made, is rare in the field of public mental health. Usually, the care providers make the decisions and then impose them on the clients. Conversely, there are consumer-run organizations in which the consumers make all the decisions. I have not seen a significant number of collaborative organizations that place themselves between these two approaches.

Also, I have never seen an anthology that brings together the perspectives of consumers as well as providers, especially in a field as specific as LGBTQ mental health. There are a lot of books in which providers speak in provider language to other providers. In my view, people who are living with mental illness are the experts on what they need and what would help them and only by engaging in active, open, mutual conversation and collaboration can we do the vital and demanding work which lies before us. My objective—after fifteen years of supporting LGBTQ recipients of care; hearing about their positive and negative interactions with other care providers; and providing trainings to and listening to the challenges, concerns, and questions of several thousand mainstream care providers—is to offer some simple recommendations that may help care providers listen better and more openly. It can assist them in pathologizing LGBTQ clients to a lesser degree and ensuring better treatment outcomes.

If you are a provider reading this book, you already have years of experience and wisdom and invaluable skills to share. You have already provided enormous benefit to many clients. And you got into this field in the first place because you are compassionate, and you want to help. But everybody needs tools and information so that they can apply their skills as broadly as possible. That's what I hope to share with you.

Here are some specific ways in which I think providers sometimes struggle to really hear and accept what LGBTQ clients have to say.

1. Some providers continue to believe, pursuant to more than a hundred years of the history of our profession, that LGBTQ development is not normative or healthy.
2. Some providers don't acknowledge the limits of their expertise or competence.
3. Some providers don't sincerely want to support their LGBTQ clients' goals.
4. Some providers overlook or fail to recognize the many strengths and positive qualities that their LGBTQ clients embody and possess.
5. Some providers assume that LGBTQ people have little or nothing in common with them, and thus fail to recognize the enormous amount of common ground and experience that they share with LGBTQ clients.

If you glimpse some of your past behavior in this list, please *don't feel bad*—these thoughts, feelings, and actions are a part of the history of our field as a whole. We have the potential to examine our assumptions and to do better in the future.

Research shows that, while LGBTQ people seek mental healthcare more often than our non-LGBTQ counterparts, we are more likely to leave care prematurely because, all too often, we do not find the support and affirmation that we were hoping to find (Cochran, Sullivan, & Mays, 2003). My goal in writing this chapter is to help providers offer more affirming care so that their clients will continue participating in care and be able to receive the care and support that they so badly need.

Since the advent of psychoanalysis, the field of mainstream mental healthcare has pathologized LGBTQ identities and behaviors, defined them as forms of illness, and offered "cures" for them, including painful electric shocks, injections of hormones, castration, and lobotomy. Although same-sex sexual attraction was removed from the DSM in 1973, many people—both mental health professionals and lay persons—continued to believe that LGBTQ people are traumatized, damaged, or underdeveloped versions of non-LGBTQ people.

As a result, it is unsurprising that, for some providers, it seems to make sense to pathologize every impulse or behavior that a client may have to explore or enact an LGBTQ identity. Too often, we mistake conformity and a conventional presentation of self and understanding of the world for mental health. A nonconforming gender presentation, sexual desires or behaviors that seem unfamiliar to a given provider, or culturally specific forms of support and defense against both physical and emotional threats may seem alien and hard to understand—and therefore crazy, something to be pathologized and eradicated.

Some providers subtly or overtly encourage their clients to reduce these culturally specific behaviors instead of trying to understand the important functions that they serve. I hope that the many contributions in this volume will vividly illuminate these aspects of people's experiences and help both providers and consumers understand their importance and value.

Everyone I have worked with has responded to treatment and been able to build stable, enduring recovery—and help others to do so—once their sexual orientation and gender identity are understood as indispensable aspects of their "well" selves. These must be acknowledged as a foundation of their health and well-being.

Not doing so has undermined people's recovery, caused their mental and emotional well-being to deteriorate, and put them at risk of relapse, hospitalization, or self-harm.

Not every expression of LGBTQ people's gender or sexuality (or that of non-LGBTQ people's, for that matter) is necessarily healthy or adaptive. But my years of experience have taught me that providers will get much further in helping their clients work through these complex issues if they take it as axiomatic that sexual orientation and gender identity are inalienable. If supported and explored in a positive, accepting way, they can be a cornerstone of enduring health and recovery—or, if pathologized and denigrated, they can put the client at ongoing risk of relapse and decompensation.

## ABLE—AND WILLING

Long checklists and questionnaires have been developed to try to define and assess LGBTQ cultural competency. I'm going to boil this issue down to several simple questions that you can answer for yourself.

Are you *able* to extend your entire skill set—what you know about healthy coping, relationships, and understandings of our limitations as human beings in a complicated world—to the client in front of you?

Are you *willing?* Do you *want* to help them reach their stated goals? Are you the right person to support them in doing that?

These are entirely separate questions. And only you can answer them. Your LGBTQ clients need your best and fullest help, so if there is some way in which you could learn more—from a book, or seminar, or Google, or more study or training—I encourage you to do that.

Clinicians' behavior toward all clients, including LGBTQ clients, is guided and shaped by our good intentions—and also, frequently, by both conscious and unconscious biases and assumptions. Our need to think of ourselves as competent, open-minded, caring professionals may get in the way of our ability to accurately evaluate our ability to work effectively with a given client. We must carefully think through these issues before deciding whether we are, or are not, the right care provider to help a given client reach his or her goals. This issue is entirely distinct and separate from the question of whether a provider is knowledgeable, competent, ethical, and professional. It touches a much deeper issue: Is the provider willing to accept, endorse, and embrace the client's thoughts and feelings about what would make them happy and well?

There are many possible reasons why a provider may feel they are not the best person to help a client explore his or her dating options, improve a problematic relationship, or explore and enact his or her gender identity. In some situations, both client and care provider may benefit from a tactful, ethical offer of referral to a more suitable care provider, whether within or outside the current clinic, agency, or practice. Three things are needed for this to happen: providers must have, or develop, a willingness to examine these issues within themselves and with their supervisor; they must be aware of, or seek out, a more suitable LGBTQ-affirming care provider to whom they can refer the client; and, finally, they must be able to discuss this issue with the client in an ethical and caring way.

The first issue—the willingness to examine these issues and discuss them with one's supervisor—requires a great deal of honesty and humility. I can offer some encouragement along the way. When I first began my training, I was convinced that I would be the ideal therapist to work with every single client who walked through my door. All budding providers likely start out with that kind of optimism, one that can verge on hubris.

But we all have human limitations. Some clients' behavior, appearance, history, behavior, or diagnosis will push too many buttons for us to be able to work with them effectively. There are likely some issues that we have a good understanding of and others for which we lack insight or have a hard time tolerating. For instance, I am comfortable hearing about and discussing clients' impulses and behaviors of self-harm, whereas I know many clinicians are not. Conversely, eating disorders baffle me. If I had a client who was struggling with an eating disorder, I would very much want to refer that person to a colleague who is skilled in that area—and, conversely, I would be happy to accept a referral of a client who has a history of cutting behaviors from a provider who found that content too difficult to tolerate.

If you work in a clinic or group practice, you will want to make sure that there's an atmosphere of openness in which clinicians can discuss their strengths and weaknesses, to ensure that as a team you are optimizing the fit between staff and clients. In my view, a clinic or agency must have *at least one* person on staff who wants to be LGBTQ-affirming—and *the other staff members must be aware of this.* Maybe that person is you. Wonderful! Please let your colleagues know that you have been learning about LGBTQ-affirming care and that if they are working with an LGBTQ client whose needs may not be a good fit for them, you are available for referrals.

You may wonder: If you do that, are you making things better or worse? Shouldn't everybody learn to be effective with all kinds of clients? If a colleague refers an LGBTQ client to you, won't they miss out on an opportunity to learn and grow?

In the long run, yes, we should all try to grow beyond our limitations—and we generally have a yearning to do so.

But the client needs help *now.* This anthology is full of stories from recipients of care who would have benefited, in many instances, from being referred to care providers who were better equipped to meet their needs.

Don't overlook the vicarious learning that occurs in staff meetings, group supervision, and rounds. If you are working successfully with an LGBTQ client, talk about that with colleagues during supervision groups, meetings, or case conferences. Make brief mention of affirming techniques—"I make sure to always call her Christina because she let me know that that's what she prefers to be called." And also any positive impact you are seeing—"And despite her three psychiatric hospitalizations last year, since I started working with her six months ago, she hasn't had any hospitalizations or emergency room visits, and her attendance at appointments has improved." Even colleagues who seem uninterested in meeting the needs of LGBTQ clients will pay attention to the impact that affirming treatment can have.

Finally, no matter what obstacle or issue may prevent you from being the right care provider for a particular client and his or her goals, you can say, "I understand that you want to work on _____. My colleague Frank has a lot of experience with clients who have goals like that. Would you like to meet him and see if you'd like to work with him?"

Of course, this means you need a "Frank" in your clinic or in your referral network to step in and work effectively with this client. To locate an appropriate referral, actively reach out, inquire, ask the people in your clinic about their present strengths and specialties as well as their professional training goals.

At the same time, make sure your colleagues and co-workers know when you have something to offer on an issue. You might be just the Frank that somebody needs to refer a client to. If you're there, but they don't know it, they won't be able to benefit from what you have to offer.

Look for and celebrate the vast areas of common ground that you share with LGBTQ clients. Perhaps you both identify as female. Perhaps you are both attracted to men. Perhaps you have both struggled with some kind of marginalized or outsider status. Perhaps you've seen how stigma and prejudice can burden hearts and minds of people you know and care about.

If you can identify with a client's struggles and connect those struggles to the struggles of other people you have helped, you will be able to share your enormous skills and talents with a broader and broader range of clients. However, if you notice yourself inwardly pulling back or recoiling, or you realize that on some level you say to yourself, "I'm not at all like *that*," it will probably be difficult to manifest the empathy to make therapy or peer support function. If you have an internal reaction such as this—and we all do at times—it can be a useful cue to go searching within for the underlying assumptions, thoughts, and feelings. We should be grateful for this valuable information and make the most of the opportunity to get a better understanding of our strengths and weaknesses. We miss an opportunity if we give in to the impulse to gloss over or minimize experiences such as this.

The awkward acronym LGBTQ does not represent a monolith. It comprises many facets and communities. Anyone who participates in an LGBTQ community, agency, or organization is already interacting with many individuals and groups who can be exceedingly heterogeneous. Lesbians, gay men, bisexual people, transgender people, and those who are queer or questioning or choose not to label themselves have vast differences of gender, attraction, identification, and background. Yet, by and large, we make the effort—not always entirely successfully—to empathize with, identify with, and unite around the struggles that we share.

My point is that the differences between LGBTQ and non-LGBTQ people are not greater than the differences among LGBTQ people themselves. We are all "more human than not," as Harry Stack Sullivan put it. You can find an enormous amount of common ground with any LGBTQ client. Just look for it.

When you look at your LGBTQ clients, don't just focus on the problems and challenges they face and the pain these can cause. Doing so can make both you and your client feel helpless. Instead, focus on the long history of resistance that your client embodies—the fierce insistence that rises up from somewhere deep inside that person, the inner voice that insists that they have a right to be healthy, a right to be well, a right to survive, and a right to thrive and to help others do so as well.

Seen in this way, it's much easier and more natural to respect our clients and to listen carefully to what they have to say. It's natural to respect their goals and either help them reach those goals or find someone else who can help them better. And, finally, it comes naturally to feel a sense of appreciation for these clients who likely have faced and surmounted obstacles and difficulties that we would not have been able to overcome. It becomes natural to support our clients, to learn from them, to help them get what they want—and to admire them for the strengths and virtues that they manifest in doing so.

## REFERENCE

Cochran, S. D., Sullivan, J. G., & Mays, V. M. (2003). Prevalence of psychiatric disorders, psychological distress, and treatment utilization among lesbian, gay and bisexual individuals. *Journal of Consulting and Clinical Psychiatry, 71*:53.

# 26

## PROBLEM GLYPHS

### *Eliza Gauger*

Problem Glyphs is a sort of occult advice column. I'm an illustrator by trade, but, four years ago, I started drawing sigils for people who sent me their problems. I tried to get at the crux of their issues; if I didn't have any useful advice, I just tried to be encouraging. The drawings did a lot of the work for me because they changed every time someone different looked at them: common symbols are personally interpreted in entirely subjective ways, and the sparse text (just a title) conveyed a meaning but did not force the interpretation. The early ones were very simple; the later ones more complex and illustrative.

There are now almost 300 problem glyphs. The authors of *Headcase* asked me to present six here.

Problem Glyphs by Eliza Gauger © 2014–2017. Reprinted with permission of the artist.

# 1.

veryconfusedunicorn asked:

April 20, 2014, 10:09:00 AM

I am trying to find out who I am. I don't know my gender identity, I'm not sure if I identify as nonbinary or what, and I'm not sure about my sexuality either. I'm afraid it will mess up my life.

FIGURE 26.1 "Baphomet's Blessings" in "Problem Glyphs," by Eliza Gauger.
Eliza Gauger © 2014–2017

[BAPHOMET'S BLESSINGS] depicts Baphomet, the famously multigendered "god/dess of witches," as a powerful figure with features of a spotted hyena leaning forward in a bow. The spotted hyena is unusual among mammals for its genitals; both males and females have penises, an adaptation that may have occurred during a time in the species' history when mates were scarce and inbreeding had to be avoided at all costs (see [INVIOLABLE]). As a representation of Baphomet—represented from antiquity with ambiguous secondary sexual characteristics as an indication of magical liminalism—the spotted hyena has a lot to offer. I couldn't possibly advise the questant directly about the extremely personal issue of their gender or sexuality. This glyph was only meant to give them a focal point, encouragement, and a nod to the existence of biological and cultural sex and gender concepts outside of the conventional or even the human.

## 2.

Anonymous asked:

November 4, 2013, 1:00:00 AM

The more time I spend with my roommates the more convinced I am that they're awful people and I'm afraid being around them so much is really starting to affect me.

FIGURE 26.2 "Grace Amidst Monsters" in "Problem Glyphs," by Eliza Gauger.
Eliza Gauger © 2014–2017

[GRACE AMIDST MONSTERS] is Red Riding Hood triumphant in the forest. The wolves surround her, branded with warning runes, but she is unperturbed and already holds one severed head in her picnic basket. A glyph for walking through a dangerous world, surrounded by people who want you dead.

## 3.

Anonymous asked:

July 9, 2014, 6:43:00 PM

I am mildly manic-depressive, and I regularly fuck up my relationships by being incredibly sweet one minute and then sinking into a depression the next. When depressed I tend to start firing emails to my girlfriend blaming her for my problems. I always regret it: she's great at helping me face my moods in person, but she's devastated when she gets my angry email tirades. I need a reminder that it is wise to take a breath, take time out, and stay away from the keyboard when I feel like shit.

FIGURE 26.3 "Half-Life" in "Problem Glyphs," by Eliza Gauger.
Eliza Gauger © 2014–2017

[HALF-LIFE] illustrates my own sense that I am radioactive, poisonous, dangerous to people around me. When that awful feeling becomes acute, I bury myself until it passes. I keep the people around me safe from myself. The spike motif is from the design document of the Waste Isolation Pilot Project—a think tank convened to brainstorm ways to store nuclear waste for the 12,000 years it will take to become inert, while communicating to future generations of humans or other sentient life that the storage site is not a tomb or a treasure, but a dangerous garbage dump. The "forest of thorns" was one of the more fanciful concepts from the project, and it always stuck with me.

# 4.

Anonymous asked:

November 4, 2013, 12:37:00 AM

I feel as though I'm having difficulty manifesting my will as far as my creative life goes—everyday stressors get in the way of my work, and my downtime, which should be dedicated to the work, becomes recuperation. Can you help me?

FIGURE 26.4 "Live Betwixt" in "Problem Glyphs," by Eliza Gauger.
Eliza Gauger © 2014–2017

[LIVE BETWIXT] proposes that we find the cracks in our wage slavery to grow between. Five minutes on a bus, two minutes on an escalator, a ten-minute smoke break. Sometimes scraping together an hour a day, out of scavenged minutes, is the best you can do. And sometimes it is good enough.

# 5.

Anonymous asked:

November 4, 2013, 12:22:00 AM

I preach about things like feeling pain is better than feeling nothing at all, yet I find myself doing nothing but lying in the stagnant puddle of what my life has become. People have stopped telling me how much I could achieve because it's been years now and I haven't lived up to anyone's expectations, most of all my own. I only keep falling even more behind.

FIGURE 26.5 "Mutatis Mutandis" in "Problem Glyphs," by Eliza Gauger.
Eliza Gauger © 2014–2017

[MUTATIS MUTANDIS] depicts an axolotl wielding the syringes that, when filled with certain hormones and injected, can turn the axolotl into an "adult" form of its natural, lifelong "larval" form. Such injections are not necessary or even humane; this amphibian simply evolved out of having to "grow up," and forcing it to do so is something only done in the context of laboratory experiments or callous aquarist hobbying. Mutatis Mutandis, used primarily as a legal term, means "what must change, must change," and the ambivalence and sacrifice of the axolotl's forced "growing up" was what I wanted to illustrate. Sometimes you must change even if it is not best for you, even if it is artificial, even if it would never happen in the wild. Alternatively, escape may be a better option than being forced to change artificially and against your own best interests.

# 6.

Anonymous said:

November 5,2013, 2:04:00 AM

I am a cam girl and I've been having a really hard time staying motivated to do my work the past month. Additionally, for most of that time, my living situation has been weird and unstable and I've probably made like under 600 dollars during that time.

FIGURE 26.6 "Sheela Na Gig" in "Problem Glyphs," by Eliza Gauger.
Eliza Gauger © 2014–2017

[SHEELA NA GIG] is for sex workers. The title is the term for a certain kind of an-cient, mysterious representation of a crouching figure holding open its legs and what is usually interpreted as a vulva. Sheelas appear on very old masonry throughout England and Ireland, and their meaning is unclear. It may be a blessing, warning, ward, or apotropaic symbol, but it is ubiquitous and powerful. I have always thought of sheela na gigs in the context of sex workers and models in the same spread pose, a ubiquitous modern image. The current subcultural sheela is probably "the Goatman"; all joking aside, his gaping anus acts as a ward, a curse, an initiation or hazing, and sometimes a "blessing" or secret sign within Internet communities. It is often directed defensively against "outsiders." I covered this sheela's spread with a laptop because the shape of their actual genitals is irrelevant to the blessing: Whatever you are spreading, it is powerful, it is ancient work, and may you be blessed by it.

# 27

## ERASURE

*Gabriella M. Belfiglio*

I. We are forbidden to bring in any lighters, matches, scissors, razors, knives, personal medications, glass bottles, glue, knitting needles, rug hooks or embroidery, firearms, liquor, marijuana or drugs, fingernail polish or remover, aerosol cans, lighter fluid, or cameras. The guard behind the front desk warns me to be careful—pointing to my belly seven months full of growing baby.

II. Lisa is happy to see us, for once. As usual, she immediately asks if we brought cigarettes. When she hugs me, I feel bone.

III. Cell by cell, I've been watching her die for more than two-thirds of my life. Longer than I've lived in Brooklyn. Longer than I've lived any one place, or than this tree that towers beyond my apartment has been growing, or than people have been dancing to *Thriller,* or watching *The Simpsons,* or Bono has been singing about streets with no names, or Madonna has been preaching to women about deserving the best in life, or people have been watching Thelma and Louise triumphantly drive off their cliff, or than Spike Lee telling us how to do the right thing, or watching William Hurt kiss Raul Julia in *Kiss of the Spider Woman* and Whoopi Goldberg kiss Margaret Avery in *The Color Purple,* or Natalie Goldberg's been advising writers to bare our bones, or we have been tasting Anne Carson's bittersweet love poems, or been lost in Toni Morrison's middle passage, or solving the six sides of the Rubik's cube, and much longer than we've been using cell phones, iPods, YouTube, blogging, Facebook, or email, and longer than Lady Gaga has been alive or Georgia O'Keeffe has been dead.

IV. We meet in the hospital lounge. My father sits next to my mother then Lisa, then her caseworker, and a social worker, around a small table. My girlfriend and I sit on two chairs with cushions along the wall close by. A team of four young interns in official white coats and nametags stand on the other side of the table.

As they discuss business, Lisa drags her chair over in between Margarita and me. Lisa tells me she's going gray in the same place I am. She tears her chair over to our mother's side to interrupt the conversation. She has something *really* important to tell her. She spins back to me and asks if I will buy her a diet Coke from the machine downstairs. She can't sit still; still, it is the longest I've seen her so contained in years. She tells me she cannot wait to get out of this place—that it's been months and they all drive her crazy. She looks hesitantly over to Margarita and tells her it's nice to meet her, not remembering when, about a year ago, she viciously pushed her out of the room.

Lisa leans closer to me and asks if I know who the father is. She tells me I can call her any time if I need to talk. Afterwards she scrapes her chair to our father's side, climbs onto his lap as if she's trying to erase forty years. His body immediately tenses.

V. How many times have I tried to write this poem?

VI. Before we leave, Lisa releases the chain from around her neck, a gift from her *boyfriend*. She says she's sorry it got a little messed up from the shower and loops it around my neck, where a rusted silver heart dangles into the hollow of my clavicle.

**Our Sisters**
Gabriella Belfiglio

Over the tenuous phone lines old implications slip out—
details that were buried like seeds
alongside her body. Today, a little green
pries through the hard ground and patience
is like rain in a drought—you want to see
what will grow, Now.

When you talk about your sister, I see
my own. You want to know how, why—
part of me shudders wondering why I can't
feel the love that you are so full of, it comes
leaking out of your eyes.

My sister is an overgrown field—
one you find fenced off in those abandoned lots
next to buildings with boards for windows.
She sprouts through concrete cracks—
around rusted shopping carts, her weary
tendrils weave in between the wires of the fence.

Walking by, people throw their empty bottles
crumpled wrappers
adding to the mess they already see.

They told you your sister died of Malaria.
But what they didn't say lingers—
in the dark, the holes are so easy to fall into
the space so full of emptiness you are left drowning
in your own imagination. You remember the nights
she came home bruised, high, or not at all.
Her nightmares waking you up first—
keeping you up last.

My nightmares bring me north Philadelphia—
row houses a porch full of cigarette butts—
the only allowed drug at the house full of addicts.
It is hard to see, there are so many weeds,
seasons of rough grass between us.
My sister is still alive, but she's been dying for years.
She collects letters—A. I. D. S., hepatitis A, B, C—
I've lost track, there are too many to follow anyway,
her body an unruly labyrinth

**While Taking This Drug**
Gabriella Belfiglio

While Taking This Drug:
Periodic Examinations
of thyroid hormone levels in blood.
bone mineral density.
and that one, which holds nothing but itself.

While Taking This Drug:
Observe the Following
the blushing one, that turns and leans
if embarrassed, toward the one that's cool,
and how that cool one won't respond, withdraws,
and how a cold one stands, wrapped in itself,
among the opening ones, that shed everything.

While Taking This Drug:
you increase the risk of bleeding;
and wind and rain and spring's great patience
and guilt and restlessness and masquerading fate
and the darkening of the earth at evening
and even the clouds that change and flow and vanish,
and even the vague command of the distant stars
changed to a handful of inwardness,
a therapeutic effect.

While Taking This Drug,
or any drugs filled with small, lit butterflies,
an increased dose may be required
to obtain proper control of the soft and breath
tossed aside in the morning shadows.

NB: A found poem comprising lines from *The Essential Guide to Prescription Drugs*
(Rybacki, Long, & Long, 1997)

**Weary**
Gabriella Belfiglio

I want to jump off.
I want to shoot.
I want to slit,
longways down veins.
It shouldn't be this hard
hard heart.

I want to shed skin
transform in
to wings
to free.

I want to not want,
to not be.

# 28

## INFORMED CONSENT

*Asher J. Wickell*

Three years along, my heart still stops a minute, some days, when you first walk in the door. I wonder if I'll look like I know what I'm doing. I wonder if I'll feel like I know what I'm doing—and whether you'll notice. Sometimes, I can hold my curiosity out away from my anxiety; those are good days. Others, all my questions collapse into panic. I can worry about anything—how shaggy my beard is getting, or whether I wore the same shirt on this day last week, or if you already know I'm trans, and what it will be like for each of us when you find out. There are still stretches when I'm not at all certain I'm doing a convincing impression of "therapist." The parts of myself I trust most are reasonably sure this is irrelevant to how much of a therapist I actually am. I try to remind myself of that, when I can't get around to eating breakfast because my stomach is so unsettled over my next intake. Don't take it personally—it's definitely me, not you—but, of course, the same hesitation walks toe-to-heel with us both.

It lives down in the narrow place, between my ribs, where panic clenches and I can't get any air. Or it's in the dark edges that cage and blur your vision; it's the throbbing roar in your ears. It's how our hearts careen away from our outstretched palms, laughing a shrill whinny as they jump the fence and leave us hollow-chested and alone. It's the cold pit under my belly. It's the cliff your feet ache to shuffle over. That's where fear lives, foreclosing everything. We both came by it honestly.

It gets better. These days, for me, it's nearly always over by the time we're both inside the office. Have a seat wherever you like. Can I get you something to drink? We have tea, water, coffee. Here's a professional tip: holding something warm in your hands will help ground you, pull your whole self out to the edges of your body. This is important in therapy. It is particularly important if you're the therapist.

What was it like for you to come in today? How does it feel to sit down across from me, and who do I remind you of? Who do you remind me of? You don't have to answer that one; it goes into this file in the back of my mind, for later use in your treatment planning and my self-care. Here is a story most therapists will tell, sooner or later: "You know, I had a client who. . . ." Sometimes, I did. Sometimes, the client is me or someone I love. An open secret in mental health is that we are not blank slates, not a single one of us. We see through the stories we carry; we are our own instruments of practice. It's not that I think you're my mother, but both my parents taught me what tone of voice helps her feel safe.

I'd like to know what basic needs have been ignored because you're bi, or trans, or gay, or positive; or because you have too much sex, or too little, or the wrong kind. I'm interested in who didn't listen to you because you're a woman or because all the doctors over there are White and rich; or because the shape of your body means no one takes you seriously. Tell me who's decided you're psychotic because the truth you told wasn't the one they preferred. Tell me who decided being psychotic meant you didn't know your own mind or have a perfect right to use it. Tell me what words illuminate your life, that get thrown back in your face because this is Kansas, which apparently means we have chosen to live forever in the 1950s, but with crueler economic policies.

I know what the lobby smells like at the community mental health center. I know how bored you get at the county health department looking for shapes in the ceiling tiles. Every time I sign up for Obamacare, I get teary-eyed and strident on social media because it means twelve months without the specter of trading a day's wages and most of my dignity for five-and-one-third days of mood stabilizers, with a two-week wait for a patient assistance plan.

I know there are some words in my file that ensure the nurse will forever speak to me like a six-year-old child if the sex on my license, taken in tandem with my haircut, didn't already. Some days, like some of my clients, like some of my friends, I fantasize about just getting them tattooed somewhere visible—not that it would help, I guess, but then I could read people right away. I could skip the tightrope performance of crazy-enough-but-not-too-crazy. But how would you do it? Medical codes only, or should you account for potential employers, educators, clinical supervisors who haven't memorized half the ICD-10? Best to do both: F31.74, bipolar disorder, type I, in full remission, last episode manic, with psychotic features; F64.1, gender identity disorder in adolescence and adulthood—one on each arm, for comparative purposes, maybe. I could keep a mood journal about which side of me people saw first.

I know once you've been manic, or psychotic, or suicidal, the odds are against anyone taking your word for your own sanity, even years later, even a decade. Even if you take all your meds, every day. Even if you are such a true believer in therapy, you go ahead and get your own master's degree in it. If it turns out that you're a guy, that may help, but definitely not until after your voice breaks. I know that, for some of us, joy and satisfaction and self-determination have been ruled unnecessary. Aren't we pleased, after all, that our own brains aren't trying to kill us, today? We've brought the ceiling down, and the floor up, and we can walk forward at a moderate pace on level ground. Aren't we happy?

The shapes of our stories are similar enough, I'll almost certainly recognize the outlines. In some ways, it doesn't matter: it's telling that's important, and bearing witness. In old trauma texts, they call it "pendulation"—planting half of yourself here, pinned to your tea-warmed hands; half there, back in all the old injury. I'm the safe, queer muse, floating ahead of you into Hell and back out until you can manage it without me, until there is consistently an out.

Tell me what feels like it might help. If you woke up tomorrow and everything was all right, how would you know? What's the first thing you'd realize was different? Tell me who you need in your life and what they should know about you. Tell me who has made a difference and in what direction.

Or don't tell me anything. Maybe there are no words for how it was. Maybe your own name was slapped out of your mouth. Maybe every breath was needed for something more urgent than speech, than self, and our beginning point is just filling your lungs with air. So now that you've made it at least partway out, enough to sit here with me—let us remember bravely. What was it we were holding out for? The first thing we did was stay alive, and now here we are to make sure it's not the last. What I mean is: a life raft can keep you from drowning, but it's no place to call home.

It may be important for you to know that my anxious heart will keep pace with yours, through the long silences or breathless rush of our conversation today. Feel your feet on the floor. Feel your hands wrapped around your drink. Feel the air rushing into you, shaping itself into speech. The most important thing is that we are both here. I am right here with you.

Try not to worry too much. This first session, most of what we're going to do is sift your life down into little boxes and make sure none of them requires immediate, safety-oriented responses. It's just like at the doctor's office. Difficulty sleeping: check. Isolation: check. Sexual concerns: check. Discomfort with your body: check. All the hard short-answer questions are on the back. Remember in elementary school, when your teacher lied that there were no wrong answers and no stupid questions? In this room, that is actually true. I'm aware that the people who taught you may not have equipped you to believe this.

It's okay to hold off on answering some of these, I tell you. It is also okay to lie, I don't usually say; plenty of people need to do that, too. I know it's weird to sit down with some stranger and spill your deep emotional stuff all over him, I say, and I do know that. I really do. There is room for all of you here, and there's plenty of time.

No, it isn't too much for me, but I'm glad you brought that up. We are together here in a relational laboratory—the serious kind, with shock-absorbing windows. You can blow up whatever you need to. You are not a nuisance. You are not a burden. But what if you were? Here is what we're going to practice believing: you teach me to regard myself more kindly by allowing me to see you. I struggle steadily deeper into the courage you are studying. Our connection is sacred. Connection is sacred. You are so very important. I am so very important.

Everything that has happened to you is yours. You didn't buy most of it, but you'll still have to pay: there are no shortcuts, there is no exit ramp. This is where we will live, until we find someplace better, and we may hit some intense terrain. I won't leave you out here on your own, but I'll alert you now that the forecast is light on sunny weather, long on the side of flash floods, straight-line winds, and range-burns run well past anyone's control. Here is a magnet with the phone number to call for breakdowns along the way. They are not altogether conversant in queer, let me warn you upfront, and they are not terribly aware or affirming with respect to trans. I won't tell you the precious name of my beloved, who they misgendered through a long night of murderous dysphoria. I won't think until tonight about the forty minutes firefighters spent trying to restart the heart of the woman I loved before him, before she finished dying of suicide; but it is in his honor and her memory that I will confirm your suspicions, or certainties, depending. The crisis intervention situation is not ideal. Think about it like having a heart attack. You know the paramedics might not speak kindly about your beautiful life, but if it gives you a chance to embrace it for a few more years, you dial 9-1-1 anyway. It isn't perfect. Sometimes it's really bad. But it's what we've got. Here's my business card—you can sign a release to me, and I'll run interference if you need me to. This is me, signing away forever the small hours of my life, but what choice does either one of us have?

Is it strange to talk about possibility now, in the middle of a long stretch of problem-talk and crisis planning and worst-case scenarios? But some part of each of us trusted this moment enough to step into it. This is the balance point from which we can lean into your life. Hope is a terrible risk; you must know that, if you're here. Our work is to help you afford it. After all, what's a crisis-line magnet to a queer client, if not a staggering, ludicrous gesture of hope?

This is what my professor said, half a decade ago, at the first night of the first class for a therapy degree: "Sometimes, you will be the only person in the therapy room who has any hope at all. You are not allowed to give up on your clients; too many of them have already been compelled to give up on themselves. It is your job to hold onto that hope for as long as necessary, your job to tend it and give it room to breathe, for however long it takes your clients to sustain it for themselves." I clenched my jaw the whole time to keep from crying, partly because someone had finally named the thing that was driving me forward; and also because the hope in my throat was threatening to choke me. If you've been deep enough in darkness, you can't always stop yourself from massing up candles. Try to remember, for future reference, that this is not a weakness.

Do you have any questions or concerns about any of this?

I'm going to have you sign and date, here, and then we should be good to go for today.

My best hopes walk with us out of the office. It takes time for the hour to wind down, to spool our conversation up and put it somewhere safe. Next, the careful work of reentry: what did I feel, today? Where was that coming from? I lace my body back into my brain, let my awareness saturate only myself, stand all the way up on my feet. All of my parts are still here. Also, I'm hungry, and I need to pee. My best friend is waiting, with beer; or my boyfriend is waiting, with dinner; or my bed is waiting, with post-apocalyptic young adult vampire fiction. How do I deal with my own messy life?

I try to speak as kindly to myself as I would to you. I don't lie to my clinical supervisor or my therapist; anyone else who wants to see into my story has to earn it. I go to therapy. Sometimes I run late. When my body feels bad, I pay attention. I forget my hormone shot until I get stomach cramps, but then I take it, and remember that other intentions have taken me years to get the hang of. I use any way I can find to move forward, even if it isn't elegant. I dodge intimacy and vulnerability more than I hope to, less than I used to. I practice saying no when I mean it, and saying yes when I want it, but I'm scared. I take my meds. I take my meds. I take my meds.

Let's go ahead and get you scheduled for next time. I'll manage my anxieties, grow deeper into myself, breathe through the raw places, and see you in a week—we can spend an hour being human together and see what that does for you. Call me if you need anything.

# 29

## BAD PENNY

### *J. M. Ellison*

My pockets always contain coins from Palestine. I keep the bills in a drawer with my passport, but the shekel coins escape and mix in with the nickels and dimes of my daily life. They turn up like bad pennies. Inevitably, I must apologize for them to unamused clerks and bus drivers. "Why do you have that in your pocket?" a friend asks, as he hands me the coin I dropped on the floor.

I don't know how these mysterious coins end up in my pockets, but I know why I keep them.

—

"Do you have PTSD [posttraumatic stress disorder]?" asks Mike. We are in a perfectly appointed home in which neither of us is comfortable. Fancy tea cups and pita cut into triangles. Running water, electricity, and flushing toilets. Mike is a member of Veterans for Peace. I have been invited to speak about my experiences working in Palestine as a human rights monitor. That's what most people call it—monitoring human rights. It means that, for three years, I lived in a Palestinian village where Israeli soldiers prevented my neighbors from constructing electrical power lines and laying pipe for running water. As a human rights monitor, I videotaped adult Israeli settlers attacking Palestinian children on their way to school and watched Israeli soldiers arrest my Palestinian friends for no discernible reason. It means, like everyone else in the village, I tried to stop the beatings and arrests, but I couldn't. It means I wrote press releases detailing the terrible things that happened to people I loved and sent them to media outlets that usually ignored them.

Because I am a White person, other White people are sometimes interested in my experiences, even if they would usually ignore the stories of Palestinians themselves. White people usually want me to keep my stories upbeat and hopeful. Mike is the only person who has ever asked about my mental health.

"I don't know if I have PTSD," I answer. Here in the United States, we are a nation of conquest. The scant resources we spend understanding and treating trauma are directed toward soldiers, not those traumatized by soldiers. Besides, I have no insurance.

"Here," says Mike. We stand next to each other after my presentation, both waiting awkwardly for our respective friends to decide it's time to leave. Mike hands me a wallet-sized photo. "This was my helicopter when I was a medic in Vietnam," he says. "See, we painted 'Why?' above the red cross." Why is a good question, I think. Dangerous, too. Asking why can make you crumble. I take the photo. "Take care of yourself," says Mike. It's an order from someone who will tolerate no bullshit.

After I leave Palestine, I move to Chicago. For a very long time, America's second city is second on the list of places I most want to be. I miss everything about Palestine, except the Israeli military occupation.

I keep in touch with my former colleague, Jessica. We are each the only person who understands the other's experiences. We talk on the phone for hours. "Do you think we're traumatized?" I ask. Jessica says, "I'm not traumatized. I'm just fucked up."

Just fucked up. Yes. Let's print that on a bumper sticker and put it on my suitcase. I want to warn the TSA.

—

For a long time, my friends hurt me badly without knowing it. "You shouldn't go back to Palestine," they say. My pain is strange and inconvenient to them. They are afraid to ask what caused it and I am afraid to tell them. I know they don't really want to know, that the knowledge would break them. I don't tell them that I still speak with my neighbors in the village. I don't tell them that Keifah is pregnant again or that Basil's father is on hunger strike and may die. I am betraying my American friends. They want Palestine to be past tense. For me, it is so present.

—

"You have trauma?" asks Samia. "Like what?" I describe my nightmares, my exaggerated startle reflex, the way I sometimes feel like vomiting. "Oh," she replies. Samia is from Syria. She hasn't heard from her family since the uprising against Assad began. She doesn't know if her cousins are alive or dead. She says, "Oh, everyone has that." She's right.

—

"How can you want to go back to Palestine when you're transgender?" I know that my American friends wonder this. I'm almost relieved that one of them has finally said it. I am a non-binary trans person. That means that my gender falls outside of the categories of men and women. It also means that I am used to answering prying questions. There are lots of answers to this one. I could flip a coin to decide which one I'll share. Will I say that my friends in Palestine have always treated me well? I work closely with a handful of queer Palestinians. Should I tell my friends that? Or will I point out that I wear the clothes that conform with the gender I was assigned at birth when I'm in Palestine, just like I do here in the United States whenever I have to go to the DMV, or see my family, or when I feel like today might not be the best day to look trans while I'm walking down the street? Or I could just say this—being trans means that I know more about violence and trauma than most White Americans. I'm already an expert in heartbreak, so why not visit the village I love?

—

"I don't know what to say," my friend Lindsey tells me. She stands over me in her purple bikini as I lie on a lawn chair. We are on vacation, but suddenly the beach has turned into a confessional and Lindsey is offering me an apology I didn't request. "I don't know what it feels like to be born in the wrong body," she explains, shrugging her shoulders.

It's my turn to speak. I can tell that I am supposed to offer Lindsey absolution by accepting her bumbling apology, but all I can do is look at her in her bathing suit. She is magnificent. I know that sometimes she believes in her magnificence and sometimes she doesn't. Sometimes she diets, plucks, and dresses out of confidence. Sometimes she does the same things out of anxiety. I do the same. I wonder who among us doesn't. Don't we all feel like the bodies into which we were born are wrong? The only difference is that some of us, we trans people, are told that the ways that we dress, manage our bodies, and understand our genders make us crazy, sick, dangerous, and wrong.

I didn't tell Lindsey that sometimes I wish that I had been born into the wrong body, to use her reductive turn of phrase. Some transgender people seek out medical assistance in the form of hormones and gender confirmation surgery to aid them in a gender transition. I'm happy for these trans people. I'm proud of them for taking control of their own bodies and for doing whatever they need to do to survive. I happen, however, to have no desire for hormones or surgery, though there plenty of things about my body that I can't help but regard as wrong. This doesn't make me better or worse than any other trans person. It is just a fact. It is also an inconvenience.

The fact that I do not want to medically transition places me largely outside of the limited legal protections offered to transgender people. The courts have placed great faith in doctors, so if I am not seeking medical assistance as I live out my gender identity, the law does not consider me to be trans. But I don't want what doctors are selling. Sometimes I wish I did.

I don't fit into the medical industry's understanding of transgender. I worry that I won't fit its understanding of PTSD either. You'll forgive me if this makes me skeptical of what a therapist could offer me as I cope with trauma.

—

I put my hand in my pocket and rub the coin I find there. Here is the reason that I keep these coins: trauma, like my bruised heart, is precious, and, like my coins, it seems to be here to stay. Doctors and psychologists say that the hardest thing about trauma is accepting that you have become a different person. But I like the person I am now. The experts say that trauma is how the brain copes, how it saves you. I say I don't want to forget the people I love.

Living with trauma is like my experience of being queer and trans. PTSD is something the experts tell me I am supposed to overcome. They tell me that I can overcome being queer and trans, too, that the medical industry can help me be less visibly gender-nonconforming, that I could be just like everyone else. Doing so would be easier for everyone, and maybe easier for me, too. But I wonder if my gender, my sexuality, and even my trauma are actually the best parts of me.

So, instead, I live with trauma. I do so as myself, a queer and trans person. I pour trauma a cup of tea and ask it if it's comfortable. I love and care for my trauma, like I love and care for myself.

—

"Have you talked to a therapist?" I'm not sure if this conversation is about my PTSD or my gender identity. Either way, the solution is the same. I'm supposed to talk to a therapist so that I will stop being sad that my Palestinian friends live under military occupation, that their children run from armed Israeli settlers. I'm supposed to talk to a therapist so that I am no longer sad that my boss harassed me until I quit my job, that I'm terrified that someone will call the police just because I am using a public bathroom. A therapist will help me cope, my friends tell me. They might be right, but I think they hope that a therapist will make me disappear. Perhaps with the help of a therapist, I'll be able to attend Fourth of July barbecues bedecked in stars and stripes and neither the jingoism nor the sound of the fireworks will make me jumpy. Or maybe with the help of the therapist, I will be able to be happy and transgender. After all, a therapist could prescribe me hormones, so I could live in a binary gender and be less confusing for everyone.

Maybe I am broken. Sometimes I feel that way, but I am pretty sure that the only cure is an end to the systems of violence that keep bruising my heart, breaking it over and over and over again. I could talk with a therapist. But my friends could work to end the Israeli military occupation of Palestine. They could stand against transphobia. Why don't they? But don't ask why; it's a dangerous question.

—

In all my years in Palestine solidarity activism, I've only cried in public once. It is July 20, 2014, during the Israeli bombing of the Gaza Strip. I am lying on the ground outside the Tribune Tower in downtown Chicago, face down so no one can see my tears. Around me, my friends are also sprawled on the ground in the attitude of corpses. It is a die-in. Someone is reading the names of the Palestinians who have been killed in this, the latest massacre. Although I have never been to Gaza and all of my Palestinian friends are far away from the bombings, I hear familiar names. Ahmed. Nasser. Jameli. Fatima. Omar. Amira. I picture the people I love running from helicopters and fighter planes. I wonder if the soldiers who killed Ahmed, Nasser, and Jameli spent a second wondering why they received the orders.

The hot concrete is wet below my cheeks. The names go on too long. When they finally stop, I stand up, pick up a coin that has fallen out of my pocket, and wipe my eyes quickly. I don't want anyone to see me crying because who am I to cry when no one else is? But then a sob comes out of my throat. The sob keeps coming up and out of my mouth, like a snake. A friend wraps her arms around me and holds me while my body shakes. She doesn't say anything. She knows there is nothing to say. She knows that in some ways, this is the only thing that can be done.

I wonder when I will cry in public about transphobia. Maybe it will be at a candlelight vigil for the eighteen transgender women of color who have been murdered this year in the United States. Maybe it will be caused by a more private experience of violence. Whatever the reason, I hope someone will be there to hold me. I hope that person will know that sometimes tears are the only possible response. Sometimes, it's wrong to be dry-eyed.

My experience of having PTSD is like my experience of being queer and trans, but it's also more than that. Being transgender in this country is a trauma. And I am surviving.

—

Cleaning my apartment, I find coins on the floor and scattered on tabletops. This is the first home I have decorated by myself, and it is an assemblage of my life. Ties in my closet and nail polish on the dresser. Teapots and rugs from Palestine. Hand-me-downs and gifts from my friends and family. Cast-off treasures from the alleyways of my new city. Posters of my trans heroes on the wall. Rocks and shells from a dozen beaches. Colors and geographies rub against each other. My bookshelves and dressers form Pangaea. I have given up on achieving any fixed look or organizational system. It is enough for the objects in my house to be beautiful and, hopefully, beautiful together. Photographs of people and places I have loved—and still love—are strewn everywhere. My little apartment is a sanctuary, a talisman, a map.

In a place of honor, I have hung a framed photo of a medic's helicopter. "Why?" is painted above the red cross. It's a good question. A dangerous one, too. But I am still asking it.

# 30

## LIBERATING THE BIG PINK ELEPHANT
## IN THE THERAPY ROOM

*Thomas Mondragon*

I have the privilege of teaching in a master's level clinical psychology program devoted to the instruction of LGBTQ-affirmative psychotherapeutic theory and practice
at Antioch University in Los Angeles. Graduate students are given the opportunity
to explore, understand, and gain a lived experience of a much-needed therapeutic
approach to working with LGBTQ individuals. Students are often surprised that this
requires going beyond viewing commonalities among client populations with similar life challenges in the human search for meaning. Both as a professor and in my
own private practice in West Hollywood, I am constantly reminded of the necessity
of vital LGBTQ-affirmative psychotherapy. Tozur and McClanahan describe this delivery of mental health services as one that "celebrates and advocates the authenticity
and integrity" (1999, p. 734) of LGBTQ clients toward greater ethical, compassionate,
and life-enhancing clinical treatment.

Developed more than ten years ago, the LGBT specialization at Antioch draws
on a unique curriculum based on the unfolding LGBTQ-affirmative literature.
It provides students with comprehensive exposure to working affirmatively with
LGBTQ individuals, couples, and families in psychotherapy. The compulsory heteronormativity embedded in Western culture means that none of us is immune to the
effects of heterosexism and homo/bi/lesbian/transphobia. In service of more compassionate and empathic treatment of LGBTQ clients, the mental health community is also ethically obligated to pay attention to how this shows up within the lives
of heterosexual and LGBTQ practitioners. Understandably, heterosexist bias could
deeply affect the delivery of psychological services, training, and research, which
goes unnoticed by many. It makes sense, then, that instruction on the principled
treatment of LGBTQ individuals in therapy requires special attention, bringing to
light the needs, challenges, traumas, and gifts that lie outside the heterosexist paradigm of "normal." This special attention contradicts the standard clinical norm of

neutrality, calling instead for a conscious effort to recognize and question hetero-sexually driven psychological theory in practice. Therapists don't usually overtly celebrate clients' identities, yet affirmatively recognizing the *meaning* and *potential* in the identities and lived experiences—physical, relational, emotional, mental, psy-chological, and spiritual—of LGBTQ individuals can provide crucial validation of experiences dating back to childhood.

Even with the Supreme Court decision on same-sex marriage in 2015, there is still much work to be done to achieve LGBTQ civil rights on the political, social, and cultural levels. Only a year afterward, we witnessed in horror the tragic massacre of LGBTQ people at Pulse, a gay bar that had been a safe haven for many in Orlando. Unfortunately, this event mirrors the hundreds of years of individual and collec-tive experience of being queer in Western civilization. Through our effortful aware-ness, we therapists can work to fully appreciate and integrate the cultural aspects of LGBTQ lives. It is on us to diligently and consciously assist clients in articulating the ongoing psychological impact they experience living in a still fiercely heterosexist society.

An LGBTQ-affirmative therapist adopts a radical notion by rejecting an en-vironment of neutrality, which can render LGBTQ experience invisible in the therapist–client relationship. From this position, a therapist would proactively en-gage in affirming attitudes, presence, and responses to elements uniquely found in the expression of LGBTQ identities—as an interventionist attempt to rectify the effects of heterosexism right there in the therapy room. Adopting an attitude that fosters identities and behaviors sourced in what could be called an "inner fire" that *celebrates* one's difference, affirmative therapy takes on a politically motivated position to bring forth corrective counterexperiences to the homonegativity and gender biases rooted in childhood that can play out in the client's current environ-ment. An affirmative therapist creates an invaluable safe space in which a whole spectrum of feelings, experiences, and unrealized potential can begin undergoing examination.

When I look back at my formative years as a mixed-race protogay boy raised in a very conservative Christian church, I see myriad forces shaping my sense of self, relationship to others, and place in the world. I was expected to be heterosexual like my parents and sister, to anticipate marriage to a woman and to have children, and to "naturally" relive out the institutional involvements modeled by my parents. All of this emerged within the particular cultural nuance of being raised by a Japanese mother and a Latino father; in this milieu, collectivity overpowered the idea of a Western sense of individualism. I experienced a clashing of values—my very being as a gay person left me uniquely unlike my family and clearly without support to bring forward my individualistic expression sourced in my attraction to other boys.

I remember as far back as age three my wish for relatedness with other boys and with men. My earliest memory is of my father, how I ran into his arms when I became frightened at a Halloween event, and being nestled and protected by his embrace. I was surprised as an adult gay man when I recalled this forgotten moment, as I had long ago also felt a deep estrangement from him with only a ghost-like memory of that night. My focus had always been on his emotional distancing, which I felt and sensed as it became more obvious that I wasn't like other boys.

I also remember strong preadolescent attraction when looking up at my Latino uncle, who loomed larger than life with his swarthy features, jet-black curly hair, and Marlboro Man mustache. I couldn't wait to see him when my family would take the monthly three-hour trek to the northern New Mexico homestead simply called "El Rancho." To me he was a mythical figure in the lineage of Zeus and Ganymede, Gilgamesh and Enkidu—archetypal imagery of the divine spark of same-sex love and meaning that were fully alive in my gay psyche, even at that young age.

In addition to being gay, I grew up in New Mexico with few other Asian people around me, magnifying an existing sense of feeling different and not fitting in. When I was fourteen, thousands of miles away on the other side of the world and another side of my heritage, I came to know one of my Japanese uncles. Becoming acquainted with him constituted another thrilling encounter with libidinal same-sex longing. My uncle seemed full of kindness and interested in me, and—in a most unexpected twinship experience—looked very much like me. Many years later I read that, in Japan, as embodied in *Partings at Dawn: An Anthology of Japanese Gay Literature*, there existed rich historical accounts of the love between men in the samurai class and those in Buddhist monasteries. That summer, thousands of miles away in the Land of the Rising Sun, I had a taste of this history via the fantasies I carried, hidden away, while with this cherished uncle.

As a gay Japanese-Latino man, I have been able to acknowledge and address the heterosexist, homophobic, and racist affronts that have stood in the way of a more holistic appreciation of myself. My own affirming gay-centered psychotherapy embodies the knowledge that my gayness is valuable, deeply meaningful, and full of possibility.

The shamanic Two-Spirit tradition buried in my Native American background references a time when sexuality, gender, and spiritual calling came together in a way often valued and of contributional import to the collective. We queer people have always stirred things up and brought a different and much-needed perspective to unchallenged heterosexist culture, mores, and attitudes. LGBTQ-affirmative psycho-therapy can bring forth a crucial understanding of the psychological impact wrought by being queer while growing up in a heteronormative world. Helping us develop meaningful relationships with ourselves and others to embark on a journey of the self, full of its own language, and its own world of symbols and images and feelings, is what truly LGBTQ-informed affirmative counseling is meant to offer clients.

LGBTQ affirmativity acknowledges the social and psychological pressure to conform socially and psychologically to heterosexual standards of human experience and the internal and external conflicts brought about by that pressure. My erotically driven memories evoked feelings in my physical and emotional selves that were threatening and antithetical to the person into which my parents tried to mold me. If we look at the whole person as a social and psychological entity, then we are asked to consider the impact of these forces on the development of the outer *and* the inner life. In my own case as a developing gay boy growing up in New Mexico, this showed up in several ways.

As a young adult seeking help to address lifelong depression, I could have easily begun taking medication, learned cognitive behavioral techniques, and developed better social skills. A competent therapist might have provided very useful interventions along these lines. Yet, without curiosity about my particular narrative as a young gay man, a provider would miss an important opportunity to more effectively address the intrapersonal and interpersonal impact of repeated exposure to heterosexism, homophobia, and racism and the resulting internalization of destructive psychological impediments to developing a healthy solid sense of self. Inadvertently and unfortunately, invisibility can easily be recreated in the therapeutic alliance with an LGBTQ client. One must see how creating a safe space that acknowledges the effects of these forces could provide profound reparative moments for LGBTQ individuals.

To enhance an optimal healing environment, the affirmative therapist is asked to explore possible unconscious collusion with one's own heterosexist attitudes and beliefs regarding sexual orientation and gender identity (McHenry & Johnson, 1993). What might be hidden and less obvious are microaggressions, described by Nadal as the "brief and commonplace daily verbal, behavioral, or environmental indignities, whether intentional or unintentional, that communicate hostile, derogatory, or negative slights and insults toward members of oppressed groups" (2008, p. 23). Examples include asking a transgender individual invasive questions regarding genitalia, making statements such as "that's so gay," asking "who's the man and who's the woman in the relationship?" or maintaining stereotypes about all lesbians having dominant masculine characteristics.

Affirmative therapists advocate for LGBTQ self-awareness "to provide a direct, politically motivated, corrective to the homonegativity encountered by LGB[TQ] people in this late modern world." (Langdridge, 2007, p. 35). This *affirmative* ethic calls the therapist to self-educate about LGBTQ culture, history, and unique developmental processes in gaining a self-caring attitude vital to fostering positive identity development and integration. Importantly, these guidelines are laid out in the American Psychological Association's *Practice Guidelines for LGB Clients: Guidelines for Psychological Practice with Lesbian, Gay, and Bisexual Clients* and in the *Guidelines for Psychological Practice with Transgender and Gender Nonconforming People.*

It is heartening to witness not only allies but also LGBTQ-identified students embracing these concepts and attitudes in their own self-reflective two-year graduate program. Many students are deeply impacted by the supportive faculty, the literature, and the experiential work that encourages them to "live" these concepts more fully, possibly for the first time. This has led many students to embark on personal journeys of self-reflection to acknowledge or embrace their queer, transgender, lesbian, bisexual, and gay identities. Students repeatedly express "being seen" through the coursework and readings and the concept of LGBT affirmativity, thus deepening their capacities to understand and appreciate themselves more fully.

Affirmative therapy importantly acknowledges and addresses the effects of homophobia. (Here, I intentionally focus on the use of homophobia but also acknowledge the experiential nuances for lesbians, bisexuals, and transgender and queer-identified individuals). Repeated exposure to heterosexism as a gay child can lead to an unconsciously embedded but fully active internalization of homophobia. This can be the impetus for someone seeking therapy, though it is rarely identified as such during initial sessions.

The term "internalized homophobia" is seen by some as pathologizing, implying personal weakness versus resilience on the part of the LGBQ person and "ignor[ing] the structural, institutional, political and normative assumptions that keep such a system in place" (Peel, 2001, p. 544). However, this term also brings important attention to complex feelings that have been introjected into one's psychic experience *because* of systemic heterosexism. Powerful feelings of fear, disgust, and shame due to societal disavowal of nonconforming erotic desire and gender identity would understandably result in a client's crushing belief that "I am unlovable because of who I am."

Discussing internalized homophobia with clients and students often reveals that the concept is not familiar to them, although on examination its effects certainly are. The article "Assaults to the Self: The Trauma of Growing Up Gay" puts forth that the constant heterosexist expectation and the equally constant erasure, to downright attack on being an LGB or gender-nonconforming child, produce symptoms that constitute psychological trauma. Consider the repercussion of *not* receiving on a daily basis LGBTQ-affirming images in childhood cartoons and movies, of not hearing bedtime stories with heroic queer characters, or of not experiencing supportive discussions around the family dinner table that accurately validate and celebrate one's unique sexual and gender expression. What starts to become clear is how the outcome of trauma to the LGBTQ sense of self is left to insidiously fester. As with any traumatic experience that does not get to be effectively processed, necessary creative psychological responses evolve to protect against a persistent lack of acceptance and recognition for developing LGBTQ youth. Defensive strategies such as projection, splitting, rationalizing, and hiding are exhibited in a client's behavior. Ultimately, these defenses are used to protect against internalized deep shame at feeling so unlovable—because of how one feels in one's body, where one's desire lies, and to whom one's erotic longing is directed.

It is no wonder, then, that by the time I was in high school, with my awareness of being different and terrified of being found out as gay (while still not acknowledging to myself that I indeed was gay), my self-preserving weapon of survival became withdrawal. I tried to be as unnoticeable as possible as I scurried from class to class immersed in deep shame and homophobia. I still feel reassured upon reading that, as Greene and Britton state, "while evidence of acceptance, integration, and pride in sexual minority identity may exist, practitioners cannot assume an absence of shame or lack of client need to address shame psychotherapeutically" (2012, p. 204). Even as the out proud person of color that I am, I am aware that the childhood indoctrination of shame on my same-sex desire cannot be fully eradicated. A more compassionate position is in acknowledging its lingering presence through the years beyond self-acceptance, sometimes creeping up in the form of depression and self-doubt. This implies that "there is still much internal work to be done; the emotional sequelae to lifelong deprivation, isolation and humiliation do not resolve themselves through social intervention alone" (Blum & Pfetzing, 1997, p. 435). Addressing toxic shame and internalized homophobia in therapy offers empowering objective understanding of these feelings, now viewed as psychic dynamics or "persons" separate from my self-worth as a gay man.

Recently, a young lesbian student came to me after a class discussion on internalized homophobia saying that she had never considered harboring this and was now inspired toward greater self-exploration. Similarly, so many of my clients have their curiosity piqued when we start to discuss their particular experience of internalized homophobia. One professionally successful gay man, always struggling with a deep need for intimacy with another man but not being able to broach this without being under the influence of some substance, found pieces of the puzzle falling into place through our sessions. We discussed how his experience of growing up gay resulted in internalized homonegativity with an emerging understanding of having needed his varied defenses, all of which were learned within the homophobic environment of his childhood.

Being terribly bullied intensified his shame and fear as a young teen. This added to the soul-crushing wounding of his developing gay sensibility secretly hidden in his wishful fantasies for love, friendship, and connection with different male classmates. To mask these confusing and powerful feelings, he feverishly worked to be the best at everything through perfectionism and overachieving and to be the most popular kid who could fit into any social circle. If he could be the chameleon that everybody liked, they wouldn't know who he really was. He was able to see that the deep feelings of unlovability he felt as a young gay boy were the result of being in a family and religious community where homophobic rhetoric was a central theme. By learning that something was done to him and was not innately sourced in him, he has begun to wonder in a more liberating way what it means to him to be a gay man. While we actively seek interventions for the substance abuse and for developing less shame-based ways of being with other gay men, this is done in the liberatory context of confronting internalized homophobia and sexual trauma as the big pink elephant in the therapy room.

Internalized oppression can manifest as depression, anxiety, relationship problems, substance abuse, eating disorders, sexual addictive behaviors, body image issues, and other self-destructive behaviors. All of these can be successfully treated in therapy with any client. And yet again, the affirming therapist is going to curiously explore how some of what the LGBTQ client walks into the room with might be also related to unexamined effects of heteronormativity.

One result of severe trauma, especially of that experienced as a child, is a deadening of feelings that cannot be effectively processed and symbolized. It becomes understandable that painful feelings generated by homophobia and heterosexism get pushed into the unconscious. This might also include erotic feelings for the same-sex other that can be confounding, overwhelming, and exciting all at once. As a result, powerful defenses can develop and maintain a grip on the LGBTQ individual long after they have served their initial purpose to protect. They now obstruct the development of rather than serve healthy identity and self-acceptance.

We know that in cases of childhood sexual abuse the defenses of numbing and dissociation frequently surface because the traumatized child is far too overwhelmed to digest or express feelings. Clients and students often relate that traumatic experiences growing up LGBTQ have had direct effects on their relationship to their sexuality and gender. Feelings of anger, hurt, rage, and fear get split off into the shadow regions of the mind and become obscured by shaming and self-judging cognitive distortions. Assisting clients in the process of befriending emotions disembodied or dismissed and forgotten is an important aspect of affirmative therapy. Lesbian activist and feminist Gloria Anzaldua describes how, as a young girl, she became separate and alienated from others and parts of herself, stating "when I got so far from my feelings, my body, my soul, I was—like other other other" (2009, p. 10). To be a truly affirming psychotherapist calls for empathic effort to create space for integration of disowned felt experience in the body and emotions impacting fervent psychological and sexual health in LGBTQ individuals.

Trauma affects one's ability to have a relationship to erotic experience on one's own terms as LGBTQ, with unique expression and meaning independent of the restrictions the heterosexist paradigm places on everyone. In support of the female and lesbian erotic, African-American author Audre Lorde wrote, "The erotic is a resource within each of us that lies in a deeply female and spiritual plane, firmly rooted in the power of our unexpressed or unrecognized feeling" (1984, p. 53) and that "the erotic is a measure between the beginnings of our sense of self and the chaos of our strongest feelings" (p. 54). The implication is that if sexuality has been deadened or repressed, then there could be a critical disruption to understanding and feeling feelings as a pathway into knowing ourselves more fully sexually, psychologically, and spiritually. Beyond sexual play, the erotic can also be seen as "psychic relatedness" (p. 65), having a conscious, even passionate interest in one's own inner life of thoughts, feelings, dreams, and fantasies.

Yet, to begin to navigate honoring one's sexuality and gender identity often means having to confront the reality of related traumatic experiences. As queer people, we often sense our difference taking us into a quest that becomes centered around the existential question "Who am I?" We can imagine this question loudly calling out from an inner voice in the psyche that yearns for authentic personhood by setting us on a path to confront the trauma of historically feeling like an alien, as less than, or apart from. As with the young lesbian student described earlier, an invitational starting place into greater self-knowing and respect can begin with questioning the powerful feelings a queer person has in response to being labeled "other," sourced in shame and homophobia.

Various models exist on LGBTQ personality development as a series of stages or phases that lead to a stable, self-affirming LGBTQ identity deemed valuable and supportive of maximal psychological, social, emotional, and sexual functioning. We can consider that healthy LGBTQ identity formation is an aspect of the process of *self-realization* for the queer person, of working to fulfill one's potential as a unique individual separate from the heteronormative collective. In that sense, another important tenet of LGBTQ-affirmative therapy can see coming out as entering into a self-becoming process of greater authenticity and integration in one's sense of self as LGBTQ.

There is currently another interesting dialectic between those claiming a value in naming an identity with those who advocate for fluidity and nonlabeling. A healthy skepticism of the impact of social structures and constructs that have rendered LGBTQ personhood powerless and inferior is certainly understandable. Rejecting those constructs can be a healthy choice—yet to deny a subjective experience of oneself *as* LGBTQ could also be a psychological vestige of the hopelessness and despair of the traumatized child whose repeated message was "Your existence is invalid." Hiding in the closet and denying one's identity is an understandable reflexive survival mechanism in the presence of profound oppression. Reenactment of this despair projected onto an LGBTQ identity that had not been sufficiently esteemed and validated may emerge in adulthood. The Two-Spirit person as a third gender in Native American culture was often sought out as the healer, ceremonial leader, or shaman. Perhaps as LGBTQ persons we are able to value our queer ability to question the masculine and the feminine, not only in terms of gender and sexuality but also as symbolic of often opposing dynamics, feelings, and experiences in the psyche. In that sense, an individuational stance could be in finding the value of exploring the *feelings* that come up in the dialectic between naming and nonlabeling. Perhaps a more queer position could also be to resist the urge to split in a black-and-white manner the *felt experience* related to the oppressive power imbalances around sexuality and gender from the *possibility* of holding forth meaningful subjectivity as LGBTQ. Could this not be a most worthwhile opportunity to explore yet another layer of the mystery of LGBTQ self-realization potential and what would stand in its way?

My own coming out as a gay man meant coming out of deeply rooted shame for my transgressive erotic longing and how I could be and live in the world, and finally taking those first steps in the direction of being more authentically true to myself. When I walked into a gay bar for the first time, I had crossed the threshold of my toxic shame and was swept up by the flashing, glittering disco ball and the magical rhythmic beat of the Pet Shop Boys and Frankie Goes to Hollywood—my world would never be the same. I had begun the process of coming out of a ravaged psychological disconnect from that whispering voice of same-sex love starting at a much younger age that I had unknowingly projected onto my father, uncles, and other men and boys. I could now instead begin to experience my erotic feelings as a source of inspiration in support of becoming a more self-respecting gay individual through a most challenging, ongoing, and yet rewarding relationship to myself. Jungian gay psychologist Mitch Walker has proposed that a "second stage of gay identity formation concerns the efficacious development of psychological awareness, the capacity to see and engage the interiorly-known world of experienced images and feelings in progressive terms of the salient developmental issues suchwise being presented for the gay person" (2009, p. 35). Fostering such exploration can be most useful for transforming what was once seen so disparagingly to building self-worth.

Through greater visibility, there is a growing understanding and acknowledgment of a wide range of queer expressions. From the lens of transgender identities, Singh and McKleroy claim we can more affirmatively "explore how individuals from historically marginalized communities demonstrate resilience in response to oppression—not to endorse this oppression, but to rather to understand how to work with these strengths in healing from these oppressive experiences" (2011, p. 35). As part of the ongoing challenge to the heteronormative binary, Rapoport affirms bisexual subjectivity in psychotherapy to create a forum where "individuals' subjective experiences are taken as the starting point, and theoretical concepts are developed in an effort to best capture these experiences" (2009, p. 293).

While words and language can be tools of oppression, perhaps "queer," "gay," "bisexual," "transgender," and "lesbian" can affirmatively be seen, by using Jungian active imagination, as persons in the psyche that can hold the position where, as Cherie Moraga says, "if the spirit and sex have been linked in our oppression, then they must also be linked in the strategy toward our liberation" (as cited in Rodriquez, 2003, p. 61).

From this affirmative point of view, being a queer person can be seen as more than a sociocultural phenomenon of modern times, by valuing the felt experience of being a "different" person in the world as a unique entryway into the emotional, psychological, and spiritual realm of one's human experience. LGBTQ visibility, communities, and rightful legal and ethical needs have been most important developments in the modern era, and there is more to be done in this regard. Following on the Stonewall Rebellion in 1969, LGBTQ individuals developed pathways to extract themselves from the imposed collectivistic confines of heteronormativity. Perhaps the momentous opportunity being presented now can be to attitudinally enter into a creative imagining that queer identities can take language, ideas, and feelings into the world of symbolic meaning within the psyche and back out again. The LGBTQ person can learn to envision a captivating relationship with the felt experience in the mind—not separate from but intimately partnered with one's daily extroverted life. In the end, perhaps the most salient and affirming gift of being a queer-identified person lies in the potential to experience psychological self-relatedness and self-fulfillment in a way that would be most useful at this moment in time. At this stage in my life as a gay Japanese-Latino man, I have a deep interest in a continuing "coming out inside" as posed by Walker (2009, p. 97), describing "gay desire as a personifying invitation by the psychological 'soul' to a life-long affair" (p. 10).

This suggests that, for me, an ongoing discovery of what it means to be gay takes homosexual expression into a deeper feltness of meaning and purpose in my existence as a gay man. I can now view the powerful attraction to a numinous same-sex other projected onto a partner or the hot man who just walked by me on the street as irresistibly symbolic of the enduring journey toward greater self-realization.

# REFERENCES

American Psychological Association. (2011). *Practice guidelines for LGB clients: Guidelines for psychological practice with lesbian, gay, and bisexual clients.*

American Psychological Association. (2015). *Guidelines for psychological practice with transgender and gender nonconforming people.*

Anzaldua, G. (2009). Spirituality, sexuality and the body. In A. Keating (Ed.), *The Gloria Anzaldua reader.* Durham, NC: Duke University Press.

Bieschke, K. J., Perez, R. M., & DeBord, K. A. (Eds.). (2007). *Handbook of counseling and psychotherapy with lesbian, gay, bisexual and transgender clients* (2nd ed.) Washington, DC: American Psychological Association.

Blum, A., & Pfetzing, V. (1997). Assault to the self: The trauma of growing up gay." *Gender and Psychoanalysis, 2*(4), 427–442.

Green, A. (2007). Queer theory and sociology: Locating the subject and the self in sexuality studies. *Sociological Theory, 25*(1), 26–45.

Greene, D., & Britton, P. (2012). Stage of sexual minority identity formation: The impact of shame, internalized homophobia, ambivalence over emotional expression, and personal mastery. *Journal of Gay & Lesbian Mental Health, 16*(3), 188–214.

Herek, G. (2004). Beyond 'homophobia': Thinking about sexual prejudice and stigma in the twenty-first century. *Sexuality Research & Social Policy Journal of NSRC, 1*(2), 6–24.

Jung, C. (1982). *Aspects of the feminine.* Princeton, NJ: Princeton University Press.

Langdridge, D. (2008). Gay affirmative therapy: A theoretical framework and defence. *Journal of Gay & Lesbian Psychotherapy, 11*(1–2), 27–43.

Lorde, A. (1984). *Sister outsider.* Berkeley, CA: Crossing Press.

McHenry, S., & Johnson, J. (1993). Homophobia in the therapist and gay or lesbian client: Conscious and unconscious collusions in self-hate. *Psychotherapy, 30,* 141–151.

Miller, S. D. (Ed.). (1996). *Partings at dawn: An anthology of Japanese gay literature.* San Francisco, CA: Gay Sunshine Press.

Nadal, K. L. (2008). Preventing racial, ethnic, gender, sexual minority, disability, and religious microaggressions: Recommendations for promoting positive mental health. *Prevention in Counseling Psychology, 2*(1), 22–27.

Paul, P., & Frieden, G. (2008). The lived experience of gay identity development: A phenomenological study. *Journal of LGBT Issues in Counseling, 2*(1), 26–52.

Peel, E. (2001). Mundane heterosexism: Understanding incidents of the everyday. *Women's Studies Ineternational Forum, 24*(5), 541–554.

Perez, R. M., DeBord, K. A. & Bieschke, K. J. (Eds.). (2000). *Handbook of counseling and psychotherapy with lesbian, gay and bisexual clients.* Washington, DC: American Psychological Association.

Rapoport, E. (2009). "Bisexuality in Psychoanalytic Theory: Interpreting the Resistance." *Journal of Bisexuality, 9,* 279–295.

Rodriguez, M. (2003). *Queer Latinidad: Identity practices, discursive spaces.* New York: New York University Press.

Singh, A., & McKleroy, V. (2011). Just getting out of bed is a revolutionary act: The resilience of transgender people of color who have survived traumatic life events. *Traumatology, 17*(2) 34–44.

Sue, D., & Capodilupo, C. (2008). Racial, gender, and sexual orientation microaggressions. In D. Sue & D. W. Sue (Eds.), *Counseling the culturally diverse: Theory and practice* (5th ed.). Hoboken, NJ: John Wiley & Sons.

Tozer, E., & McClanahan, M. (1999). Treating the purple menace: Ethical considerations of conversion therapy and affirmative alternatives. *The Counseling Psychologist, 27*(5), 722–742.

Walker, M. (2009). *Gay liberation at a psychological crossroads: A commentary on the future of homosexual ideology.* Los Angeles: Uranian Institute for Contemporary Psychoanalysis.

Williamson, I. (2000). Internalized homophobia and health issues affecting lesbians and gay men. *Health Education Research Theory and Practice, 15*(1), 97–107.

# 31

## GLEAM

*Nikkiesha N. McLeod*

**Nicodemus and the Metallic Mechanical Whale**
*There is sterility in travel.*
In the life of a transient
flyers are more attentive
more available than a mother
they cling even while you pretend to slip
their salutations through the sweatiness of a smug
refusal to their hand-out
smiling aimlessly into guilt.
Xeroxed remindful-ness
nonsensical rhymes like the gossiped
3 little pigs
waiting for wings
with the at last wolf's huff
puff
scatter
lift
fall
litter
In some states, the crack Nicodemus cooks
over an imagined 3D fire,
Peddling flyers is illegal.
A private high to renegotiate with useless ribbons
dyed in cheap concoctions
breaking the pattern of dancing alone
2 left feet in clowning lady bug red slippers.

# I.

After their journey is done with refinement, sugar pops. Sugar pops, because they look like granulated sweetness, and then I swallow and wash down. Such sweetness of theoretical arbitration, statistics that are yet to be unfolded, tumbling with glorified as an aftertaste. Then, defeated by more theories of difference; cascading through veins, scampering to the heart.

Am I going to work now? And the blunders, the random blurs, the ones that are particularly strong with their pinch, somehow sensing something else, are they going to tingle with joy? My lover, Paramour, angrily disapproves of my disposition. She said I had to have some faith. I laughed at her, because faith has just been a place I go when there's nothing else to believe.

This is my second week, and apparently the sugar should have kicked in. I can't say that I've noticed an unlikeness, but then again, maybe I'd have to dissociate myself from myself to really see what I look like.

Did that sentence make sense? Am I making sense?

*You must be.*

(Hmm...)

This is just a draft anyway. I'll return when I have another fever. With fresh dying eyes, I'll imagine a field filled with the abundant gleam of futuristic flowers and rainbows.

*There's no reason to get upset with the future... It has not done anything to you.*
(Not yet, haha...)

What was I talking about? Oh yeah, dissociation.

*But aren't we doing that right now? Maybe the key is to look at how people around you react when you do something, anything.*
(Maybe you should periodically make yelping sounds, hahaha.)
*Ah, now that can be informative.*

Even if it's based on assumptions, it's informative?

(Okay, this is boring).
*There's some level of knowing, there are tells.*

Maybe I should talk about my visit to the Cognitive Corrective Repair Clinic (CCRC), and the three words to remember: red, shoe,...?

*Yes, Yes, Yes!*
(Like you remember the third word, yeah, what's the third word? Come on now, don't disappoint, Haha.)

It was the analyst's recommendation that I visit the CCRC. (Like that would change anything. Solitary, maybe. Insular, always. Vacuum, yes! But what's the third word?)

*The analyst worked really hard, do you remember how small your eyes were? The precipice?*

The precipice. . . With all those thorns, tearing into miles of enduring. They were red at first, a rose bed, a red shedding into decades of shameful scars... (Yes, don't forget!) It may have been, in its recall, telling me what I need to know with its years of revealing, ridiculing blossoms. But I still believe in what is unexpected, happens next, if anything I'll have more data than before. (Yeah, but what type of data: spam or recycled ideations?)

*Idempotent, Idempotent, Idempotent!*

**Nicodemus and the Metallic Mechanical Whale**
*There is sterility in travel.*
Balancing the morning's potential
Nicodemus takes another sip on a foamy avoid
and another automatic take leads to a non-seductive pull
pushing out a fog of little things
then freestyle walking with the others
to the metallic mechanical whale in leather
Italian shoes--a hurtful gift to walk into—
an awkward promise
too expensive for a puzzle
too complicated by childlike bawlings
too put together for an unfinished look:
should Nicodemus get a gentleman's hair cut
some new gentleman's clothing
maybe a recycled saran wrapped ear-piece
a hobo's cup maybe?

Nicodemus finds a gigantic white suit to walk behind
a gorilla godzilla weaving through the crowd of modern mules
with galloping torsos
the elephants leap over the zebras
shitting on themselves
racing to the elevator
where the monkey grins
an inaugurated show of white teeth desperations
drones away
pushes the button
to the metallic mechanical whale
we go
we go
we go
they sing
hung-over

asthmatic
xenophobe claustrophobics
zip locked into nooks and knots
there is no air left in the X-box
the shouldered remains are an exchange
borrowed perseverance
sweetness to lull sensibilities senseless.

## II.

At the CCRC, the receptionist with her four screens; two for maintaining the live records of all old and new seekers that's directly linked to the Health Corp--the global health cartel--, and the others for calendars, directories, notices, announcements; she didn't believe my clean suit was exactly that, clean. I was the best well-dressed seeker ever. Unfortunately, I didn't win a prize for looking functional. She could care less that I wanted to look good, especially if they were going to probe my mainframe.

WELL, MAYBE IT'S BECAUSE THE RECEPTIONIST THOUGHT YOU WERE A GUY . . .

(Come on now, no more sidetracking, and who is this talking? There's no more room for You! The room is filled!).

FOCUS, FOCUS. HOCUS, POCUS!

Okay yeah, the receptionist did label me "sir." But it could be that she's a Neo-Luddite, against all forms of advancement, technology or otherwise, and refuses to do an upgrade.

THEN, HOW IS SHE NOT RELIEVED OF HER POST? HOW IS SHE NOT RELIEVED OF HER PAST? SHE'S NOT RELIEVED OF HER POST? RELIEVED OF HER POST? HER PAST? POST?

(It's the CCRC, and no one gives a shit.)
Maybe she apologized... At this point, I don't really care!

SHE DIDN'T. DIDN'T SHE? DID, DID, DID, DID, DID, DID, DID, DID, DID . . . .

(Whoever you are, shut the fuck up!)

CAN I AT LEAST SAY, MOST FUN ALL WEEK!

This is beside the point! The receptionist didn't listen to the sound wave sent to her, which said loud and clear--I was on my best behavior!

(Haha, I guess cheating, and by that, practicing using a simulation, rehearsing a script does not guarantee anything. Haha.)
I was there to see the Scientist. But the receptionist heard what she saw, and I was chased by wild geese. (Wild geese? Sure.) They were pecking my calves as I tried to escape through the double locking doors. (You never had keys for anything anyway. Lol.) With the aid of a lost janitor, I survived the trap doors and came right back where I started: at the receptionist's desk.

"I'm here to see the Scientist," I waved. The receptionist informed me that I had given her three different characters, "Each of them are unique you see," she informed me. Defending myself was useless, even in my clean suit.

HONESTLY YOUR HAIR WAS STILL QUITE MESSY.

I was waiting since 8:00am, and it was now 3:00pm, and because I was gone for awhile and the reprimand from the receptionist after, I lost my place as just a spectator. I had to sit next to an elderly lady, whom, every five minutes sent a loud wave to no one in particular, "How long have you been waiting? I've been waiting all my life. I've given up on my mainframe." I decided to move to another empty space.

There was now a prosopopoeia waving to the receptionist. His eyes were bloodshot. His wave was loudly impaired as it kept buffering. Like all of us, he came because he wanted answers. A Scientist arrived and gave the prosopopoeia a survey:

1. When was your last...?
2. How much....?
3. Do you get the...?
4. Have you ever....?

The Scientist waved that there wasn't sufficient grounds to conduct an experiment, because this seeker, the prosopopoeia, did not have any toxins seeping out of his pores like vapor. I instinctively went up to him, the prosopopoeia, and offered him some Prosecco, the good kind, because he had a reason to celebrate.

(Like that happened. You couldn't even look at "prosopopoeia." And where exactly were you hiding the "good kind" of Prosecco?)

If I had Prosecco, I would have offered it to "prosopopoeia" just so toxins could seep out of his pores like vapor!

(Stop with the superfluous lies, and get to the point.)

WHERE'S THE POINT? THERE'S A POINT? ISN'T "IS" A POINT?

A woman about my age approached me. She looked normal, I guess. (Oh come on! She seemed too content.)

*How can someone seem too content?*

I wondered if she was on sugar too. She waved, "Excuse me, sorry, but I don't think you should sit there. There was this guy sitting here, bugs were falling off of him. I think they were living on him."

I leapt up immediately, as the elderly woman like clock work chimed in, "I've given up on my mainframe. How long have you been sitting here?!"

I then thought, perhaps she (the mirror, the true normal one, that you could never aspire too, and can't!) accidentally broadcasted a corrupted simulation. Sometimes if the software is corrupted, simulations can become infected, and things like bugs may appear to be visually real. I guess the corruption might just be that good, but it will simply torment if it isn't applied to a particular purpose. (Maybe the sole purpose is to "simply torment?" And you had already decided to believe that bag biter. Spaz!) Of course I was scratching myself. (You're such a compooter! If it wasn't for me, you'd still be scratching, ha!) By the time the Provisioner came, I was over stimulated and couldn't focus.

FRUIT LOOPS, YOU'RE SO COOL

TRICK OUT YOUR HU-LA HOOPS

*Hahaha, I love that song! Where did you get the feather boa, and the hula hoop?*

GIRRRL, YOU DON'T WANT TO KNOW.

(Faggot!)

YOU'RE JUST JEALOUS BECAUSE YOU COULDN'T LOOK THIS DAMN GOOD IN A PINK LEOTARD WHILE DOING PIROUETTES!

(I'm going to swat you, I'm so going to swat you!)

HOCUS! POCUS! SHAZAM!

I was hoping for a Provisioner maybe to come instead of The Scientist... (Repeat after me: Maintain eye contact. Simulate before you wave. Make sure it's logic and not the absurd.) I wanted a Provisioner here. (Even while you shouldn't trust anyone? *Introducing: The Provisioner, right here, and right now.*) Fuck You! I'm still telling the story. I'm still in control. . . (Hahaha, somebody is upset. What makes them exactly different?) Provisioners are the middle ground, genuinely kinder and seemingly interested in more than control supplements. (Let's not forget that they are "people" with falsities of their own, and are learning from a book on how to care, yay!)

"Can you just shut-up! Shit!!" I said out loud. The Provisioner looked at me, and then continued inputting.

(You're such an asshole! They're locking us up. Now asshole. Get out. Now!)

Don't make me panic. It would just be worse, don't! I just need to smile.

The Provisioner did some tests (Dummy, are you a car?), and gave me a survey (hopefully you won't be like Prosecco prosopopoeia, haha). I'm not going to fail. Not going to end-up here again. (You will. They're going to get you, watch, just watch.)

"These are always the questions: when will the crash happen? Is it gradual, or just an immediate complete collapse? Did you prepare? And if you did, how well did you prepare? Can you quantify it? Is it qualitative once quantified?" There was a pause, and then, "Are you transitioning." I laughed. The Provisioner apologized for making me uncomfortable. I wasn't in the way that she thought, but I appreciated her attempt at inclusion. She prompted those three words to remember. I said, "Red, Shoe, ...?" I couldn't remember the last word. I must remember the last word.

## Nicodemus and the Metallic Mechanical Whale

*There is sterility in travel.*

Nicodemus makes perfect penmanship:
One last cry to say goodbye...
Those left behind
with bed sheet creases to line their faces
forever looking for that mirror
to say, to say
goodnight sun
say goodnight.

Descending deliberately deeper into the belly
an impatient metallic mechanical whale
gives many times to prepare
assorted ornaments for listlessness
discarded in a jungle of little things.
Words to blacklist, like Polished
error free sentences.
Can words collect filth
can they take a bullet?
I'll wash, then, hang them out
on my bambooed words line.
I'd like to hang ORIGINAL out to dry.
Now BRILLIANT is a word
worth moving your lips to
Drunk
ard
bRIL
LI
ANCE!!

To lose all your teeth—
Just BRILLIANT!

A day can conceive a Jezebel—
BRILLIANT!

A day can turn on a not so clever Jezebel—
BRILLIANT!

To Jump like Christopher Robbin's Tigger—
BRILLIANT!

Sing Hoorah like a Pooh Bear—
BRILLIANT!

We all fall down—
Absolutely BRILLIANT!
The metallic mechanical whale comes
just whimper like a Piglet
RED LIGHT
GREEN LIGHT
We all fall deliberately further
into the belly of the whale
it eats up time
racing through a riptide void
it comes up for air on 125<sup>th</sup>
then dives back into
BRILLIANT!

# III.

Not sure of *what* or *which*, since there are many tiny variables involved with the infliction of a spark. Just a spark of the uncomfortable, that leads to a notoriety of importance. Maybe it's the weather. Maybe it's an id-logical form for weather: a meteorologist's methodological attempt for predicting and thereupon facing a stream of fluctuating accidents to collect alongside a hyperbolic view for what was meant to be proven. There's going to be sun tomorrow, even while being chased by vampires.

(Good for you that you're so smart and everyone else is stupid! Maybe everything that you believe, that makes you so fucking smart, or fucking stupid will be a lightning bolt once you're dead and leading you to whatever! Gleeful sounds everywhere, because you're so fucking smart, and everyone else is fucking stupid. . . Dumbass!)

I overheard on Good Morning World, that there was a cure, that for most, the change in spells and owning a pet will xandu, xerophagy these times of caustic, dysphoric Black Bile afflictions. Or maybe sugar pops will be the cone's coin for the end, and its recurring nightmares. Maybe there's a mixture for all these things: Weather, Black Bile, Vampires. Nightmares of a panoramic dysphoric? (Dumbass!)

All I remember was my heart and mind were in a race together, which can go faster than my motions in real time. And all I could hear there, louder and angrier than ever before does not have any sympathy, nor any trace of my love for the things I learned while I was most broken. There was not any space for that.

(Of-course, you believe when it is occasional. Like a season you have plums. You don't feed in half belief when you know there won't be any plums. You don't believe in something that does not exist. Why would you?)

That's because you wouldn't stop talking.

(It's what I do best darling… You wouldn't clip a bird's wings, or lock him up in a cage when flying is the best thing he can do? Or would you?)

Paramour was already dressed and trying to ignore the pace I was going at. I was rambling something with conviction, and she casually agreed. I felt her kissing my cheek as I laid on the sleep levitator with my eyes closed, head hot with information. I then heard the front door opened and closed. I wanted to beg her not to leave me alone with him. But I didn't want her to worry. I told myself to suck it up.

He was rummaging through all of the clouds of possible infinites. Like a defined motion, he swung and laid eggs on each cloud. Until festooned on the rotting ones, he felt sure I couldn't escape their viruses.

(First, you'd be relieved from your paradox, and replaced by many small, but very distinct diversiform fragments. After a month or so of no harvest moon, Paramour will leave you for Atlantis, the Information Scientist. LOL! You'd have to move out, but where to? You'd probably end up like the homeless woman you see everyday at the teleport. Hair all in a mess like it never ever saw a comb. Dirty with duck tape wrapping around your infected leg. And yes, you'd scream, dance, and do whatever for anything. You know, she's probably around your age. LMAO, destitution really sucks. Eventually, you'd lose it and assault a pedestrian. Then finally, you'd be banished. Now if you listen to me, things won't have to go this far, don't pass go, don't collect $200 won't even have to apply to you ever again.)

Knowing what his solution was, I decided to wave the analyst,

"Hello, hello…," and then my sonic Bluetooth chip lost the signal. I waved again, nothing. And again, until finally the analyst waved me back.

"Hello, Nicodemus?" Here is where everything becomes a blur. All I remember is my head overheating. And the door was letting in five Robo-commandos. I offered them coffee, and waved, "Do you like micro-organic eggs, scrambled micro-eggs?" They were indifferent. But really, was it me, or him offering Robo-commandos coffee, waving if they liked micro scrambled eggs? (What does it matter now who offered them coffee, and who gives a fuck about micro fucking eggs? That future is dead.)

Getting down to the console hub area, the built-in support was waving with five more Robo-commandos. I wasn't embarrassed then. No, in a strange way I was excited, but I wasn't sure what I was excited about. We were getting close to the door, and I was trying not to trigger my flight simulation program, where I run up the block as fast as Neo from the Matrix. So, I created a simple pop-up code in my mainframe, a cute funny distraction that waved, "I feel like one of our luminary deities needing protection from the Web-Paps with their web-cam eyes waiting to take 'The Picture'." One of the Robo-commandos, however, read deeper in the code of the cloud, and overrode the code I was using to distract them. He demanded that we wait in the lobby for the airbus's arrival. (Ha, like anyone ever outran a Robo-commando, at least not all 10 of them in a hail storm.)

On the airbus, I was incredibly chatty with the Robo-Emergency Action Figures (R-EAF). I was hoping to overload their inboxes with instant messages. I've never been that chatty even in a chat room. (That's because you could never cloud that up by yourself. Using your tabs as an evasion tacit to open up chat windows instead of going into a sleep mode which you cloud could stop them...ROFL. Don't fret my darling, we've been through this before.)

Oh my darling
Oh my darling
Oh my darr-ling alkaline
You are lost and gone forever
Oh my darling alkaline

*I do not know what this folk reference is suppose to mean, and when did you learn guitar? Either way, you may not want to be involved here.*

I'mma just lightening up the clouds chica! Just lightening up the clouds.

And did that really help? Like we could stop their advanced cookies from tracking those cloud waves, as they ran a diagnostic on our cerebral cortex. Even with all the pop-ups, they read those cloud waves and they made their assessment, and gave no reply to my invitation for coffee that day.

At some point, one of them asked if I had anyone they should contact. I sonic waved Paramour. She was in high court when I interrupted with my inappropriate euphoria. She panicked as I laughed nonsensically.

Once I arrived at the Panopticon, I waited for my preliminary interview. Robo-takers (RTs) did the interview. RTs never make eye-contact. The first RT ran a diagnostic on my mainframe. Questions that I rudely re-routed to the RT's inbox. Useless. I was becoming more anxious, looking for ways to escape. Once the preliminary interview was over, they took me to my second (oh yeah, this is a job interview!), where I was asked the same questions again. I gave them shit (good for you for showing, demonstrating your worth, idiot!) for the obvious lack of communication between their servers. I was becoming less charming and entertaining, and more irritable and a nuisance. I kept pushing escape buttons while the RT scanned my body for any irregularities. They wanted to make sure I was healthy enough for the experiments that the Scientists were to perform. They discovered that my heart rate was unusually high. I joked that my unusual heart rate was due to probing overload. They asked if I used any accelerant RAM. "Never, only elixirs. Accels would completely overload my mainframe, and I'd crash," I giggled. It was becoming difficult to sit still and to hold back the laughter.

They took my Earth shoes (Earth shoes? Haha!) and gave me their socks with traction at the base. Then, they escorted me to the hermetic cluster, where the others were. ("Hermetic cluster?" "Others?" You're just like who they are!)

The Panopticon was exactly what you'd think a Panopticon to be: with us, there were RTs locked inside the circular space of the Panopticon, and even though the watch tower wasn't high above the clouds, the eye was still capable of seeing everything. Somewhat like the eye of Sauron from Lord of the Rings.

(Glad that this description is so depictive in its details of what exactly what a Panopticon looks like. . . Maybe we need the guy who actually thought of this first to be resurrected and draw a better picture of what it looks like. Maybe, just maybe we need a prison inmate's perspective?)

I was introduced to the head RT on shift. His face was emotionless and cold (what happens can never be predicted by what you assume or expect! You can continue to try however, haha). I timidly walked into the cluster, where everyone was downloading. There was a woman waving loudly in a thick New York accent,

"I'm not going to stand this sort of treatment anymore. For 20 years they've been probing me. I know the Governor, wait until he hears about this."

Then this kid, who couldn't be more than 18, yells back, "Shut up already!"

"All these probing and experiments... For 20 years... I refuse this non-sense."

"Well then go, no one wants to hear about it. Damn yo!"

"Do you want an apple?" A guy with a huge scar across his face waved me. I was startled by his sudden appearance, and didn't dare look him in the eye when I waved no. (Hahaha, that's because you were afraid. Why are you afraid?)

I maintained all of the impulsive neurons signalling that I should start singing a song, like the one my mother sang everyday, "*Oh what a friend we have in Jesus.*" The giggling was insatiable, the worst to subdue. But I was still in control. I wasn't going to give up. I remember the old woman at the CCRC. I started to giggle a little. I took a deep breath and mumbled. "I'm not going to give up on my mainframe." (Maybe your mainframe gave up on you, chuckles.)

"Just shut-up, alright." One of the RTs tried to scan my clouds, but I caught her eyes just in time to divert to another page.

Knowing was terrifying, knowing that anything could happen here in the Panopticon. I had to get out and before sleep mode sat in. My head was throbbing, like the walls of the skull were closing in on everything pertinent for a muscled escape. I waved to the nurse, "How long are they going to keep me?"

"If you do exactly what we say and take your control supplements, you will be out of here in no time." I got the feeling that it was a hologram I was speaking to not a real nurse.

In the Panopticon, you're allowed 15 minutes on a regular payphone. I called the analyst, "You have to get me out of here. I don't belong here, my mainframe is salvageable, but if I stay here it will die." "Nicodemus, do you remember our agreement. Do you remember the contract you signed?" Pause.

"Well, do you?" "I do, I do, but this isn't the time for contracts and who waved what. I can't stay here." "I'll see what I can do, but I'm not hopeful. The things the R-EAF discovered on your mainframe were disturbing." "Just try!"

I heard my entire title being waved, "Nicodemus of South America," I turned, and it was the head RT.

"You have a visitor," and he escorted me to the visitor room that was covered in spy-ware. It was Paramour. We embraced. She looked like she was about to break down. I held her firmly.

"Are you ok?"

"Yes, I just need to get out of here."

"I spoke to the analyst... She doesn't think they will let you go. The things on your mainframe make it less likely. Do you remember what you waved?"

"No. I lost all the footage for some weird reason. It's there but as soon as I try accessing those scenes, my memory starts skipping or freezes up."

"Your mainframe is getting worse." "I know," I snapped, and then quickly held her hand apologizing. She started to cry. "Para, please don't... Not here... I'm sorry you have to see me like this."

### Nicodemus and the Metallic Mechanical Whale

*There is sterility in travel.*

To avoid everything shameful

in a little thing as a look can reveal

while riding the metallic mechanical whale

Nicodemus discovers the wonders of anonymity.

When asked why the dark shades

Nicodemus, irritated, takes them off and renders:

*There's nothing worse than a loquacious eye*

*blinking when they're unsure of what's coming*

*backstabbing eyes*

*darting back into tortoise shells of*

*Of Course, Of Course!*

*Indeed, Indeeds!*

*One day*

*we'll congregate in the metallic mechanical whale*

*wearing nothing but baby powder. And in a circle of all of us*

*we'll each have turns*

*Saying, "TADA! Think Josephine Baker."*

Wearing necessary discoveries

Nicodemus becomes a fly

on a wall in a room

the whale's hard plastic mirrors

gives many eyes as a fly
on a wall in a room
witnessing the fleeting speed of gossip
spying for secrets:
knickers exposed
mouths open
buggered noses

Nicodemus the ethnographic scientist:
*What's the difference between*
*a zombie in a zoot suit and a bullfrog*
*hoping, hoping, to make it to the nearest exit?*

Hushed! into a little thing
fitting nicely in a palm, in a pocket
iPods, disc men, walk men hands
bury the most imitated moment
the intoxicating high of death.

Hushed! into a little thing
Nicodemus mediates electric
staring at Billy Graham's poster
"God. Loves. You." Next to graffiti scribbles
"Are you a sinner? I'm afraid so!"
Magnetic in the fingers
toes
weird looking circuits
hungrily standing bold
burning on the chest.
Caught in fitful fantasy
the main event explodes
as shoulders are gone first
showing off an offering
tap
tap
tap
yes
yes
yes of the feet and head in deserted praise.

# IV.

"I do not think watching Star Raiders is going to change the chemistry. For the time being, I may find appeasement, but am I to propitiate that I'm suppose to watch or do something constantly throughout the every millisecond of existence, something outside of what is "real," in order to stay in that moment of changing that chemistry? Maybe I should be a Star Raider if that's the case. It says by the way that you are an enabler of fallacies, and you have not fully understood anything. Just to be clear, since everything is repeated in a vastness of pick and choose jumble: the *which* and *what* are going to end, and *supposed* will be a happenstance for those severity of *which, what, when, why*? As again and again, even *while* it is *supposedly* over, in the after awaken-ness of dreams perhaps, so it is locked in mainframes as a touchy space. That still reboots along with the semblance of progressive ideology? When blankety-blank dirt is never silent, nor captive to accursed, ill produced amnesia.? The idea of sleep is not even a possibility, unless in complete death. You might want to differentiate, or possibly rethink these ideas? These long held ideas of what relativity truly exhibits: an unknown form, which we make up as walking and trying to understand the language of a bird. Because it is a necessary illusion of many allusions to what is *supposed*. Resting is maybe a better thought. Daily resting. And clearly I have rested on this idea of sleep, and if you cannot provide something other than watching Star Raiders to the most simple of a long list, then I proved my point of why I should not be here. Also, if I am going to have to depend on fictional pictures as a means for escaping my own friction, then those champions should at least know how to act honest. Like an actual human being. . . Not like an android, but a human being or whatever that is. That's just my first thought to your recommendation."

*There is nothing kind about existence. What you ascribe as not being a human being is exactly what is human, maybe you would have better success saying adult: learned, learned, learned . . .*

(Exactly!)

*Certainly do not agree with your solution, Eye! Certainly not, and Trevor is on my side by the way.*

Wait? What? First of all, I don't go by that name anymore. I am Shangó . . .

(Found yourself, lately?)

Excuse me . . . ? I was not finished, and I will use my double-edged axe to cut you!

*There is no need for that Trevor. . . I mean Shangó. There is a thing called logic.*

Glad you got it right the second time bitch! As I was trying to say, I have no alliances to anyone, and that clearly seems more logical to me, Claire!! . . . There is no remedy for chaos, and that is why I'm going dancing. If you want to come, and I mean CLAIRE!! Not you Eye, you're welcomed to join.

(I am THERE, dumbass!)

"All of this is exhausting."

"What do you mean?" The Scientist asks.

"All of this fighting."

"Who is fighting?"

"No one . . . "

I am not here to prove anything. What I really want does not live here or any of your places. (Oh, so special. Maybe make a story time special for everyone?)

I don't want it. I don't want yous, because all that is awful lives in yous. . . I don't believe in after. . . I don't, but I want to be burnt, just so I know for sure that I will never come back here as anything. (So, so pure, and such innocence derived? But anyway, glad though that you finally realized what I was saying.)

### Nicodemus and the Metallic Mechanical Whale
*There is sterility in travel.*
In the belly of the metallic mechanical whale
it eats up time
blue lightening
thundering through caves.
Another whale rides next to Nicodemus's.
Looking in
seeing nothing but an overpriced pastry dish

Nicodemus diddles:
*Just as neighbors ought to be*
*this is yours and this is mine*
*we'll be pleasant in the living area*
*and say, "How do you do?"*
*We'll each have our own cupboards*
*to put the complaints in.*

# NOTES

Seeker became self conscious once brought to her attention that she was sweating. I believe this is related to the question on the subject as to why and what she believes led up to her arrival here. As much as she tried to hide her agitation, Seeker seemed to be in an array of dialogs with herself. Seeker inadvertently mentioned the following characters: Trevor, Claire, and I believe Paramour. Also mentioned, CCRC, Robo-commandos, Scientists, and something regarding either her physical eye or "I" as in herself, which apparently plays a key role? We examined Seeker's eyes and they were completely intact and functional. Seeker seems fearful of revealing the most common of things, such as domestication. It seems Seeker is mostly disturbed by the past, and tries to dissuade any questions that are related to the past? I believe that is a starting point, as Seeker's thoughts were clearly interrupted, and she seemed to have struggled with an answer when asked again, "What brought you here?" Seeker is apparently aware of some sort of pattern on avoidance, and clearly has trust issues. I believe we will find most of the painful things for this Seeker to reveal with this question. As it is also obvious that Seeker is not telling us everything. Seeker blurted out stop randomly several times throughout the interview when there was no one there. She however immediately looked at me when I made her aware that I heard her, and that was the first time Seeker actually was capable of maintaining any eye contact. My assessment is that Seeker is hiding what is really happening internally in order to get out. My recommendation is that we keep Seeker here for more assessment. I think Seeker Z10101010101010101010101010 1010 . . . is a great subject for our research!

## PART V

# The Poetics of Mental Health and Wellness

# 32

## OUTLIER
## THE AGORAPHOBIA FRAGMENTS

*Kevin Shaw*

The spontaneity must now be rehearsed, doctors order.
I should tell my friends and lover:
surprise me next Thursday.

To learn to whim takes practice.
*

Monday:
"Try taking the bus,
try not taking the pills, and
if you're feeling up to it,
buy groceries, try
not to abandon the basket in the aisle—"

Is today mundane or Tuesday?
*

To call the hinge of light a morning, a choice:
I can stand in line or stay in stanzas.

But there's beauty on the early bus:
bricolage of coffee cup and waxed moustache.
*

Overheard: "The word
'agoraphobia' means,
like, literally,
the 'fear of the marketplace.'"
From the open textbook on a lap, the answer
for the test.

And if I didn't speak on the cuff,
and go in on limbs,
I'd tell them a good day means
like, literally,
an unspoiled carton of cream.
*

Anti-explorer, I chart in reverse
marking the known places as the ones to fear.

I write *here be monsters*
across an ocean of empty hours
blue as the iPhone's porny glow.
*

Does a guy still exist when he leaves his square on the grid?
*

The artist at his opening says
he's really getting into ideas of space lately.
I say I'm working on getting out more.

And after the opening: a bar
where a drunk guy keeps
proclaiming himself, unfashionably,
the bomb.

It's the pseudonymous double
agents of the after-hours
who put the fear of your blood
in you, but—

"You're always so negative."

Above the urinal, a lipstick scrawl:
*Too much cock,*
*not enough action!*

Take cover and cologne for a dollar.
I know I'm not the bomb,
but the shelter.

# 33

## WERE YOU CONFUSED AS A CHILD?

*Stephen Mead*

As with everything else in my life, I was a late bloomer in actively pursuing mental healthcare for depression, anxiety, suicidal ideation, and agoraphobia stemming from years of bullying. When I was growing up, these terms were not in any sort of common lexicon, and I was taught my mental/emotional suffering was something weak, to be ashamed of, and kept hidden like homosexuality itself. This image is a good starting point for understanding the dialogue at that time. The title "Were You Confused as a Child?" employs something of a gallows humor in regards to what a therapist—or a proponent of conversion therapy—might ask a person. The mixed-media imagery of the piece plays with that, as well as with the central detail of a little boy putting on lipstick while also pointing a gun to his head while, on either side of him, two bare-chested cowboy figures are looking down at their genitals as if pondering what *that* might all be about. It is a semi-comedic, lyrical piece meditating on years of pain brought on by societal straight-jacketing.

FIGURE 33.1 "Were You Confused as a Child?" by Stephen Mead.
Stephen Mead

# 34

## PLEASURE-BASED PARENTING

### Crista Anne

I never planned on being a mother.

Came of age as a queer woman in the late Nineties, listening to Ani Difranco while tirelessly updating Angelfire sites with my angry ranting against the patriarchy long before the term "blog" was invented. Finding a home for myself at the dawn of queer porn on the Internet, learning to love myself as I surrounded myself with other queer naked people breaking boundaries and fucking with conventional beauty standards. Sneering at heteronormativity. I was childfree, staunchly anti-marriage. Proud black sheep of my family. My sister could provide the grandchildren, I was on my own path. Happily fucking my way through life, my ultimate dream was to spend my days with a revolving door of friends and lovers.

I came out of the womb depressed, but I also came out of the womb with a hand on my clit. My sexuality was my power. Masturbation was my coping mechanism. After stepping away from queer porn—it had gone too mainstream for me—I found my calling in life behind the counter of sex shops. Preaching the power of masturbation, of owning your sexuality, owning your orgasm. I was a force to be reckoned with—if I had a dildo in my hand, my depression and anxiety melted away. A sexual superhero. Carol Queen's brand of sex-positivity became my gospel. A gospel I proudly spread to any and all who would listen to me.

My stores were located deep in the heart of Texas, where, at the time, selling sex toys was illegal. The possibility of jail time for selling a vibrator was absurd to me and I embraced my new label of "outlaw dildo peddler." I was here, I was queer, I had a vibrator on my clit. Unstoppable force. The power of my work kept my depression at bay. It was easy to push past my brain's desire to never get out of bed when I knew that people needed my passion and expertise to find the perfect sex toys for their bodies. There was nothing else I wanted to do with my life but spend every waking moment surrounded by dildos, working with my customers, picking up beautiful women along the way.

My plan was blown to bits, though; circumstances changed and I was no longer able to stomach the "boys club" that ran the sex shops. Burned every bridge possible as I left my career in a blaze of righteous rage. Their refusal to carry LGBT-friendly products, binders and packers, to make trans clients feel comfortable within the walls of my sanctuary was too much. I refused to be complicit in the exclusion of those I viewed as my people.

Without my career, the beast of depression ate me alive. After an extended hazy period of not being able to get out of bed, feeling the devastating loss of identity to my very core, I packed two suitcases and ran away from my life. Taking a "vacation" to see my mother across the country from which I would never return. Suddenly I was adrift, feeling homeless and without any sense of self.

Depression lies. Depression lies to you endlessly, and eventually all I knew were those lies that depression told me. I was worthless, useless, my dreams had shattered, and I would never find the happiness I'd known again. All I had left was a powerful libido, which I overindulged in by hooking up with an ex-boyfriend from my teens. He was drawn to my queer identity, taking pleasure that this queer woman was interested in fucking him. Mistakenly, I took his silence in response to my queer politics as agreement. That he understood where I was coming from and respected my desire to never be tied down. Respected my stance on open relationships, that I would never be owned as a wife. We were having a grand time together, and through an endless stream of orgasms I began to see the light of myself returning.

If I couldn't run sex shops, I'd combine my love of blogging with sex. Sex blogging brought me closer to myself again. The depression was starting to ebb, and more and more I was feeling myself return. I could breathe again.

Then my period disappeared. My depressive recklessness meant that I had not been as careful with safe sex as I always had. After my offhand comment about being late, we made a midnight trip for a pregnancy test (which I thought a waste of money) and menstrual supplies. That second line appeared before I had finished peeing.

I was pregnant.

After staring at that fucking pregnancy test for what felt like hours, I let him in to see. While I was filled with shock and dismay, he filled with expectant father pride. Within an hour he'd called everyone he knew to share the joyous news that we were having a baby.

We were having a what now? I stared blankly at the phone in his hand. We're having a baby? Oh no, an abortion is what we're having. Have you met me? I'm not having a baby. I'm not cut out to be a mother. This isn't happening. Slow down.

Those words hit deaf ears. We weren't aborting HIS child. It would be fine! I could still write with a baby! He'd be up at night with the child, he'd be there for everything! It wasn't a change of identity, it was a new adventure! Obviously though, we had to get married. There was no way that prenatal care would be affordable unless I was on his health insurance. People get married for the benefits all the time! It's no big deal. Nothing would really be changing.

Nothing would be changing, except everything would be changing. Depression mixing with pregnancy hormones? The gains I'd made at finding myself again were gone. More lost than I fathomed someone could be, I stopped fighting and gave in. Okay, motherhood. I guess that's something I haven't done before. Getting married? Whatever. Yeah, health insurance would be nice, I guess.

In a blink of an eye I was in a white dress, saying "I do" in my grandmother's back yard with an almost-showing baby belly. I was a "wife." Looking at the pictures from the wedding, you can clearly see the blank terror in my eyes. I was no longer living my life, I'd stepped into this mirror universe. The only input I made to the wedding was to pick out a thrifted wedding dress, an absurdly over-the-top gown. Everything about my life was suddenly laughable, so I might as well go with the most unbelievable dress possible.

While the pregnancy was uneventful, uncomplicated, I was horrified by the changes to my body. Quiet horror at my life. As shocked, scared, and horrified as I was, my husband was ecstatic. He was at every prenatal visit, speaking twice as much as I did. The baby's heartbeat was unreal. Ultrasounds looked nothing like a baby, an oddly shaped blob that was now dictating my every action. As my stomach expanded, it felt like an alien had taken hold of my abdomen. Once she started moving within me my husband admitted that he no longer saw me as a sexual creature, but as the beautiful mother of his child.

The last bits of my sense of self shattered to the ground. My queerness, my sexual power, my ideals were all gone. I now lived in a suburban apartment, a stay-at-home, soon-to-be mother. My words left me. Everything left me. All I had left was this ever-expanding belly and a husband who day by day became an even more proud father-to-be. Each and every day I fell more and more into that life by which I had always been horrified. From queer sexual superhero and outlaw dildo peddler to the very picture of perfect heteronormative suburban life.

Oh, how I tried to embrace it. I was going to be a mom, but I'd raise my child to be an open-minded oddball like me. An unconventional weirdo who'd eventually work with me to smash the status quo! Once I got through the pregnancy, once I had my little weirdo in person, then I could start to get back to myself. Plenty of parents have careers! All was not lost. We could move into the city, I would find other unconventional parents. All was not lost.

Halfway through the baby baking process, we moved cities for my husband's job. He was the only person I knew, and my alienation grew. Folks that I met in my upper-middle-class apartment complex seemed to each be more cookie-cutter than the last.

Depression grew, hormones became more intense. As my belly expanded to the point that I could only waddle, my husband morphed from a fellow radical into a Fifties-era father. The house had to be kept up, I was expected to cook the meals, wash his clothes, put together the perfect nursery. Keeping up appearances took all my time. My identity was gone. Lost forever. This was all I had, so make the best of it.

My daughter exploded into the world just before midnight. I'd taken all the drugs they'd give me through her labor, I birthed her as an out-of-body experience. During my hospital stay, my husband changed all the diapers, showed her off proudly to all our visitors while I smiled through a haze of Percocet. Worry creeping up my spine as the time to take her home drew closer. I had this beautiful baby, but I had no idea what to do with her.

One of the few parenting decisions I felt strongly about was breastfeeding; I was adamant she'd not have any formula. Upon getting home, she nursed every forty-five minutes, refusing to latch unless I was sitting up. Sleep deprivation began to eat away at the little bit of sanity I had left. Five days after her birth, I was sitting on our couch trying to get her to latch upon a breast while panic filled me. This was the worst decision I'd ever made, but there were no take-backs. Blissfully, continued sleep deprivation soon ate away at my ability to feel panicked, to feel depressed, to feel anything at all.

My husband quickly returned to work, family left to go back to their lives. The first day I was alone with my daughter, I sobbed for ten hours straight. For the first six weeks of her life she continued to nurse every forty-five minutes, and I never slept for more than fifteen to twenty minutes at a time. My husband became obsessed with being the "provider," throwing himself into work. I zombied through my days. There was nothing within me but Mom Bot, milk machine. Everything was lost, but I didn't have enough within me to care. I could no longer feel powerful, no longer could remember anything before my life was endless diapers and nursing sessions.

Three months into her life, I realized that I was more than "just" depressed, that postpartum depression was eating me alive. Telling no one, I monitored my thoughts for signs of being suicidal or wanting to harm the baby. Those did not manifest; I was too exhausted. Feeling suicidal took more energy than I had.

I have almost no memory of the first six months of her life beyond the realization that I was lost to postpartum depression. Magically, at this point, she began to sleep for extended periods. Thus I did, too. Awoke from my haze, married to a complete stranger, living the life that I'd always railed against. I was trapped in the perfect picture of my personal hell, feeling that I had no idea how I'd gotten there, knowing that I had to get out.

First, I tried to regain some sexuality. Even if it was heterosexuality, I needed to be a sexual creature again. My husband only saw me as the mother of his child, and our sex life was virtually nonexistent. He found my attempts at sexiness to be amusing rather than arousing. He'd lost interest in touching me. I consoled myself with the fact that I'd never really liked dick all that much anyway.

Masturbation and fantasies of having queer sex again were my first steps at finding myself again. Baby sleeping? I'm in the other room jerking off to queer porn. Soon I began sex blogging again, reaching out to my friends working in the sexuality field. Talked my husband into covering my re-entry to the sex toy world via sex toy parties with a company that my mentor and favorite educator started.

I was still deep within postpartum depression, still lost in the bizarre life I was leading, but sparks of my true self began showing. I cut my hair short again. Went back to wearing heavy eyeliner, threw away my "mommy clothing" in favor of short skirts and tank tops. Reached out to sex toy retailers who had progressive politics like my own so I could review toys for them. Attended conferences covering sexuality and feminism. Wrote daily about sex toys, sexuality, promoting sex-positive causes. Thrilled beyond words that there was some of me left inside.

This alienated my husband further, but I'd given up on our relationship. The first local friend I made, someone who had also worked in sex toy retail, became his mistress. I pretended that I didn't know because, for the most part, I didn't care. She and I had a falling out over her attraction to him, and I knew that they'd continued a relationship behind my back. He was happier and easier to deal with during the brief periods he was home. Their affair gave me more time to write, more time to escape into my world, talk to my people.

As my daughter grew, began showing her personality, I fell deeply in love with her. Mothering became more enjoyable. Sure, my marriage was a sham, but it turned out that I was an awesome mom. More of myself grew. The more I grew, the more I wrote, the more I was able to escape into educating about pleasure-based sex education, the happier I became. Postpartum depression was still there, but it was finally manageable. Finally, I felt ready to get into the world again. I identified as a Queer Mom, finally a label that I could embrace.

So, I stepped out of my house and began finding other alternative mother groups in the area. I jumped into these groups with both feet, expecting to find other queer moms like me. Oh, how wrong I was. Once inside their world I discovered that while they claimed open-mindedness, they were advocating heteronormative life with intense shaming of anyone who parented differently than they did. Upon discovering that I both fed my child baby food from the store and had a queer sexual identity, I was quickly expelled from their ranks. I was both too conventional and far too weird for them. I might infect their children with "the gay" or feed them nonorganic food. Goodness knows which of those was the greater sin, but I was certainly unwelcome.

Once expelled from the alternative moms, I began to seek out other queers. There is a vibrant LGBTQ+ community in my city, so I had hopes that I could push through my deep depression and find some acceptance within their ranks. There was acceptance to be found, until my status as a married mother was disclosed. Again, I was unwelcome—this time as a fake queer. It didn't matter that my marriage was a sham, I was now too straight to be trusted. Again, I was expelled.

Depression ate me alive again, the gains I had made were washed away. Poured every ounce of energy into being the best mother I could be to my wonderful daughter, completely neglecting myself. I ate because I was breastfeeding, but neglected any self-care that didn't impact my ability to mother. Completely stopped reaching out to anyone for friendship, I felt hopeless and unlovable. Lost between worlds, feeling that no community would ever accept me. Too queer for straight moms, too straight-passing for the gay community.

For the first time in more than a decade, I loathed my sexuality. Climbing back in the closet wasn't an option, but I desperately wanted to. Felt that my queerness would forever keep me an outcast from the straight world, that my being a mother would forever keep me from the queer community. Suicidal thoughts took over, but thankfully the demands of a toddler kept me too busy to act on my impulses. I hit one of the darkest points of my life, alienated on all sides.

At the deepest of that darkness, I did reach out to an online friend. He was also a poly queer with small children. Discovering that I was not completely alone, that there was another outcast from the various spheres, saved me. As he and I grew closer, my marriage came to its natural end. After years of depression and self-loathing, finding another queer parent gave me the courage to reclaim my life. I left my husband; we divorced amicably with a shared custody arrangement.

That other queer parent became my life partner during the next few years. We've built a vibrant blended family together. We both battle depression, we both have deeply felt like outcasts in both queer communities and straight alike. Together we've built a strong support system for each other. Helping the other out of the darkness. Recently, with his help, I decided to try medication for my depression again, wanting to be the best parent and partner I can be. Amazingly, it works wonderfully for me. For the first time in my life, I am not actively depressed.

As I'm finally experiencing life without active depression, I've found a vibrant community of "Queer Slut Moms" hiding under the surface of social media. Wonderful, supportive, and understanding folks who can relate to the challenges of parenting as a queer with mental illness. As I continue down this unconventional path, their support gives me the confidence that I'd so lacked before.

I still harbor a lot of grief that I spent so much of the early days of my daughter's life so lost to depression. She's grown into an incredible little person, compassionate and powerful. As my depressive symptoms have lifted, she's noticed a difference in Mommy. We've started talking about how brains can get sick just like bodies do, that Mommy has an illness in her brain and that she's on medicine that's helping it get better. That Mommy has always had this illness and that she probably always will, but that none of it is her fault.

As she grows understanding, I hope that the open dialogue between us will mean that if or when she feels the symptoms of mental illness, she'll be able to talk to me about it. We've covered my sexuality in the same way. She's grown up in a world surrounded by people of all orientations who love her, where people are appreciated for who they are above all else.

Antidepressants obviously are not the solution for everyone, and I'm very aware that this may not keep my symptoms at bay forever. For now, I am enjoying this break from the darkness as much as I can, while nurturing a strong support network that I can lean on if it returns. Most importantly, I know above all else that I am not alone in my situation or my struggles. You are not alone either.

# 35

## DOCTOR ANONYMOUS
## A PLAY, AND A LESSON IN MEDICAL ETHICS

*Guy Fredrick Glass*

I believe there is something to the idea of our being drawn to the mental health field as a result of our own issues. As a psychiatrist, I know that my own coming out felt like having a tremendous weight taken off my chest. Afterwards I experienced a sense of liberation that was so profound I knew I wanted to spend my life helping other people feel the same way. I was fortunate with my own psychoanalyst in that I found someone progressive and open-minded. However, as an older heterosexual man, he was not the role model for whom I was looking, and I lacked direction. Somehow, in the days before the internet, I managed to find out about the Association of Gay and Lesbian Psychiatrists, and I showed up at a meeting in San Francisco. It blew my mind to find dozens of young shrinks there just like myself. I became aware there was something new called "gay affirmative psychotherapy." I then got permission to invite Richard Isay to address my residency class, and as a result Isay became a mentor who urged me to come to New York. My direction was clear: I hung out my shingle and practiced in Manhattan for many years.

Time went by, and I needed to find a means for creative expression that was not being fulfilled by my clinical work. When one makes one's living talking to people, it's not surprising to discover that one has a facility for writing dialogue. So I began to write plays. While at first I kept psychiatry separate from my playwriting, gradually I sought a topic that would enable me to integrate my two personas. Enter John E. Fryer, a gay psychiatrist who, under the name Dr. H Anonymous, had famously outed himself at a 1972 meeting of the American Psychiatric Association. A year later homosexuality was removed from the DSM. These events provided the inspiration for my play *Doctor Anonymous*, ultimately produced at the Zephyr Theatre in West Hollywood in 2014.

*Doctor Anonymous*, by Guy Glass, published by Heartland Plays, Inc. Excerpt reprinted by permission of the author.

When a production ends, most plays are forgotten. Finding a way to make the message of *Doctor Anonymous* thrive has become a preoccupation. In a nutshell, I have given up my practice and am now an educator who specializes in synthesizing theater and medicine. As such I use *Doctor Anonymous* to teach bioethics as it relates to the mental health treatment of LGBTQ individuals. In addition to the Dr. Fryer story, other themes are developed; for example, Matthew Goldstein, a young psychiatrist, undergoes gay conversion therapy. The following snippets from *Doctor Anonymous* (the complete play is published by Heartland Plays, 2014) give one a sense of Matthew Goldstein's journey. In my teaching I use video excerpts from my production alongside vintage images and video to set the historical context.

At the play's outset, we find ourselves in the Philadelphia office of Dr. Edward Bergman, where Matthew is being interviewed as a candidate for psychoanalytic training. His credentials are impeccable, but the interview turns into an ordeal when Bergman unearths something very personal. In 1968, psychoanalysis was the predominant treatment modality, and a young psychiatrist really needed the training to get ahead. Some managed to get through by misrepresenting themselves; others were weeded out. At this point in the scene, Matthew's efforts to evade his interviewer have become futile, and he drops his façade:

EDWARD

You have been keeping an iron grip on things for such a long, long time. Hoping it would make the feelings go away. But they haven't, and they won't. Haven't you? Haven't you?

MATTHEW

(*In a whisper*) How did you know?

EDWARD

My son. You don't have to feel as if you're carrying the world on your shoulders.

*MATTHEW holds back tears and turns his head away. EDWARD goes to him and puts his hand on his shoulder.*

EDWARD

I cannot accept you into the program.

MATTHEW

(*Gasping*) I can't believe this is happening to---

EDWARD

But if you are willing to change, I can take you into treatment. You have a personality disorder that is eminently treatable. You will be in the most capable hands in Philadelphia. Conversion therapy is the bread and butter of my practice.

MATTHEW

I have never not done well at something in my life. How will I face my colleagues, my friends? If there is some way I could audit, I would---

EDWARD

You really want this.

MATTHEW

I want it with all my heart and soul.

EDWARD

And you are a mensch. Anyone can see that. It will be as simple as . . . getting a vaccine.

Four years have passed. Matthew has long since dropped out of therapy. In spite of his indoctrination, he manages to enter into a romantic relationship. However, his personal progress comes at a price, and he remains deeply conflicted. At a low point, he turns up one evening at Dr. Bergman's doorstep. Against his better judgment, he lies down on the analyst's couch. This selection raises the question of whether it is ever ethical to enlist a patient in treatment by preying on their vulnerability, fellow psychiatrist or not.

EDWARD

I want to show you something. Just relax. You remember my wife, Judith?

MATTHEW

Uh..sure.

*EDWARD flips a switch on his desk. We hear a machine turn on.*

EDWARD

Take a look at these slides of our trip to the Grand Canyon. I'm dying to show them to someone.

MATTHEW

You keep a projector in here?

*We hear a click. We see a scenic slide of the Grand Canyon.*

EDWARD

What do you think of this?

MATTHEW

It's very nice. But---

*We hear a click. We see a slide of EDWARD and his wife at the Grand Canyon.*

EDWARD

You were like a member of the family, you know. And what do you think of this?
*We hear a click. We see a slide of a sexy, naked woman. MATTHEW gasps.*

EDWARD

How does that make you feel, Matthew?

Psychoanalysis is all about self-expression, no? Rest assured there were many analysts who freely applied aversive techniques. Some even delivered electric shocks along with the erotic images.

Later in the play we see our subject one step further along in his conversion therapy.

*As the scene opens, EDWARD and MATTHEW sit together looking at slides of naked women.*

EDWARD

Does she excite you?

MATTHEW

I don't really feel anything.

EDWARD

Perhaps she's just not your type.
*We see a slide of another naked woman.*

EDWARD

This may be more to your liking. Which do you like better?

MATTHEW

It's possible. Just possible I may be getting an erection. Well, maybe not.

EDWARD

What about this?
*We see a slide of a naked man.*

MATTHEW

Definitely not.

EDWARD

No? Well, then. I call that progress.

Still later, Matthew's transformation is nearly complete. In the following monologue, spoken during a therapy session, he imagines the letter he will write to sever ties with his boyfriend. Unfortunately, the events set in motion by the letter result in tragedy.

MATTHEW

I am not gay. I repeat, I'm not gay. I went through a phase. And I realize I made a mistake. I'm sorry if I hurt you, or anyone who thought I was something I'm not. That's what I'm going to say. I thought I loved you. But I was deluded. Now I'm ready to make up for lost time. There's a woman. Her parents go to the same temple as mine. We'll make lots of babies, and she'll stay home with the kids. Her parents are already planning the bris, which is pushing things ridiculously fast, don't you think? After all, our first child could be a girl. I'll give up my office on Rittenhouse Square and open one that's more masculine in Bryn Mawr. I won't have to walk past the park on my way to the car. (*Scornfully*) It's brimming with faggots, especially at dusk. We'll go into the city now and then, but our lives will revolve around the country club. I'll be like everyone else. I'll be happy. And I hope you'll be happy too. Please don't call me at home. Ever. Drop me a line, at my office, once a year, and let me know how you're getting on. But don't come after me in any way. And don't try to make me change my mind. I am not gay. I am not gay.

> *Still lying down, MATTHEW turns around. EDWARD,* taking notes, nods.

MATTHEW

Are we finished now? There's nothing left to say.

Without completely giving away the ending of *Doctor Anonymous*, I feel compelled to say that Matthew eventually manages to free himself from Dr. Bergman once and for all, and like the real John E. Fryer, vindicates himself in a dramatic gesture.

In conclusion, medical students are sometimes shocked to learn that this "therapy" actually happened. They are even more shocked to learn that, in some places, it still happens. It was sobering to learn that, on average, medical schools spend less than five hours on LGBTQ health issues in the entire curriculum. Therefore, I feel privileged to know that I play a role in educating the next generation of physicians, whether they become psychiatrists or radiologists. I can also vouch for the effectiveness of theater in helping to make a lesson come alive in a way that a textbook or a lecture does not.

# 36

## JEKYLL'S LOVER

### *James Penha*

It's not so much waking up to Hyde
as it is wondering, after a day
giggling about Henry's failed soufflé,
singing the old tunes around the piano
(he recklessly pounding the keys)
and making love no less passionately
than when first we met,
with whom I shall wake.
My eyes blink fitfully through the night.
I stare at the ceiling and listen to him breathe:
his rhythmic exhalations, snortless, ease me
to slumber. And at daybreak, if he slips quietly
from our bed, wary of disturbing me, I can
be certain fairly that Henry will soon return
with my tea and a kiss and a smile. But
if I feel the covers swept like tides from my body
and the mattress depressed with careless
exertions—stretches and scratching—then
I am in thrall to Edward. It will be bad, of course,
but not so bad as the worry of the waiting. He
will hate me, blame me for his predicament,

The following poems were written, and are owned and copyrighted by James Penha: "Jekyll's Lover" was originally published in Devilfish Review 11 (2014). "T is for Them" was originally published in A Quiet Courage 8 April 2015. "Fool's Gold" was originally published in Quail Bell Magazine: The Unreal 22 June 2015.

accuse me of spreading lies of beatings
and broken bones. And, yes, he is more victim
than villain, I tell myself in mantra. And he is
too the Henry whom I love.

## T IS FOR THEM

*James Penha*

*You slow all existence down with your call / Nobody notices, only you've known,*
*you're not sick, not crazy, / not angry, not sad—*
*It's just this, you're injured.*
—Claudia Rankine, Citizen, *An American Lyric*

I swallow the anger
but it does not settle;
my mouth reveals
reflux and dismay.

Your face purses
knowing the they
of your nightmares
have cornered you

again, and I
collude, or am
at best a dupe
of these enemies

as long as I believe
silently in paranoia,
plead for a better life
through chemistry,

as if they were never
real, they who live

I know, but not with
the divinity you bestow

on them
and I am left alone
to wait them out
with you.

## FOOL'S GOLD

*James Penha*

what luster i have amassed,
mining silently my soul
and the poetry breezing
through us,
i want to gleam
in his eyes, but
he picks at the pyrite
i have yet to scrape away
and at the gilt
he hammered
onto me flaking aureate
atop aureate
until i don't know gold
for the pain
of the burnish.

# FEATHERS

*Benjamin Klas*

*"Hope is the thing with feathers . . . "* – *Emily Dickinson*

## I.

I saw the skeleton
on the way to English class. It had
been a bird once. Now its hollow
frame rocked back and forth on the cold
sidewalk. One mangled wing
stretched out, a few soiled feathers
still piercing what was left
of the flesh. *Hope is the thing
with feathers.* It was dead.

## II.

*This is a Christian school, she said. We shouldn't
have to read novels with queers
in them. I can't believe that's on the course
list. There is just no reason we should have to
read about someone with disgusting issues like that.*

## III.

Disgusting. I laid the broken
glass in my shoe, arranging
it so each step would pierce
me with the knowledge of what I was.

## IV.

*It's not you, he said. Whether or not*
*we think you would do anything*
*to the children, we need you*
*to step down. We need parents*
*to feel safe. Sunday school should*
*feel safe. And someone like you . . .*

## V.

Dangerous. I pinched the skin
between the twin blades of the scissors
until they closed, leaving a hollow
beneath them. Open shut. Open
shut. Until the back of my hand
was covered in trenches.

## VI.

*What am I supposed to tell*
*your sisters, he asked. Do I say*
*God made you this way? That God wants*
*you to be "queer?" Benjamin, you*
*will destroy this family.*

## VII.

Destroyer. I held a razor
in my hand. I pulled long, red
lines up and down my leg
until it was covered
in minced hair and blood.

## VIII.

*You need to leave, she said. This*
*is a Christian institution. You are*
*the immoral brother the Apostle*
*Paul talks about. If you don't, you*
*will unleash demons on this school.*

## IX.

Demonic. I picked up the razor
which had become so comfortable
in my hand. I looked over
the battlefield of my body.
Disgusting.
Dangerous.
Destroyer.
Demonic.
Somewhere, from outside,
I heard birdsong. Slowly,
I put the razor down.

## X.

It was springtime. I was walking
through the park when I saw
the bird. It was tiny. It hopped
feebly through the grass. Fluffy
down stuck out from its pink skin. The thing
with feathers. It should be dead.
It couldn't fly. It could barely
walk. But somehow, at this moment,
it was still alive.

# RESOURCES

## CRISIS AND SUICIDE PREVENTION RESOURCES

**Befrienders Worldwide**
https://www.befrienders.org/
Befrienders provides crisis helplines in many countries; callers can receive free and confidential emotional support.

**National Suicide Prevention Lifeline**
https://suicidepreventionlifeline.org/
**1-800-273-8255**
24/7 free, confidential support for people in distress, prevention and crisis resources, and best practices for professionals.

**Trans Lifeline**
http://www.translifeline.org/
**US: 1-877-565-8860**
**Canada: 1-877-330-6366**
A nonprofit run by and for people of transgender experience with a hotline staffed by volunteers. Trans Lifeline operators are available eighteen hours a day, every day.

**Trevor Project**
https://www.thetrevorproject.org/
**24/7 Hotline: 1-866-488-7386**
Crisis intervention and suicide prevention for LGBTQ youth. Text and chat support available in addition to voice. TrevorSpace is a social networking site for LGBTQ youth aged thirteen through twenty-four and their friends and allies.

## MENTAL HEALTH CARE AND REFERRALS

**LGBT National Help Center**
http://www.glbtnationalhelpcenter.org/
Free and confidential peer support, including online peer support chat and online groups, and local resources.

**The Icarus Project**
http://www.theicarusproject.net/
The Icarus Project is a support network and education project by and for people who experience the world in ways that are often diagnosed as mental illness. They advance social justice by fostering mutual aid practices that reconnect healing and collective liberation. PDFs of helpful publications can be found at: http://www.theicarusproject.net/resources

## National Alliance on Mental Illness (NAMI)
http://www.nami.org
info@nami.org
Helpline: 1-800-950-NAMI
The nation's largest grassroots mental health organization. Founded in 1979, NAMI is today an association of hundreds of local affiliates, state organizations, and volunteers who work in communities to raise awareness and provide support and education to those in need. NAMI offers many programs and support groups via its local chapters. The Helpline is available Monday through Friday, 10 AM–6 PM ET.

## Gay and Lesbian Medical Association
www.glma.org
A search engine is available through which you can find LGBTQ-competent doctors, including therapists and psychiatrists.

## Psychology Today Find a Therapist
https://www.psychologytoday.com/us/therapists
You can refine searches for psychotherapists by using criteria including accepted health insurance plans, sexuality and gender, language, and more.

## MindOut
https://www.mindout.org.uk/
UK-based mental health services by and for LGBTQ people. Counseling, peer mentoring, online chat and support services, and advocacy help are available.

## Rainbow Heights Club
http://www.rainbowheights.org
25 Flatbush Ave., 4th Fl.
Brooklyn, NY 11217
1-718-852-2584
Rainbow Heights Club (RHC) is the only LGBTQ-specific psychosocial clubhouse program in the United States. It offers socialization, support, and peer advocacy for LGBTQ consumers requiring mental health services. Membership is required to participate, but is free.

## Association of LGBTQ Psychiatrists Referral Search
https://aglp.memberclicks.net/index.php?option=com_content&view=article&id=14&Itemid=74

## LGBTQ Peer Counseling Services
http://www.lgbtpeercounseling.com
lgbtpeercounseling@yahoo.com
1-215-732-TALK (8255)
A program of Philadelphia's William Way LGBT Community Center. Free one-on-one confidential peer counseling (peer counselors are *not* therapists) via phone, Monday through Friday, 6–9 PM. Also available by appointment or walk-in, but is short-term counseling only and located in Philadelphia.

**Pride Institute**

https://pride-institute.com/

Located in Minnesota, Pride Institute provides LGBTQ+ residential and outpatient treatment for substance use. Most major forms of insurance, self-pay, and Minnesota state funding are accepted. For information on residential treatment, visit: https://pride-institute.com/programs/residential-treatment/

## SUICIDE POSTVENTION (POST-LOSS SUPPORT)

**Samaritans NYC**

http://samaritansnyc.org/wp-content/uploads/2015/11/2016-Survivor-Guide-Active-Links.pdf

Samaritans NYC's resource guide for both suicide loss survivor resources and suicide prevention services; many resources are online or national rather than NYC-specific.

**American Foundation for Suicide Prevention's Survivor Outreach Program**

https://www.afsp.org/coping-with-suicide-loss/find-support/survivor-outreach-program

This program facilitates visits to newly bereaved individuals from survivors who have spent some time healing from their loss and want to help others.

**American Foundation for Suicide Prevention (AFSP)**

The AFSP's Support Group Listing is available at:

http://www.afsp.org/coping-with-suicide-loss/find-support/in-person-support-groups

AFSP also has information for facilitators of survivor support groups: http://www.afsp.org/coping-with-suicide/for-support-group-facilitators

**Alliance of Hope**

http://www.allianceofhope.org/

Alliance of Hope has online community forums, referral information for in-person services, and more.

**American Association of Suicidology**

http://www.suicidology.org/suicide-survivors/suicide-loss-survivors

The American Association of Suicidology has a list of books and resources for survivors, and provides links to PDFs.

**Suicide Prevention Resource Center**

http://www.sprc.org/basics/about-surviving-suicide-loss

This Resource Center provides many postvention resources.

## RECOMMENDED READING

*My Almost Certainly Real Imaginary Jesus*
Kelly Barth
*Headcase* contributor Barth's memoir of growing up Christian and discovering her attraction to other girls addresses the disconnect between the radical and human Jesus of history and the church's supernatural savior.

*Live Through This: On Creativity and Self-Destruction*
Ed. Sabrina Chapadjiev
A collection of original stories, essays, artwork, and photography by women exploring the use of art to survive abuse, incest, madness, and depression and the often deep-seated impulse toward self-destruction.

*The Motion of Light in Water: Sex and Science Fiction Writing in the East Village*
Samuel Delaney
Science fiction and nonfiction writer Delaney's memoir of living and writing in bohemian New York City while in an open interracial marriage. Winner of the 1989 Hugo Award for nonfiction.

*Marbles: Mania, Depression, Michelangelo, and Me: A Graphic Memoir*
Ellen Forney
Forney's memoir of living with bipolar disorder, with which she was diagnosed shortly before her thirtieth birthday, in a graphic-novel format.

*Queering Sexual Violence: Radical Voices from Within the Anti-Violence Movement*
Ed. Jennifer Patterson
A thirty-seven-piece collection of multigendered, multiracial, and multilayered voices in the anti-violence movement that disrupts the mainstream conversations about sexual violence.

*The Last Time I Wore a Dress*
Dylan Scholinski (written as Daphne Scholinski) with Jane Meredith Adams
Scholinski's 1998 memoir of being institutionalized for three years with a diagnosis of Gender Identity Disorder. A Lambda Literary Award winner.

*Beautiful Wreck: Sex, Lies, and Suicide*
Stephanie Schroeder (*Headcase* co-editor)
A chronicle of Schroeder's 1990 move to NYC with undiagnosed bipolar disorder and of her queer political activism, forays into experience with corporate America, intimate partner violence, unwilling parenthood, erotic discovery, 9/11—and three attempted suicides.

*The Noonday Demon: An Atlas of Depression*
Andrew Solomon
An examination of depression that entails details of the award-winning author's own struggles with the illness along with interviews with fellow sufferers, doctors and scientists, policymakers and politicians, drug designers, and philosophers. Winner of the National Book Award.

*Riding Fury Home*
Chana Wilson
A memoir of *Headcase* contributor Wilson's relationship with her mother, who made a suicide attempt in the 1950s and was subject to psychiatric treatment to cure her of her lesbianism. Wilson, a psychotherapist, came out herself in the 1970s, and the book explores the healing that took place between her and her mother.

*Why Be Happy When You Could Be Normal?*
Jeanette Winterson
A memoir about a life's work to find happiness and how Winterson's painful past rose to haunt her later in life, sending her on a journey into madness and out again, in search of her biological mother.

## WEBSITES AND BLOGS

Autostraddle's Guide to Queer Mental Health
https://www.autostraddle.com/the-autostraddle-guide-to-queer-mental-health-306921/
Queer feminist website Autostraddle's archive of mental health-related posts.

Queer Mental Health
http://queermentalhealth.org/
A community-based support and resource site for LGBTQ+ people with mental health issues.

Let's Queer Things Up
https://letsqueerthingsup.com/tag/mental-health/
Sam Dylan Finch's blog exploring queer/trans identity, mental health, self-care, stigma, social impact, cats, and whatever else pops into its writer's brain.

Centre for Clinical Interventions (CCI) Self-Help Modules
http://www.cci.health.wa.gov.au/resources/consumers.cfm
CCI provides free "information packages" for various mental health issues consisting of a number of modules that can be completed online.

## CLINICAL BIBLIOGRAPHY

Anderson, S (2009). Gays, lesbians more likely to seek mental health services, study finds. Retrieved from http://newsroom.ucla.edu/releases/sexual-minorities-are-more-likely-98582

Arthur, H., Rubin, J., & Huygen, C. (2016). Behavioral health, the LGBTQ community, and managed care. *Behavioral Health News, 4*(1). Retrieved from http://www.mhnews.org/back_issues/BHN-Fall2016.pdf

Bieschke, K., Perez, R., & DeBord, K. (Eds.). (2007). *Handbook of counseling and psychotherapy with gay, lesbian, bisexual, and transgender clients* (2nd ed.). Washington, DC: American Psychological Association.

Haas, A. P., Rodgers, P. L., & Herman, J. L. (2014). *Suicide attempts among transgender and gender non-conforming adults.* Los Angeles: Williams Institute.

Hash, K. M., & Rogers, A. (2013). Clinical practice with older LGBT clients: Overcoming lifelong stigma through strength and resilience. *Clinical Social Work Journal, 41*(3), 249–257. doi:10.1007/s10615-013-0437-2

Hellman, R. E., & Drescher, J. (Eds.). (2004). *Handbook of LGBT issues in community mental health.* Binghamton, NY: Haworth Medical Press.

Israel, T., Gorcheva, R., Burnes, T. R., & Walther, W. A. (2008). Helpful and unhelpful therapy experiences of LGBT clients. *Psychotherapy Research, 18*(3), 294–305. doi:10.1080/10503300701506920

Johnson, S. D. (2012). Gay affirmative psychotherapy with lesbian, gay, and bisexual individuals: Implications for contemporary psychotherapy research. *American Journal of Orthopsychiatry, 82*(4), 516–522. doi:10.1111/j.1939-0025.2012.01180.x

Levounis, P., Drescher, J., & Barber, M. E. (2012). *The LGBT casebook*. Washington, DC: American Psychiatric Publishers.

Lucksted, A. (2004) Raising issues: Lesbian, gay, bisexual, and transgender people receiving services in the public mental health system. (Contract with the Center for Mental Health Services Research, SAMHSA, DHHS). Retrieved from http://www.rainbowheights.org/downloads/FINAL_VERSIONAlicia%20Lucksted.pdf

Meyer, I. H. (2003). Prejudice, social stress, and mental health in lesbian, gay, and bisexual populations: Conceptual issues and research evidence. *Psychological Bulletin, 129*(5), 674–697. doi:10.1037/0033-2909.129.5.674

Meyer, I. H. (2014). Minority stress and positive psychology: Convergences and divergences to understanding LGBT health. *Psychology of Sexual Orientation and Gender Diversity, 1*(4), 348–349. doi:10.1037/sgd0000070

Pachankis, J. E., & Goldfried, M. R. (2013). Clinical issues in working with lesbian, gay, and bisexual clients. *Psychology of Sexual Orientation and Gender Diversity, 1*(S), 45–58. doi:10.1037/2329-0382.1.S.45

Park H., & Mykhyalyshyn, I. (2016, June 16). L.G.B.T. people are more likely to be targets of hate crimes than any other minority group. *The New York Times*. Retrieved from http://www.nytimes.com/interactive/2016/06/16/us/hate-crimes-against-lgbt.html

Su, D., Irwin, J. A., Fisher, C., Ramos, A., Kelley, M., Mendoza, D. A. R., & Coleman, J. D. (2016). Mental health disparities within the LGBT population: A comparison between transgender and nontransgender individuals. *Transgender Health, 1*(1), 12–20. doi:10.1089/ trgh.2015.0001

Vaughan, M. D., & Rodriguez, E. M. (2014). LGBT strengths: Incorporating positive psychology into theory, research, training, and practice. *Psychology of Sexual Orientation and Gender Diversity, 1*(4), 325–334. doi:10.1037/sgd0000053

Vaughan, M. D., Miles, J., Parent, M. C., Lee, H. S., Tilghman, J. D., & Prokhorets, S. (2014). A content analysis of LGBT-themed positive psychology articles. *Psychology of Sexual Orientation and Gender Diversity, 1*(4), 313–324. doi:10.1037/sgd0000060

# INDEX